The Low Countries

Cover:

Beethovenstraat, Amsterdam, 1967 (Detail)

© Ed van der Elsken /

Nederlands Fotomuseum

TLC

2017 The Low Countries

ARTS AND SOCIETY IN FLANDERS AND THE NETHERLANDS

25

**Published by
the Flemish-Dutch
cultural institution
Ons Erfdeel vzw**

Contents

Chronicle

—

Next page:
The Sixties (Knack, 1988)
© GAL (Gerard Alsteens)

On page 112-113:
Models show 'Mondrian fashion' from Paris in the
Gemeentemuseum Den Haag, 1966.
The dresses were designed by Yves Saint Laurent
Photo by Eric Koch © National Archief, Fotocollectie Anefo

'Be Realistic. Demand the Impossible'

The Ambiguous Heritage of the Sixties

We will not make the mistake of mythologising the 1960s. Imagination never made it into power; beaches did not emerge in the streets from under the paving stones and something always remained prohibited. But between the late 1950s and mid-1970s Western society and culture undeniably experienced great changes, which also affected the Low Countries.

The first symptoms of protest culture originated in the 1950s. The most frenzied events took place at the end of the 1960s and the far-reaching consequences of their various changes became clear in the 1970s.

Power and authority, at least the traditional forms of authority (that of government, educators, teachers and the churches) sustained serious damage. Young people freed themselves from all kinds of shackles. Fear was gradually removed from sexuality. People experimented with new social customs, new forms of society. Narcotics were still seen as expanding the mind. Women slowly but surely became emancipated, gaining awareness of their own bodies and rights. Music was the expression of a personal world, raising its middle finger at anything seen as bourgeois. The times smelt of romance, of the grand gesture, of frivolous activism. Self-expression became an aim in itself. The sky was the limit. The impossible became reality, or at least had the potential to do so.

But perhaps this is mythologising by the back door.

After years of rebuilding following World War II, at the start of the 1960s prosperity had arrived. Consumption was definitively on the up. It was that prosperity and optimism which made much of the above possible.

What remains of all that in the Low Countries half a century on? Let me quote just two sentences from the answers you will find in the following pages: 'There was plenty of narcissism and ego-tripping in the "Golden Sixties", but this period also introduced a feeling of solidarity from which twenty-first-century advocates of a new sense of community still have a great deal to learn,' (Geert Buelens); and, 'There is no need for more flexibility, discontinuity and extravagance; there is, however, a need for non-paternalist forms of authority, based on a deep, confidence-inspiring knowledge of affairs and the power to delegate them to others' (Cyrille Offermans).

In this book, we discuss student uprisings in Amsterdam in 1969 and 2015, and Boudewijn de Groot, iconic singer-songwriter of the Low Countries who is still singing today. We discuss the sexual revolution and the price revolution always entails. We ask what the happenings of pop art have to tell us now, and investigate the extent of secularisation in the Low Countries in the last half century and to what degree today's sharing economy is indebted to initiatives and practices which emerged in those years. We close the theme with a refined literary anthology: Harry Mulisch as fellow traveller of Provo, an ode to erotic vitalism (which now sounds sexist and neo-colonialist to some) and the positioning of a poet who was a committed outsider in the 1960s.

We were not a poetic theme by Mao.
We thought, we'll make our own poem.
We thought, we'll make history here
On the sly.
(Leonard Nolens)

LUC DEVOLDERE | *Chief Editor*

An Era of Early Globalisation

The 1960s in the Low Countries

[GEERT BUELENS]

Until the 1960s, you might have been forgiven for seeing your home as the entire world. Of course, parts of that world were being colonised in your name, but an ordinary citizen would generally be fairly oblivious to all that. You might repeat-edly see war on your territory, as any Belgian knows, but although the most important conflicts were called 'world wars', most Europeans experienced them as regional battles, extremely violent encounters between neighbouring countries. The breakthrough of television as a mass medium and, almost simul-taneously, accelerated decolonisation and mass immigration of 'guest workers' brought the world in the 1960s both concretely and symbolically into the lives of many Western Europeans, in the Low Countries as well as elsewhere. This made it possible for matters which were essentially internal American affairs – the civil rights movement and protests against the Vietnam war – to inspire po-litical, social and cultural movements in Europe, and vice versa, with the Provos – speaking terrible English and writing in Dutch – becoming an international media phenomenon, inspiring their contemporaries from Sweden to the United States. Vietnam and the counterculture determined to a large extent the image of this decade, but, all things considered, they occupied only a minority of the population, even among young people. However, the pop culture which broke through in the 1960s – the Beatles, the mini skirt, informal styles of clothing and interaction, in relationships and sex as well as elsewhere – transformed the lives of a whole generation and their descendants.

Times feel open

In the Low Countries, the 1960s probably really began in 1958, in Brussels. The World's Fair catapulted Belgium back to the forefront of modernity, not only through radical infrastructure works, but also by bringing together the new, the exciting, the visionary and in some cases the utopian from almost all of the rest of the world and demonstrating that an era of *possibilities* had begun. De-spite the violence and crises – in full swing in the 1960s, in the Low Countries as well as elsewhere – that might be the most important feature of this time: it felt open, a preparation for the future.

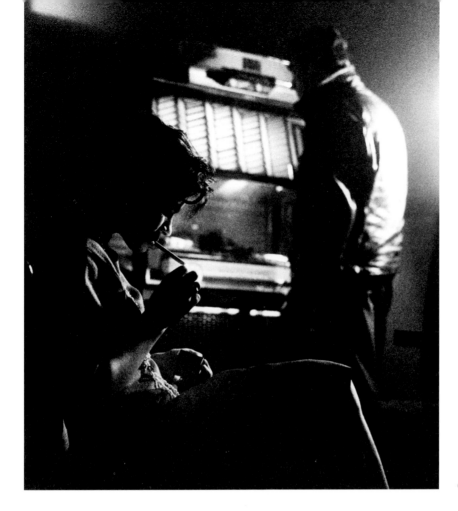

That openness was undoubtedly supported by economic growth and the conspicuous youthfulness of the population after the baby boom, but in retrospect probably also depended on the government having less of a tendency to protect citizens from themselves in their daily lives compared with today. Despite a startling rate of traffic deaths by current standards, car seatbelts were not compulsory. Smoking was so generally accepted that it went on without question in TV studios, offices and cars. Campaigns against alcohol were similarly unheard of. Those freedoms still take a high toll today, but the fact that everything was possible back then undoubtedly contributed to a carefree feel which is largely absent from today's society, with its health and safety obsession.

Glocal

In the carrousel of opinions continually doing the rounds today, the story goes that the left (or terms applied synonymously: the 'cultural elite' or '1968') set this early wave of globalisation in motion or at least embraced and encouraged it, and, blinded by cosmopolitan notions, threw the baby out with the bathwater when it came to the culture and individuality of the population. This

Jimi Hendrix,
Brussels, 1964
© Herman Selleslags

Frank Zappa, Palais des Beaux Arts, Brussels,1974
© Herman Selleslags

Pink Floyd,
Brussels, 1967
© Herman Selleslags

Paul McCartney, Magical Mystery Tour, Torquay, 1967
© Herman Selleslags

John Lennon, Magical Mystery Tour, Torquay, 1967
© Herman Selleslags

misses the simple fact that mass immigration of 'guest workers' happened on the initiative of business, when employers went in search of cheap labourers who would not turn up their noses at dirty, dangerous work. A newspaper such as *De Telegraaf* supported this project and in the summer of 1965 sent a reporter to follow a Turkish labourer on his way from Rotterdam to visit the village where he was born – another sign of globalisation. It was observed with satisfaction that not only was the man delighted with his job, assuring the reporter in broken Dutch that he worked hard and earned lots of money, but that the entire operation was a civilising mission ('What can these two young girls from Çaykent expect from life? [...] Perhaps these girls will be able to benefit from Western European ideas, which the Turks will take home with them.') The European Economic Community was another project of the administrative elite. During the 1960s, no new member states joined, but in 1965 the so-called 'Merger Treaty' was signed, laying the foundation for a number of the central European institutions (the Commission, the Council of Ministers) which come under so much criticism today. The development of popular culture undeniably had internationalist if not cosmopolitan features. That had always been the case in modern times and developments in media and communications technology accelerated that process after World War II. At the same time so-called global trends (in practice almost all Anglo-American, occasionally French) exhibited conspicuously local variants with different emphases, and individual characteristics were not automatically sacrificed for the general or supposed universal.

Lange Houtstraat, Amsterdam, ca. 1965 © Ed van der Elsken / Nederlands Fotomuseum

Against uniformity

Folk music appears to be a genre which reflects individual roots and community by definition. The fact that it suddenly flourished in the Low Countries in the 1960s, however, was due to international trends; specifically its exceptional success in the United States, with new voices (Joan Baez, Odetta, Judy Collins) and new songs (by Phil Ochs, Tom Paxton and particularly Bob Dylan) giving this music an unprecedented boost. Flanders and the Netherlands also had their protest singers (Armand, Ferre Grignard, Fabien Collin), but they did not just refer to local events (like Miek & Roel in 'Te Leuven'); in Flanders in particular dialect variants flourished. In the various provinces musicians sought to establish a connection with the language and heritage of the region and with local concerns. In Antwerp Wannes Van de Velde was involved in early 'happenings' to make parts of the city centre free of traffic; in his songs he also protested against the mindless destruction of the medieval core of the city. To the elite of that time (promotors of the construction industry and politicians) this certainly came across as anti-modern, perhaps even reactionary contrariness, but in retrospect it is as clear as day that Van de Velde with his ecological and urban concerns was ahead of his time in one of the most important public debates of the past decades, internationally too: that of town planning and keeping vulnerable local communities liveable. The choice of dialect was also loaded with significance: singers such as Van de Velde used this to counter the impersonal uniformity which seemed to be paired with this latest phase of modernity, whether it was American, European or Dutch.

Demolition of the *Galerij* on Frederiksplein, former site of the *Paleis voor Volksvlijt*, now *De Nederlandsche bank*, Amsterdam, 1961 © Ed van der Elsken / Nederlands Fotomuseum

Oppressed peoples

Another aspect of globalisation which seems very topical is the conspicuous revival of nationalism in the 1960s. Unlike today, it was a largely left-wing (sometimes even left-revolutionary) variety. From Quebec to the Basque Country and from Scotland to Flanders, nationalist movements weighed on the political and social climate, in the former two cases through bombings and other violence, in the latter predominantly by marches and political writing. Significantly, the way these movements flourished among young people was often seen in the light of decolonisation and the battle against big business. A progressive Flemish radical newspaper such as *De Nieuwe* (1964-1984) argued that the Flemish people should be emancipated both in spirit and politically, but they wanted the same thing for the people of Angola, Vietnam and other oppressed nations. During the notorious student protests in Leuven people first shouted 'Out with the Walloons!' (directed at the francophone elite in the Flemish university city), but soon added, 'Out with the bourgeois!' In that climate the University of Leuven eventually split (with construction starting on Louvain-la-Neuve in 1969) and the federalisation of Belgium was also formally placed on the political agenda – 1970 brought an end to the unitary state.

Adieu to the smell of boiled sprouts

For the Netherlands, the 1960s almost appear to be the beginning of contemporary history. Of course, the Golden Age is an endless source of national pride and for many ethical and political discussions World War II remains the reference point, but for the country's self-image as a liberal, progressive nation we largely draw on the 1960s. That was when, tradition has it, the nation of hard-working, pragmatic tradesmen finally took a step back from the 'smell of boiled sprouts' which had always defined the atmosphere of the Netherlands and the world was embraced as a magic globe full of possibilities. The core of the transformation took place in Amsterdam, which described itself at the time as the 'magical centre' of the country and the world. Of course, that was very much a relative matter. Liverpool, London, San Francisco and Paris in fact exhibited slightly stronger powers of attraction, and for the vast majority of Amsterdammers (not to mention the rest of the country) the new washing machine, first television or car, and for young people the latest Beatles record, were rather more important than what a group of crazy Provos were getting up to on the Spui square. Moreover, in this version of the facts it is conveniently forgotten how the 1950s with CoBrA and the Vijftigers had already caused a profound revolution in high culture.

© Herman Selleslags

In the light of the later history of the country and of the current climate of intellectual debate in the Netherlands, what happened in the 1960s around the Provo movement was nevertheless of great importance. The international image of Amsterdam changed so radically that in early 1969 *The New York Times* was able to describe the city as a spot for hippies, Provos, rebels, homosexuals, drugs and tolerance. A year later, a reporter for *Rolling Stone* incredulously related how the prices of various sorts of drugs were read out on VPRO radio as if they were stock market results. It all seemed so natural in the new Netherlands, but of course it was not. Even if, as James Kennedy convincingly showed, the Dutch elite went along remarkably comfortably with this cultural revolution, beneath it all something raged which today we would call a culture war. Broadcasting companies such as VARA and VPRO intentionally sought out the boundaries of decency and the consequent commotion was expertly exploited in consultation with prominent intellectuals and publishers. While this was certainly about religion and sex, perhaps the more important point was the tone with which the new media elite distanced itself in these discussions from what was tellingly referred to as the 'klootjesvolk' or 'hoi polloi'. In the apparently so-tolerant Netherlands, people with different views were sidelined as stupid or dangerous. In *Bericht aan de rattenkoning* (Message to the Rat King, 1966), a book-length analysis and insider history of the Provo movement, Harry Mulisch did not hesitate to contrast cosmopolitan Amsterdam, radiating freedom, with 'the province, where the feudal spirit of AUTHORITY rules', a spirit which was politically interpreted as the Boerenpartij or Farmers' Party of Farmer Koekoek, the first clearly Poujadist party in the country. Koekoek led a campaign with the slogan 'For Right, Freedom and Authority' and the fact that he succeeded in gaining considerable parliamentary success shows that the regular parties were no longer seen as defenders of those values. Above all, of course, it shows that even in the large cities, where many of the party's voters resided, contrary to expectations raised by its name, a substantial proportion of the population really did want to see these values defended and wanted nothing to do with the radical liberalisation of the Netherlands. The fact that the party still never succeeded in achieving more than seven seats in the House of Representatives illustrates the extent to which Mulisch exaggerated when he suggested that Koekoek spoke for more or less everyone outside the sanctuary of Amsterdam. By making the enemy out to be bigger than it really was, he may well have made the Provos more heroic, but of course, that did not change the fact that there was indeed an enemy; besides Farmer Koekoek, the popular newspaper *De Telegraaf* in particular convincingly adopted that role.

In Dutch history it is rarely pointed out how much rhetorical violence was involved in all this and how much the heralds of the cultural revolution presented the actual use of violence as an obvious option in their writing. Mulisch compared Koekoek's supporters with the Ku Klux Klan, and, based explicitly on the translation of Mao's *On Guerrilla Warfare*, published in 1965 and much read at the time, he also saw the Provos as the shock troops which introduced the urban guerrilla into the Dutch political establishment. The fact that the German Red Army Faction later found both sympathisers and actual support in the Netherlands is in that light less remarkable than the fact that there was

no native domestic terrorist movement in the country itself. Although Koekoek is seen today with good reason as a forerunner to Pim Fortuyn and Geert Wilders, opponents of the Provo movement continue generally to be represented as the losers, as reactionaries and neo-fascists who for that very reason found themselves on the wrong side of history. As long as that is the case, the Provo movement appears to have won the culture war, but it is by no means certain that it will remain in the lead.

Globalisation of culture under the influence of mass media can also be illustrated by the relative ease with which this in fact rather limited group of miscreants of the Provo movement reached the world press with their ideas and happenings. Vincent van Gogh and Piet Mondrian also succeeded in reaching the top of the international avant-garde, although they did so from France. The members of CoBrA and Vijftig had already given the scene a thorough shake-up, but Appel, Corneille and Vinkenoog too had built up their networks and much of their wisdom in Paris. Thanks to the speed of the television and their own media savvy, however, the Provos succeed, albeit very briefly, in becoming world famous from Amsterdam. Indeed, they quite innocently put into practice an idea which terrorists would later perfect: the quickest way into the news is throwing a bomb. The Provos' bombs were minor affairs: a pineapple bomb in one of their

Near the Waterlooplein, Amsterdam, ca. 1965 © Ed van der Elsken / Nederlands Fotomuseum

magazines and in 1966, at the wedding of Princess Beatrix to the German Claus von Amsberg, smoke bombs. Those images went around the world, as did the White Bicycle Plan, as mediagenic as it was original, if not visionary.

Happenings

In fact, the Provo movement was far from the only one to touch a sensitive note abroad. The world of free jazz and modern classical music retains a very special place in the Netherlands (and Belgium too thanks to Fred Van Hove). 'Jazz + Classical Music + Absurdism', states the cover of Kevin Whitehead's book *New Dutch Swing* (1999), and along with the title of Robert Adlington's *Composing Dissent* (2013) that nicely sums up the unique contribution of Misha Mengelberg, Willem Breuker, Han Bennink, Louis Andriessen and co. They proved how exciting freedom and crossing boundaries could be; how jazz, classical music, theatre and poetry could overlap and how democratic and artistic engagement could touch folk and pop music as well as the avant-garde.

Avant-garde movements had also often been extremely mediagenic in the first half of the twentieth century, but due to a lack of moving images most citizens only became acquainted with their ideas and exhibitions through the written word. In the era of television that changed in two ways. Artists and musicians increasingly sought out their audiences and art came out of the museum or gallery. Happenings in public places also often led to spectacular images, raising eyebrows among some sectors of the public, which was ideal for news or current affairs programmes. This method reached millions of viewers who would never go to happenings or similar activities themselves. The effect was not limited to dissemination of culture. Since these were also the years in which art subsidies were substantially expanded, this mass confrontation with extreme art must certainly have increased feelings of aversion and alienation among many viewers towards what the so-called silent majority saw as an overly permissive society.

The 1960s can therefore be seen as an early moment in post-war globalisation, but the Low Countries themselves performed rather awkwardly on the world stage. The decade marked the final moment in history when the foreign policy of both Belgium and the Netherlands really carried weight and formed the subject of continuous international attention, sometimes even irritation. The overly hasty decolonisation of Congo, the remaining troubles in resource-rich Katanga, and the transfer of New Guinea to Indonesia, forced by the United States, led to scepticism and criticism abroad. However, the Low Countries only came to a political and public examination of conscience long after events such as Hugo Claus's analysis of colonial ideology in his play *The Life and Works of Leopold II* (1970), or psychologist and war veteran Joop Hueting being forced into hiding following his 1969 television revelations about Dutch war crimes during the Indonesian war for independence.

The '70s are the real '60s

It might be a cliché to say that the 1960s really took place in the 1970s, but there is some truth to it. It was only then that the Netherlands gained a real left-wing cabinet (Den Uyl, 1973-1977), the country became known internationally for its policy of tolerance for abortion and soft drugs, and a generous budget became available for development cooperation, including support to Cuba and liberation movements in Angola and Mozambique. Here the government manifestly attempted to stand on the right side of history. At the same time these were also the years in which the wagging left-wing finger of caution, later so much criticised, came not only from activists in anoraks but also from members of government. Ministers joined in marching in protests against Franco (which mattered little if at all to the average Dutch citizen), as well as making motor-bike helmets compulsory and introducing breathalyser tests.

Left-wing philosophy, however, was more deeply anchored in society than might have been suspected purely on the basis of election results. In Flanders, too, in the course of the 1970s it became clear how much the social movement and the movements for peace, women, youth, ecology and the Third World were communicating channels, in which the significance and weight of Christian-inspired civil society was not to be underestimated. Yes, in Flanders too the churches were quietly emptying, but spirituality and a deep sense of connection with the underprivileged nearby and far away created a generation which perhaps experienced the ideals of Christian charity more deeply than their devout forebears. Even when the economic crisis of the 1970s and 1980s hit hard, these movements kept the ideas of the 1960s alive. There was plenty of narcissism and ego-tripping in the 'Golden Sixties', but this period also introduced a feeling of solidarity from which twenty-first-century advocates of a new sense of community still have a great deal to learn. ∎

Translated by Anna Asbury

The Search for Lost Authority

The 1960s – Again

To be honest, I did not expect that *Les Aveugles*, a one-act play by Maurice Maeterlinck, with its heavy pessimistic symbolism and theatrical minimalism, would ever be performed again. I was wrong. Guy Cassiers staged it in 2014 in a translation by Erwin Mortier. Whether this proves *The Blind* can really be performed remains debatable. Some critics described it with some justification as a *tableau vivant* and an installation. Nevertheless, as an artistic statement about the seemingly hopeless and ungovernable problems of our time, the play undeniably has some contemporary relevance.

A group of blind people, left alone by their priest, wander about aimlessly and hopelessly until they discover that the priest, who was also their guide, is dead. Then there is a blind mad woman with a child who cries but who alone can see. Is that child the new seer, the prophet for whom everyone is yearning? But then the question is: does it cry because of what it sees? Clinical psychologist and psychotherapist Paul Verhaeghe concludes his new book *Autoriteit* (Authority, 2015) with an apposite reference to the play. He sees *The Blind* as 'a metaphor for our time which carries a clear warning: there is no longer a leader; he is dead and his return is pure fantasy. We shall have to do it all ourselves.'

It is scarcely possible that Maeterlinck did not know of Nietzsche's doom-laden pronouncement to the world, eight years earlier, of the death of God. His blind, aimlessly wandering characters are a vivid reminder of Nietzsche's madman in *The Gay Science* (1882) who, in broad daylight, lit a lantern and went into the marketplace crying out incessantly 'I seek God! I seek God!' – although it might strike the modern reader as less of a search than an example of alarmist political street theatre. The public also needed to be persuaded. God may be dead but for Nietzsche, contrary to what is often believed, it was not necessarily something to celebrate. God's death left an immense existential void. 'Where are we moving?.. Are we not plunging continually? Backwards, sideways, forward, in all directions?.. Are we not straying as if through an infinite nothing?'

Neither did Nietzsche's readers, it seems, receive the announcement of God's death with unmixed joy. On the contrary, they needed a convincing alternative, a less absolute and dogmatic but nevertheless super- or non-human source of meaning, and this took many forms at around the turn of the century, also attracting many highly educated Europeans. After one and a half millennia of monotheism, a complete metaphysical vacuum was difficult to accept. Particularly in literary and artistic circles, surrogates were sought and found in a new broadly based mysticism that embraced a colourful mixture of (semi) religious and other spiritual and irrational beliefs and practices.

The influential Maeterlinck who published in French was crowned the 'apostle of mysticism' while the even more influential nobleman Leo Tolstoy was known as 'the mystic count'. Following the latter's example, communes were set up in the Netherlands with anti-modernist and puritanical Christian leanings. The new mysticism, fed by an aversion to the prevailing urban, technological and materialistic culture, was so ubiquitous that there was scarcely a single writer who was not influenced in some way, being either inspired by it or driven to oppose it. The most succinct criticism was probably formulated by the Flemish writer Herman Teirlinck (1879-1967) who bluntly dismissed the

A priest opposes the leftist
demonstrators against the
'Eenheidswet', 1961,
Brussels
© Herman Selleslags

Riots during the wedding of Princess Beatrix and Prince Claus, Muntplein, Amsterdam, 1966
and Provo-Happening against police action at the wedding, Prinsengracht, Amsterdam, 1966
© Ed van der Elsken / Nederlands Fotomuseum

'strange symbolism' and 'obscure allusions' in Maeterlinck's *Pélleas et Mélisande* as a 'great fraud', despite being very impressed by Claude Debussy's operatic adaptation of Maeterlinck's misty fairy tale.

The First World War marks the sharpest break in Western civilisation on all fronts. Never before can there have been such extreme disillusion as when it became apparent that the almost collective enthusiasm for war in Germany and elsewhere had not culminated in a joyful march towards the bliss of nationalist self-determination, but had instead led to total destruction.

In radical circles, God had already been done away with; but now all the alternatives faced the same fate. The Cabaret Voltaire, founded in Zurich by the Dadaists Hugo Ball and his life partner Emmy Hennings, became the stage on which the 'flight out of Time', as Ball called his fascinating autobiographical intellectual exercises in 1927, was given its most radical form. His absurdist performances had no literary pretension ('you can't turn a caprice into an artistic movement'). Rather, they were rituals of exorcism: any elements of language relating to sense, content or communication were discarded; what remained were loose, meaningless, elemental sounds to which any rational reaction was impossible and which therefore could never lead anywhere. Absolute discontinuity and unfathomableness walked hand in hand.

However, living permanently without seriousness or meaning proved too much. In 1920 Ball looked for more solid ground in of all places the strict asceticism of the early Christian hermits in the deserts of Syria and Egypt.

Cultural confusion

The 'Sixties'[1] saw a remarkable repetition of the cultural confusion of the late nineteenth and early twentieth century, though of course with obvious differences. The most important difference was one of scale. Whereas the initial announcement of the death of God had been heard primarily by a social and cultural elite, now after half a century's delay it reached broader sections of the population. The Catholic Church made frantic efforts to limit the damage. It tried to make contact with doubters by doing away with its traditional Latin and hallowed Gregorian music, but all in vain. Indeed, the very attempt to be progressive did much to undermine its authority.

At best, this dilution of faith contributed to the spread of 'isms', which in all their variants are mainly a compensation for unbelievers who dare not confront their unbelief. We have been witness to an enormous growth of spiritualism, often of oriental origin. Nietzsche's sobering insight that we are wandering through an infinite void is clearly unsettling to many. The escape from one-dimensional materialism has led to the world-renouncing dogmas of Hare Krishna and Timothy Leary, to the artificial paradise of alcohol and drugs, to the idolatry of mass culture and sport, to faith healers and charlatans. The Dutch essayist Rudy Kousbroek (1929-2010) found it all highly entertaining, perhaps too much so, particularly in *Het avondrood der magiërs* (Sunset of the Magicians, 1970). For irrationalism, however amusing it might be, is ultimately more than just irrational; it always contains a diffuse yearning for a different more meaningful life, for something to hold on to, yes, even a longing for authority.

But not in the most radical areas of the visual arts. There, Dadaism made a dramatic comeback in spite of Ball's aversion to the institutionalisation of his symbolic dismantling of the institutions. But its influence on daily life was minimal. The obstinate refusal of the 'neo-Dadaists' to learn anything from Europe's cultural heritage in the second half of the twentieth century led to few, if any, new and possibly fruitful scandals, but rather to utter indifference, and galleries that were even more empty and cold than the churches.

Something of Dada's original vitality did survive in the metropolitan sub-cultures of hippies, Provos and other 'anarchists', who gave content to their anti-authoritarian attitudes with witty, humorous and often highly practical proposals for improving the social environment. But not surprisingly, their un-conventional attitudes created tensions not only with the establishment which often reacted to their light-hearted provocations with an absurd lack of under-standing and mindless police violence, but also with the more conventional members of their generation who were often tempted to satisfy their frustrated need for leadership and certainty by surrendering to the doctrines, which were as dogmatic as they were murderous, of Mao, Ho Chi Min and Fidel Castro. In defiance of all the empirical evidence, those self-declared revolutionaries remained blind to the fact that the working classes had a great deal more to lose than their chains.

Farewell to meritocracy

Nowadays the 'Sixties' often find themselves in the dock. The anti-authoritarian youth of those years supposedly paved the way for the ill-mannered citizens of today who refuse to accept any form of authority whether it is that of the

Living Theatre
© Herman Selleslags

scientist or the politician, the doctor or the teacher, the social worker or the police. They already know it all and brag noisily about it to the world. Politicians in particular have a tendency to hang on every word of the presumed popular will, which is constantly being enflamed by an alarmist media. They are finding it increasingly difficult to decide whether this manipulated 'will of the people' is also an expression of their own 'popular' convictions or merely useful to their political strategy.

Anyway, we are faced here with a vicious circle. Cowardly and blind conformity on the part of politicians strengthens the irrational, narrow-minded and often xenophobic reactions of the masses to the deep crises of the early twenty-first century – and vice-versa. Ironically, the force by which the popular will becomes the uninhibited and unhindered master of the lines of communication is rarely seen as 're-infantilisation of the masses' which leads to a desire for an omnipotent leader, as Freud analysed so penetratingly in his later writings after fleeing to London from the Nazis. On the contrary, it is described rather as a demonstration of maturity and emancipation, the origins of which should be looked for in of all places the protest culture of the 1960s.

But that is fundamentally wrong. That kind of maturity is an affront to maturity in the Kantian sense of courageously relying on one's own power of reason. The avant-garde of that culture of protest – Provos and artists, students and intellectuals – were distinguished by a highly developed sensitivity to any form of illegitimate authority. They knocked every authority off its pedestal which they regarded as a living, at times grotesque, proof that it was only there thanks to the dubious privilege of birth or tradition, and not on the basis of indisputable and continuous excellence in parliament or the lecture theatre. Meritocracy, an early bourgeois, primarily Dutch, principle directed against the arbitrary powers of church and nobility, had long been showing signs of wear. The economic and demographic developments of the 1960s laid this bare for all to see.

This is not the place to explore in detail the complex contradictions and relationships between the diverse anti-authoritarian subcultures of the past and the much more homogeneous commercial mass culture of the present. However, it is fairly safe to conclude that the latter is exercising an unprecedented degree of coercion and conformity on all sectors of society. Where that influence is weaker, the voice of the people, echoing through the mass media, can give the impression of genuinely having a say. At the same time, it illustrates more clearly than anything else how far the meritocratic principle, which Europe has so much to be grateful for, has fallen into decay. It is not talent, apart from a talent for self-promotion, but a combination of networking and luck which decides a person's success and status. Nietzsche's fear that with the death of God all vertical tension would disappear from society, removing the desire for self-improvement, has proved completely justified.

The limits to growth

It is dangerous to speak of *the* protest culture of the 1960s, considering how diverse groups were in their methods, motives and direction. Nevertheless, there is a discernible common thread, whether it involves anti-authoritarian poets, students, conservationists, antimilitarists, feminists or urban dwellers.

In all cases, they were reacting to socio-economic developments which in a short space of time had changed the whole face of the Low Countries and the developed world in general.

In the early decades after the Second World War, Western Europe enjoyed unprecedented economic growth of around 5% per annum. It was accompanied by an equally unprecedented growth in prosperity: a car, TV, contraception, washing machine, fridge, holidays, cameras (still and movie). All these luxuries were now within everybody's reach and the challenge was to outdo the neighbours. Furthermore, the post-war population explosion led to a stampede to set up educational establishments, especially from the middle classes. The welfare state was built up, churches emptied, and the class struggle continued only in the dreams of stubborn students.

But that is only the success side of the story. Consumerism and economic modernisation went hand in hand with large-scale reorganisation which brought demolition, dislocation, deforestation and social coercion. Consolidation of landholdings, increasing mobility, urban expansion and shopping centres changed the urban and rural landscape – drawing protests from students, women's organisations, urban residents and farmers.

It is not surprising that the Netherlands, Amsterdam in particular, became the centre for protest and progressive reform, and also for peaceful cooperation and toleration. The seafaring Hollanders have an anti-authoritarian streak in their blood. On their voyages to unknown and hostile regions, often lasting several years, they had to fall back on their own courage and resourcefulness. There was little need to stand on ceremony let alone indulge in the lengthy rituals of courtly manners (which Norbert Elias rather one-sidedly interpreted as the origin of Europe's culture of modesty and etiquette). Later anti-authoritarian movements could therefore, even if not always consciously, draw on a centuries-old tradition which reached back to the illustrious maritime past of the Dutch Republic in its revolt against corrupt Catholicism and the feudal Spaniards. And it surely goes without saying that the bluntness of the Dutch which foreigners often find so off-putting can to some extent be attributed to their ruthless brutality during the colonising years of the Dutch East India Company (VOC)?

At the time, protest culture became identified with its most spectacular forms: in the Netherlands, these were in particular the Provos and the musical underground. But there was also social experimentation and the 'liberation' of sexuality, the euphoria of democratisation and solidarity, the student protests and their sit-ins, the anti-imperialist and disarmament demonstrations, and in particular the violent and criminal offshoots in Germany and Italy.

But viewed from a later perspective, when it is more difficult for media coverage to be exciting, inflammatory or shocking to bourgeois sensibilities, the most important effect of the 1960s by far was the emergence across the globe of environmental awareness. The importance of the Club of Rome which was set up in 1968 and its report in 1972, *The Limits to Growth*, in which for the first time a plausible link was established between economic growth and its disastrous effects on the environment, cannot be overestimated. Its clear message, despite later criticisms, was that planet Earth does not have infinite resources and requires sensible management, which will have inescapable consequences for our whole way of living.

That message was formulated most concisely in the Netherlands by Prime Minister Joop den Uyl in 1973, the year of the oil crisis and the year in which the sharp and still ongoing decline of the Western economies began. 'Seen in that light, the world of before the oil crisis will never return.' That had been foreseen much earlier by Provo which was discontinued in 1967 for fear of paralysis in becoming too institutionalised. Roel van Duijn (a founder of the Provo movement) and his fellow activists directed their energies in theory and practice against 'the consumer society' with all its 'addictions', no matter how much the *plebs* might delight in them as luxuries. The most spectacular in this respect was the absurdist street theatre – at the time, referred to as 'happenings' – of the anti-smoking magician Robert Jasper Grootveld on the Spui in Amsterdam. After the fiasco of communism, which had signally failed to achieve its original goal of a life freed from the domination of alienated labour but on the contrary had everywhere become bogged down in bloody dictator-

Sit-in on the Old Market in Louvain: students fighting for a
'Flemish' (i.e. Dutch-speaking) University but also for left-wing ideals, 1968
© KULeuven, Universiteitsarchief

ship, Van Duijn argued, as had the non-violent and pragmatic Peter Kropotkin before him, for the small-scale, for horizontal networks of cooperation, for a sober life style which respected nature, and a morality that would also include the lives of animals.

New forms of authority

It is one of the ironic quirks of history that some of the core concepts of the anti-authoritarian movements of the 1960s should re-emerge unchanged a couple of decades later, though pointing in the opposite direction, in the publicity and command centres of deterritorialised, supranational concerns. The artistic *avant-garde* of the time directed its repertoire of critical concepts – flexibility, mobility, without limits, without identity – against relationships in which people seemed to be permanently defined by the circumstances in which they had first entered the world. Their goal was liberation from the rigidity of indefensible conventions and hierarchies, and a vision of new unknown worlds. But they also described unwittingly and with great clarity a postmodern world in the making which had broken free from its historical social and cultural ties and its traditional sources of meaning and motivation, with fatal consequences.

This receives its clearest statement in the grandiose and visionary 'unitary urbanism' that the visual artist Constant Nieuwenhuis developed in *New Babylon* (1956-1974). In numerous sketches, drawings, watercolours, graphics, texts, films and particularly architectural models, Constant's by definition unfinished project provides a tangible picture, not of buildings, houses, dwellings, which have become outdated in his futuristic world of the contented unemployed, but of permanently changing neighbourhoods, of an artist's colony that spreads in all directions, in which people drift constantly without ties or obligations. Life is completely decentralised and dematerialised; just as in Ball's Cabaret Voltaire, deeds have neither cause nor consequence. There is an obvious relationship with Guy Debord's *Situationist International* and the later anti-oedipal, rhizomatic philosophy of Deleuze and Guattari, which became so popular in arts faculties. There too we can see, broadly speaking, the hyper-romanticism of a permanent revolution of nomads in mobile undefinable spaces.

Meanwhile, the neoliberals' adopted concept of the immensely flexible human being has been as convincingly falsified in the psychiatrist's chair as in numerous philosophical works such as Richard Sennett's *Authority* (1980) and *The Corrosion of Character* (1998), Paul Verhaeghe's *Autoriteit* and the colossal *Sphären trilogy* (1998-2004) by Peter Sloterdijk. Architects, in their scarce free time, may still freely float around dreaming of a New Babylon but in their actual work they are experiencing more than ever the gravitational force of their employers' strict, profit-oriented programmes. There is no need for more flexibility, discontinuity and extravagance; there is, however, a need for non-paternalist forms of authority, based on a deep, confidence-inspiring knowledge of affairs and the power to delegate them to others.

The word authority comes from the Latin *auctoritas* which does not indicate power but moral force, dignity, reputation, influence. An authority is someone who in uncertain situations can offer certainty, protection and direction to all those who, because of their age, development or position, desire them. Its absence in childhood can create a painful lack of self-confidence, ego weakness, a gnawing dissatisfaction which can lead one later, like Maeterlinck's group of blind people, to search for a saviour. But we know that such a saviour embodies the authoritarian principle in its most shameless, irrational and repressive form. To prevent that, depending on circumstances, learning and work processes must be long-term and as horizontally structured as possible in order to encourage the full development of that authority which already resides within every human being. ■

Pupils of a Catholic college demonstrating for a 'Flemish' University, 1968
© Université catholique de Louvain, Service des Archives

Translated by Chris Emery

Revolt of the Students

1969 versus 2015

[CASPER THOMAS]

'The university has become a difficult element in our society. The students have risen up. They demand democratization of higher education and society. The antiquated university edifice is about to collapse. The rest of society looks on in fright. The Minister of Education takes action.' If you asked someone to pinpoint this quotation to an era, the answer would be more than likely 'the present one'. At universities all over the world a wave of protest has arisen, driven by students and lecturers united by a common agenda: against cuts in research and education, against a culture of management that has been copied from the business world and against their lack of influence on the future direction of their institutions.

Yet the quotation with which this article opens comes from an earlier period in history. Describing a turbulent academic world, the above statements are taken from *De lastige universiteit. Over democratisering en politisering van onderwijs en wetenschap* (The Difficult University. About Democratization and Politicization), published in 1970 by Universitaire Pers Rotterdam, and written by a pair of sociologists – Bram Peper, the later PvdA-politician and mayor of Rotterdam, and the academic Willem Wolters – to interpret 'current and controversial issues around the university' which had already 'for quite some time' been at 'the centre of attention'.

De lastige universiteit (The Difficult University) contains a wonderful portrait of the era. When it was published, the Netherlands was only just saying goodbye to the decade which the authors, even then, described as 'the Roaring Sixties'. In the opening chapter the young sociologists shower us with words that were fashionable at the time (today they would be turned into a word cloud): 'Participation, democratization, autonomy, teach-in, hearing, grassroots support, joint management, right of consultation, are probably the terms most often used during the second half of the 1960s', Wolters and Peper write. A decade that reacted against 'the Boring Fifties' when only the 'Rock-and-Roll explosion' livened things up a bit. Through books like this, the image of the 1960s, which due to a generation of articulate young people has come to be seen as a watershed in history, was immediately provided with a solid foundation.

I came across *De lastige universiteit* on my father's bookshelves, which, like so many personal libraries, reflected that the desire to buy something new was always stronger than the need to get rid of old stuff.

In the early 1970s, my father was active in Amsterdam student politics and was inspired by books such as this one, and others on his bookshelf like *Studentenprotest en universiteit* (Student Protest and the University) in which the Tilburg 'social ecology' professor R.A. De Moor asserted that the student protest of the 1960s was a symptom of the 'political alienation of the younger generation'. This discovery made it possible to compare the university revolt of the 1960s and '70s with the present one: it also served as a lesson that history to a certain extent will repeat itself.

In the name of the 99 percent

As for lessons learnt, a few months before I emptied my father's bookshelves, I had published a book myself: *Competente Rebellen. Hoe de universiteit in opstand kwam tegen het marktdenken* (Competent Rebels. How the University Revolted against the Ideology of the Market). In it, I reconstruct how for six weeks in the spring of 2015, the Maagdenhuis, the administrative centre of the University of Amsterdam was occupied by angry students. They were motivated by the precarious financial situation in which the university found itself. Because

Occupation of the Maagdenhuis, 1969 © Ed van der Elsken / Nederlands Fotomuseum

Occupiers of the Maagdenhuis, 2015

of real estate investments, the university was heavily in debt. At the same time there had to be cuts both in staff and in research funding, while whole degree programmes were threatened with closure for being 'uneconomic', according to the administration.

During the occupation, the Maagdenhuis became an open platform for a debate about the purpose of the university as institution and about how it could be won back from its administrators who, according to the demonstrators, were in the grip of 'efficiency thinking', that is, in terms of numbers, quantification, supply and demand, cost-benefit analysis. This market ideology, according to the demonstrators, was the wrong starting point for a public institution that is there for the acquiring of knowledge.

I wrote *Competente Rebellen* (Competent Rebels) in the conviction that the 2015 university protests were a symbol of a broader societal discussion. The collision at the University of Amsterdam fitted in with the ideological divide of our time regarding the foundations on which institutions are based, be it the health care, banking or university system. That was the most important reason to take the Maagdenhuis occupation seriously: the dissatisfaction with the market ideology in the public sector runs deep, but the debate about an alternative model was still in the beginning stage. At the Maagdenhuis, this discussion had begun in earnest. I suspected that the 2015 student protests could become a benchmark of a broader revolt against the market ideology of public institutions.

I saw the Maagdenhuis occupation as an expression of a new political phenomenon, that the world had already had a glimpse of with the Occupy movement which, in 2011, had occupied ('appropriated' as they preferred to call it themselves) squares all over the world in the name of 'the 99 percent'. Occupy started as a reaction to the 2008 financial crisis and demonstrated against 'supercapitalism'. Just like in Occupy, the heart of the Maagdenhuis occupation was the general assembly, a 'horizontal' meeting without leaders, that would only come to an end when there was complete agreement between all participants.

One source of inspiration for *Competente Rebellen* was Moisés Naim. This Venezuelan economist had already written the book *The End of Power* in which he describes the erosion of traditional power as a result of technological progress, increased mobility and changing opinions about politics. According to Naim, the way in which we make political decisions is changing, after staying the same for more than a hundred years. Social movements and NGOs are much more successful, he thinks, in bringing up issues and engaging the public.

The Maagdenhuis occupation is a perfect illustration of this theory. It knew how to put issues on the table, both in and outside the university. In their distaste of a financial economy, efficiency thinking and the desire to make everything quantifiable, the university protests are a mirror of a society in which at least some part of the population hopes to end a phase in the history of capitalism and to be able to start a new one.

First as tragedy, then as farce

When I wrote all this, in the summer of 2015 shortly after the riot police had put an end to the Maagdenhuis occupation, these insights seemed extremely relevant and topical. Then the doubt came: was this really all so very new? Restless students complaining about the debasement of the university and demanding more participation, isn't this a constant in academic history? In an article related to my book, *De Groene Amsterdammer*, the weekly I work for as an editor, printed photographs of the first 1969 Maagdenhuis occupation, underneath photos of the recent one. The old photographs were in black and white, the new ones in colour, but for the rest they appeared identical: groups of students, debating in a circle.

Permanent dissatisfaction at universities even turned out to be the subject of an academic study. Shortly after I finished my book, I came across *The Question of Morale: Managing Happiness and Unhappiness in University Life* by historian of ideas David Watson, who spent the last part of his career at Oxford. According to Watson, deep dissatisfaction is an ineradicable facet of university life. Showing dissatisfaction is, he thinks, a 'rhetorical instrument' that strengthens the solidarity between the students and puts pressure on management. And this instrument, Watson showed, has been used as long as universities exist.

Opening *De lastige universiteit*, which appeared nearly half a century ago, the penny dropped. Here too, a university revolt was presented as a symptom of discontent with the dominant societal logic. Where I wrote about market ideology, Peper and Wolters talked about the 'neo-capitalist system' that had penetrated every capillary of society and against which the universities were protesting. Their observation that business and the university become interwoven because 'next to capital, knowledge has also become an important production factor' could easily have been recorded during a meeting at the Maagdenhuis last year. Moisés Naim's theory, that power is challenged from below, is also

Occupation of the Maagdenhuis, 1969

Occupiers of the
Maagdenhuis, 2015

noted, in slightly different wording, in *De lastige universiteit*. Peper en Wolters described how the new student unions and action groups succeeded in firing up the debate about management culture in universities among the burgeoning student population. It made me think of Marx's pronouncement that history always repeats itself, first as tragedy and then as farce.

The similarity in how the student protests of the 1960s and the present ones are interpreted show how history can cling to people. Ideas and frameworks for getting a grip on the world around us are mostly ready to be let loose on unexpected events. And as long as they apply, there doesn't seem to be an urgent need to come up with a new vocabulary. The student protests of the last half century illustrate this. Apparently, the language about democratization and economic values versus academic values was just as applicable in 2015 as it was in 1969.

And as it is with thinking, so it is with acting. Everyone who has ever occupied the Maagdenhuis is in fact referring to their recent past. The angry students who broke open its heavy wooden door in 2015 were aware that they were treading in the path of earlier Maagdenhuis occupations, eleven in total since 1969. If the walls of the building on the Spui in Amsterdam could talk, they would tell of identical scenes: noisy students congregating in the main hall, turning the offices into bedrooms and covering the walls with banners.

Does the recent Maagdenhuis occupation, as a symbol of academic discontent for the present time, therefore inevitably stand in the shadow of the very first occupation, a symbol of the legendary 1960s when young people provided society with a new foundation? Perhaps for the moment. Although the 2015 Maagdenhuis occupation lasted a month and a half, compared to not even a week in 1969, so far no big changes can be discerned in the Dutch university system as a result of the protests. Despite almost everyone in the administration of the University of Amsterdam having by now stepped down after sustained pressure for the university to change course. Nor have politics and society suddenly distanced themselves from a market ideology.

A post-crisis generation

Still, comparing the 1960s' protests with those of the present is a bit of a stretch. One only has to look at the way the 1969 Maagdenhuis occupation made its way into the history books. For nearly six decades people have been referring to this event and it has become synonymous with every memory, cliché and analysis of the 1960s. In left-wing circles, the Maagdenhuis still symbolizes the moment when the Netherlands had it out with its 'regents'. The right is still of the opinion that the Maagdenhuis occupation marks the moment when the Netherlands capitulated to a generation of hedonistic pseudo-revolutionaries. It's like a screw that keeps getting turned and gets more and more stuck all the time. Every referral to the 1969 Maagdenhuis occupation in a debate or the media, every historian who mentions it, adds to the importance of this event. The recent past simply hasn't had enough time to become that stuck in the collective memory.

And although the student protests of the 1960s and the present ones are similar in form, rhetoric and symbolism, they definitely have a different context. Historian James Kennedy put it aptly in an interview in *De Groene Amsterdammer*. 'The demonstrations of the 1960s were in line with rising expectations: there was more money, students had more time, they had more freedom and they wanted to extend that freedom. Now the demonstrations are taking place amid lowering expectations: the present students and lecturers do not want to break open the university, they want a recovery, a restoration, they have the feeling that all the lights are going out and that some should be left on.'

Indeed, the present discontent among students is one of a generation that came to adulthood in the world after the 2008 economic crisis. The generation with the experience that more and more money had to be borrowed in order to study, since the underlying idea was that study was of specific benefit to the individual who therefore had to invest as well (and run the risk that the investment wouldn't pay off). The generation that enrolled at universities judged on economic performance rather than the degrees they offered in which they stimulated critical, independent thinking, with the result that the humanities in particular have become hard pressed.

Once we take this difference between the 1960s and the present into account, we get a totally different picture. In the 1960s, the Netherlands was a thriving welfare state with endless possibilities to climb the social ladder. The Maagdenhuis occupiers of that time were a product of it: mostly first generation students with social backgrounds to which the ivory tower had been closed for a long time. In 2015, it was a post-crisis generation that occupied the Maagdenhuis, the product of a society that had become uncertain after a severe economic crisis. In this light, there is now much more at stake than during the mythical 1960s.

One who dismisses the 2015 student protests in advance as an event of less societal importance than the one of the 1960s, also underestimates the fundamental uncertainty about how the past will be ordered in the future. Once sufficient time has passed, it is quite possible that an era of regularly occurring university protests will be drawn up, in which the 1960s are perhaps presented as a warm-up exercise and the 2010s as its climax.

A public sector playing the market

We must not forget that the myth around the 1960s has been mainly driven by the generation that was young itself in those days and that later, due to its social influence, had the opportunity to shape our view of the past. And now that this generation is slowly losing its grip on society, making way for younger generations, the interpretation of the past is also opening up. A lot as well depends on which societal changes will occur, either suddenly or gradually, of which we have as yet no clear picture and in how far the recent Maagdenhuis occupation will be the obvious choice as a symbol encapsulating those changes.

In this light, the recent student protests raise the question of how far the present is aided by the past or actually hampered by it. The answer, as usual, is both. Because the 2015 Maagdenhuis occupiers stepped into a framework that had already been shaped by the 1960s, there was little they had to explain. Everybody understood that an occupied Maagdenhuis was the equivalent of a demand for more participation. But at the same time there is the risk that we forget that this is a new group of students who have reinterpreted the role of demonstrator for the present. In any case, the academic discontent, that boiled over in the 2015 Maagdenhuis occupation, has enough points in common with a societal undercurrent that is important *now*. These protests occurred at a moment when not only at universities, but also in health care and education as a whole, aversion to the market ideology is growing.

This administrative logic, that became dominant in the 1980s and 1990s, is based on quantification, numbers, costs and profits. It was supposed to be an answer to the cumbersome, expensive and bureaucratic public service in governmental hands. Meanwhile, the conviction is growing that this has not led to less bureaucracy, less intricate procedures or fewer rules in the public service. Let alone that it would be cheaper. Many hospitals, schools and universities struggle with debts and spend a big part of their budget on secondary activities like management, real estate dealings and communication. The central task (in the case of universities: doing research and providing education) is losing out this way. If in the coming years the public sector gradually distances itself from playing the market and behaving like a business, the 2015 Maagdenhuis occupation will be eligible, for the Netherlands at least, as the event that marks the turning point. ∎

Translated by Pleuke Boyce

Surviving Changing Times

The Singer-Songwriter Boudewijn de Groot

[WIM CHIELENS]

I was very surprised when for the purpose of this article I revisited Boudewijn de Groot's discography. The man is an institution in the Dutch-language musical genre and anyone in Flanders or the Netherlands who has a small record collection always has something of his on their shelves. He made twelve albums. Just one dozen, less than 150 songs and yet you have the feeling Boudewijn de Groot wrote at least 50 classics! When he turned seventy in 2014, he said farewell to his old repertoire. He would never sing it on stage again. For his faithful public this was something of a shock. Meanwhile De Groot has a new album out and hence again a repertoire to perform. The fans secretly hope that the classics will sneak their way back in, even if it is only as a third encore. And they don't get too worked up about it, Boudewijn has already bid farewell to, even renounced his old repertoire at least twice before. Everything comes back, because that's what he likes singing about most, about what is past and how it, whether you want or not, shapes the present or even obstructs it.

A child of sixteen

In 98 percent of cases, anyone talking about the classics of Boudewijn de Groot is talking about songs for which his fellow student at film school and contemporary Lennaert Nijgh wrote the lyrics. The first of them date from 1963, the latest are on his eleventh album *Lage Landen* (Low Countries) from 2007. It all began with an 8 mm film that Lennaert Nijgh made in which his friend Boudewijn de Groot played the part of a troubadour. He sang two songs, written by himself. Nothing happened with the songs, but it did put them in contact with a record company that made singles. They were touching protest songs that pleaded for free love and gently kicked the shins of the conservative bourgeoisie. The singer accompanied himself on a classical guitar. The singles flopped, and the EP that collected all four numbers on one disc also bombed. Just as Phonogram was about to give up the duo, producer Tony Vos suggested recording a commercial song. The choice fell on a translation (by Nijgh) of 'Une enfant' by Charles Aznavour.

Boudewijn de Groot on the left and Liesbeth List on the right

© Herman Selleslags

Protest singer

The single became a modest hit and with the LP that followed, Boudewijn de Groot was immediately labelled a Dutch protest singer. 'Een kind van zestien' (A Child of Sixteen) was the only song from French, the rest were translations of songs by Paul Simon, The Kinks, Bob Dylan ('The Times They Are A-Changin'') and two by Donovan. But there were also songs of their own, completely in the style of the covered artists. 'Welterusten, Mijnheer De President' (Good Night, Mr President) was the song that put Nijgh and De Groot on the map as a duo. Nijgh wrote it at the request of De Groot who wanted to do *something* with the Vietnam War. It came out in 1965, long before the great European protests against American actions in Vietnam. The song is an open letter to President Lyndon B. Johnson:

Mr President, good night to you and yours
Sleep tight in your nice white home.
Don't think too much about those distant shores
where your boys are sitting lonely, far from home.
Especially don't think of those forty-six dead,
That recent mistake with that bombing raid.

No more protesting

All through his life, Boudewijn de Groot will be unable to deal with turns in his artistic career that seem imposed upon him. Whenever he feels the slightest pressure from his public, he will do precisely the opposite to what is expected of him. For example, in 1966 he already wanted to be rid of the label protest singer. On their second LP *Voor de overlevenden* (For the Survivors) there was not one song that suggested any social commitment. Cover versions were a thing of the past and lyricist Nijgh displays the full range of his classic themes: unattainable loves, heartache, friends, the past won't come back. In a rather cryptic way, they also literally take their leave of the protest song:

> They've said new times are on their way,
> they've fought for a new morality then.
> They've not heeded what others had to say,
> I don't feel like doing it over again.

'New times are on their way' refers here to Nijgh's translation of Dylan's 'The Times They Are A-Changin''. Indeed, doing things over again is not something for Boudewijn de Groot and Lennaert Nijgh (Bo and To as they called each other). *Voor de overlevenden* (For the Survivors) became a classic album in the Low Countries. With the carnivalesque 'Het Land van Maas en Waal', he scored his first number one and the whole LP went gold. Of the twelve songs on *Voor de overlevenden*, perhaps seven have become part of the canon of Dutch song. Although Lennaert Nijgh was only twenty, he was already writing songs where nostalgia had the upper hand.

Album cover, *Voor de overlevenden*, 1966

Album cover, *Picknick*, 1967

Musically and socially, Boudewijn de Groot was a sponge who absorbed every-thing he heard and never imitated it but did his own thing with it. After *Voor de overlevenden* the duo already wanted to bring out a new record the following year. It is 1967 and in Amsterdam flower power breaks out with full force. De Groot has caught the bug for psychedelic music and he produces the Dutch an-swer to the Beatles' concept album, *Sergeant Pepper's Lonely Hearts Club Band*. The Beatles organised a kind of musical circus, so Bo and To would organise a picnic, because in flower power everyone wanted to be connected with nature.

> *We're giving a picnic,*
> *for the elves and fairies here,*
> *for the cattle and the deer,*
> *for the livestock and everyone*
> *must be nice, pluck a flower.*

The sleeve alone is a sample of flower power art in colour, typography and themes, of which few better examples can be found internationally. Not sur-prising, since it was designed by Seemon & Marijke (the Dutch artistic duo Si-mon Posthuma and Marijke Koger), who had previously worked for Procol Har-um, the Incredible String Band and sure enough, the Beatles! In some songs, the reference to *Sergeant Pepper* is very clear: an Indian sitar can be heard; the second number is bathed in a jazzy Charleston atmosphere, like the Beatles' second number 'When I'm Sixty-Four'; and just like 'Day in the Life', 'Prikke-been' concludes the LP with a piano chord lasting for a number of seconds. The psychedelic world of lyricist Lennaert Nijgh acquires a special Dutch variant, by linking the fantasy images of a drugs trip with the mythical scenes from the paintings of Hieronymus Bosch. In *Voor de overlevenden* (For the Survivors), the Hieronymus Bosch Circus had already put in the occasional appearance, now his best-known triptych, *The Garden of Earthly Delights* became a song title, 'De tuin der lusten'. Nijgh wrote texts like hallucinatory trips. De Groot himself only half-understood what he was singing, but it worked perfectly.

> *Yellow's the colour of remembered wheat*
> *here in the steppes of molten glass,*
> *blue is the fruit that's hard to eat,*
> *the slivers taste sharp and bitter sweet.*

- from 'Glazen stilte' (Glass Silence)

Picknick (Picnic) became another classic album, the single 'Prikkebeen' be-came a hit and the duo was awarded an Edison (a prestigious Dutch music prize) for the album. And he could scarcely keep up with requests for per-formances. The sky seemed to be the limit and then ... you can be sure that Boudewijn de Groot was looking for a back way out.

Album cover , *Apocalyps*, 1970

English beat music

Nacht & Ontij (At All Hours) became an experimental record, a kind of *film for the ears* as Boudewijn calls it. He wrote the lyrics himself and there were only four numbers, including 'Heksensabbath' (Witches' Sabbath), which lasted over twenty-five minutes. The fans hated it, but perhaps they didn't mind that much. They could make do for quite a while with the golden songs from the previous records.

With the Provo movement Amsterdam has become, after Paris, *the* hippy city in Western Europe, and De Groot is now completely on a higher plane. He leaves his wife and children and heads to a commune in the countryside with friends, where he wants to make English beat music. The Tower and Session are two groups with which he tries to work in English, but it is a flop. The music is pedestrian, and Boudewijn's English is rather poor. In the commune, everyone seems to be living at the expense of the *troubadour who had done well for himself*. In 1970, disillusioned, he seeks out his old companion Lennaert Nijgh. In the first instance, they write a whole series of songs for the Dutch singer Rob De Nijs, who was never able to choose between rocker, crooner, chansonnier or pop singer. These became his most chanson-orientated albums, with huge hits all of which flowed from the pen of the brilliant duo Bo and To.

Back again

Gradually the desire grew once more to make an album of their own. The opening song could not have been more frank: 'Terug van weggeweest' (Back Again). The public takes note with great relief: Boudewijn de Groot is back again and he's singing songs like he used to. Lennaert Nijgh is able to put exactly into words what both Boudewijn and his fans sense:

> But on New Year's Eve
> The scythe of the critics awaits.
> And I'm ashamed of myself,
> I destroy my music.
> I was on the wrong track again,
> again I dared too much.
> Again I offered nothing
> and asked for far too much.
> And I forget,
> I forget what went before.

'Hoe sterk is de eenzame fietser' (How Strong the Solitary Cyclist Is) was a warmly welcomed comeback. 'Jimmy', the single from which the album title is also taken, again became a top-10 hit, the album went platinum and won them a second Edison. There is plenty of hit material and merriment on the record, but there is also plenty of room for the melancholy De Groot: the songs 'which are closest to my character and my basic mood,' he himself writes reflecting on the disc. The Christmassy song 'Onderweg' (En Route) is the prototype of these and the translations of two child's verses by William Blake are in the same vein. The record ends as it opens:

> Get bottles from the cellar,
> let music fill the rooms.
> Let everybody hear it:
> the traveller is home.

That was what the whole of the Netherlands and Flanders felt. They also wanted to hear him play live again and if at all possible with the songs from the classic albums. But in that you are barking up the wrong tree with Mr De Groot...

Album cover, *Hoe sterk is de eenzame fietser*, 1973

Déjeuner sur l'herbe with the singer, his wife and child and Lennaert Nijgh in the background.

Chilly reception

Lennaert Nijgh was again thanked for services rendered and Boudewijn struck up a partnership with another friend of his youth from the same film school where he and Nijgh had studied. Renee Daalder wanted a record that represented a definitive break with the past. The record must finish with 'the old Bo' and the new one must reveal all. The title spoke volumes: *Waar ik woon en wie ik ben* (Where I Live and Who I Am). In 'Travestie' a girl becomes the personification of 'the old Bo' and he rapes her until she has forgotten everything. An amateurish girl's voice also sings literally snatches of his best-known songs from the past, but he is merciless:

> *You're singing old stuff there at least.*
> *You are Beauty, I'm the beast.*
> *I undress you.*
>
> *(...)*
> *My self-delight's seduced you quite*
> *and your singing's worthless to me.*
> *I want you now, here on the mat,*
> *won't stop till you forget where it's at.*

Thousands of fans in the Low Countries felt offended by the song, for didn't everyone occasionally sing or hum a song by their favourite singer in an unguarded moment?

The record sounds very empty, even the luscious colour palette of Bert Paige was to no avail. The recordings are made in a studio in the Netherlands, but mixed in Hollywood. The technician there scratches his head about the poor quality of the recordings. The result is that the singer has to re-record all the vocals and guitar parts. The reception of the record was as chilly as its sound. Then five years of radio silence. The following album has many faces and many different lyricists. *Van een afstand* (From a Distance) it is called and Lennaert Nijgh seems to understand what it is about:

> Hey listen to what I say.
> It has gone, I've gone away.
> You can no longer take it or leave it.
> No, it's just too late for you.
> Turn around and go quick too.

Boudewijn leaves behind his three children and current girlfriend in the Netherlands and goes to America, where he plans to attend a course on song writing. The record *Maalstroom* (Maelstrom) is created there. He writes almost all the lyrics, but still asks Nijgh for one song text. Nijgh knows exactly what is going on in the doubting head of his pal Bo.

> I worry about everything,
> is what I'm doing
> good, let me know.
> Are times changing yet again
> and then where am I to go?

> High above there goes a plane
> towards the sea below.
> To LA, or even Rio.
> Should I stay, or should I go?

'Are times changing yet again?' is not a coincidental question, it refers to one of the pair's first collaborations: the translation of Dylan's 'The Times They Are A-Changin''. The record is completely ignored by the public and on the radio. It is 1984 and it seems Boudewijn de Groot may forever be associated with a few improbably powerful songs from the 1960s...

A new autumn

The silence lasts a long time. In showers and round campfires, Boudewijn's songs are still occasionally sung, but the artist has been forgotten. Boudewijn earns his living doing translations. For example, for a while he becomes the regular Dutch translator of the thrillers of Stephen King. Eight years after *Maalstroom* (Maelstrom), twelve years after his departure, he again winds up, this time literally, on Lennaert Nijgh's doorstep. The American adventure is over and he's looking for a roof over his head and perhaps... also a lyricist, because he has an appetite for music again. Without Boudewijn, Lennaert has forgotten how to write. It takes forever. But in 1996, eleven years after the previous one, a new album appears: *Een nieuwe herfst* (A New Autumn). The title paraphrases the opening of a famous Dutch poem, 'Een nieuwe lente' (A New Spring). The long hair of the *hippie singer* has meanwhile gone grey and after such a long time both the press and the public are suspicious. Perhaps this is just old wine in new bottles. But no, after a few hearings it was clear that the partnership between De Groot and Nijgh, thirty years after 'The Times They Are A-Changin'', is still a magical synergy. Yes, they were still talking about lost and impossible loves, about friends, about the past and what has been won't come back. But both lyrics and music had gained a maturity which deeply moved a public that had grown old with him. For Lennaert the return of Boudewijn had something sacred about it, on this the last song is absolutely clear:

> Tell the whole of town
> and shout in every ear:
> the deaf will start to see,
> the blind begin to hear.
>
> Take the masks off now,
> let all your tears now pour.
> The rain's passed over now,
> the angel's at the door.

Lennaert will not live to see *Een nieuwe herfst* (A New Autumn) also become a classic album. He dies in 2002, leaving Boudewijn orphaned...

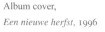

Album cover,
Een nieuwe herfst, 1996

'Orphaned' is a more substantial choice of words than one may suspect at first sight. But it is of course true: Lennaert Nijgh is the father (or mother?) of the successful career that Boudewijn de Groot had in the Low Countries up to then. And as befits an artist, Boudewijn had a few attempts at patricide, but the facts remain the same. He brought out two further CDs with clever numbers, partly to posthumous texts by Nijgh; a man of his status also has the occasional nice text passed in his direction. 'De Vondeling van Ameland' (The Foundling of Ameland), for example, with lyrics by Freek de Jonge was again played endlessly on the radio in the Netherlands and Flanders. But Boudewijn realises that he must stand up and be counted and how difficult that is, with the legacy of the duo Nijgh/De Groot.

> *Now you can no longer write*
> *I've got to write myself:*
> *new times are on the way*
> *I know nothing else.*
> *(...)*

> *Writing a thousand ditties*
> *I do it painlessly*
> *but a thousand lovely words*
> *how wise must you be.*

He tries almost convulsively to write a song, but gets no further than quotes from Lennaert's songs, since as you know by now: 'new times are on the way', was his translation of Dylan's 'The Times They Are A-Changin''.

> *Now you can write no more*
> *I've got to try myself:*
> *now you can write no more*
> *my god... this is a song.*

Movingly honest.

Boudewijn starts touring again and sings mostly his old repertoire. 'I shall always hold it dear,' he writes in an unguarded moment as a reflective comment on the tabula rasa of the LP *Waar ik woon en wie ik ben* (Where I Live and Who I Am).

And then, suddenly, that definitive farewell, on his seventieth birthday. The final end? Not at all. Just as Dylan, five years after the fairly weak disc *Love and Theft*, surprised everybody in 2006 as a reborn mischievous, swinging daddy with *Modern Times*, in 2015 Boudewijn de Groot's *Achter glas* (Behind Glass) was suddenly in shop windows. Except for two collaborative pieces and one Lennaert Nijgh quote, what else would one expect, all the texts are by Boudewijn himself. It is accordingly a very personal record in which for the first time he sings about some biographical passages of his life. About his father, for example, who left him along with his brother and sister with (a kind of) aunt to set out again for the colony of the Dutch East Indies. He never found out how a father can do such a thing and later (when he returns to the Netherlands) never say a word about it. He never really knew who his father was and he sings about it in 'Anamorfose'.

> the picture jumps
> the voice distorts
> what's left is always the framework
> don't stand hidden
> in the shadow of time
> come closer
> don't hesitate come closer
>
> you were my father.

Much earlier, he had already written a moving song about his mother, who died in a Japanese concentration camp in the Dutch East Indies during the Second World War, when he was one year old: 'Moeder' (Mother). Now it is a tough text that makes a forceful entrance: 'Ik ben een zoon' (I am a Son).

> I am a son of western beaches under dark-grey skies
> Although the sand where I was born has reddish tints
> To this day I still feel those vague ties
> They form the beginning of what's happened since.
> It was the most vulnerable time of my mother's life
> There she had me amid the filthy drains
> And while those scarcely alive gratefully clung to life
> Into a pit the Jap tipped her remains.

De Groot, unlike many writers and other artists who were born in the Dutch East Indies, has never been back to Indonesia ('the country of origin'), precisely because the trail to his mother leads no further than to her name on a monument.

> All that they could put on it was her name
> I know her name – I might as well stay home.

A song about his father, a song about his mother and then everything comes together in the title song: 'Achter glas' (Behind Glass). Now his parents are dead, he sees them only behind the glass of a photo frame, but he also sees himself under glass, we can simply only see ourselves in the mirror or in a selfie behind a glass screen. The title of his 1975 LP is as it were given a question mark: Where do I live and who am I? *Achter glas* (Behind Glass) is a new chapter in the rich career of Boudewijn de Groot and there is nothing to suggest that we must wait another eight years before the next one. In the song 'Witte muur' (White Wall) he surveys, in quick tempo in a typically De Groot rhythm, his whole career. We see him *high on the barricades*, we hear snatches of texts by Lennaert and now he sees *how the clock moves to winter time*. But the end is reassuring: *I wait and know that what I want to write / will come in good time*. The singer has found his own voice. It still sounds as boyish as in 1964, but at last they are all his own words and they sound almost as fluent as those of his old companion. He just needs to wait a little and he will realise himself how faultlessly an evening song like 'Schemering' (Dusk) can move into that old winter song 'Onderweg' (En Route). In Boudewijn de Groot's career there is only one certainty: sooner or later 'times will change'. ▪

www.boudewijndegroot.nl

Translated by Paul Vincent

Album cover, *Achter glas*, 2015

The Price of Freedom

On the Sexual Revolution

'Everyone boozed and fucked / All Europe was one big mattress,' Remco Campert wrote of the post-war years, even if this flush of liberation remained restricted to a small, marginal group of artists and writers living from hand to mouth in distant Paris. The rest of Europe, poverty-stricken, was preoccupied with restoration, leading a traditional life under the umbrella of pre-war values and norms. Only in the course of the 1960s did the focus on the mattress, along with the associated drinking behaviour, take on outside bohemian circles, reaching full bloom in the 1970s. Two elements lay at the foundation of what is now known as 'the sexual revolution': money, or economic growth, and reliable contraception (the pill). Without those two conditions the mattress idea would not have had the remotest chance. That was far too dangerous for girls and women.

I myself (born in 1954) am at the tail end of the baby boom generation and have never experienced anything other than sexual freedom. When I went to university at seventeen and took a room in a student flat, total freedom prevailed. It was a newly mixed flat (having previously only housed men) with a single toilet, a urinal, a shower and a small kitchen for sixteen inhabitants. A couple lived in a room of three by three and a half metres, and the place was full of girls who did not live there but stayed the night with their boyfriends. Nothing in all this struck me as remarkable or inappropriate, although unmarried cohabitation and fooling around with friends certainly did not belong among the values I had been brought up with at home. I was mainly glad of my new-found independence and the freedom to come and go as I pleased without having to account for my movements. Sex was not on the cards for me in that first year of university, but when the moment came, there would be the freedom for it – there could be no misunderstanding about that.

It is sometimes said that the Paris student protest of May 1968 was really about the abolition of gender segregation in student accommodation, free access for the boys to the girls' rooms and vice versa. Of course students throughout the Western world were angry about authoritarian structures, demanding a say in all areas and a year later occupying the Maagdenhuis, the administrative centre of the University of Amsterdam. In America the protests arose from the civil rights movement and rage at the Vietnam War, but apart from that students also demanded the abolition of restrictive regulations relating to their accom-

Couple Making Love, Edam, 1970
© Ed van der Elsken / Nederlands Fotomuseum

modation. This was quickly and quietly granted, because how can you keep on forbidding sex to young adults who are allowed to drive cars, vote and be conscripted to perish on the other side of the world? With sensible use of contraceptives, no one needed to fear unwanted pregnancy anymore.

The free sex and relationship market

The availability of the pill to unmarried women (later even underage girls without the knowledge of their parents) meant control over one's own fertility and therefore constituted an enormous boost to the sexual liberation of women. Simply by taking a pill a day a woman could indulge in sex as men had been accustomed to: the pleasure without the pain. Not that that meant equal partnership in sex and relationships. Relationships between men and women were far from modernised. I saw that in my student flat, where the female half of that live-in couple stood stirring pans at the stove, after which they ate together in their room. The routine disgusted me – not so much the fact that the girl did the cooking as the clingy married couple act, which struck me as stiflingly tedious. Surely people did not leave home to lounge around on the sofa (or in their case a single bed) like their parents?

Feminism came a couple of years after the sexual revolution. It is no coincidence that the two liberation movements took place separately, unlike the civil rights movement for black people and the general resistance of youth towards authority. Besides an autonomous battle by women to wrest themselves free of patriarchal structure (discrimination in education and the job market) and for self-fulfilment, feminism was also a reaction to that previously joyfully embraced sexual revolution. The pill had emerged as a double-edged sword which might allow women the freedom to have sex whenever and with whomsoever they wanted, but at the same time made it more difficult to reject men. Fear of pregnancy, for centuries a tried and tested excuse with which to parry unwelcome advances, was suddenly no longer an argument for saying no to sex, neither in stable relationships, nor on the free sex and relationship market, where every young woman who followed modern trends was assumed to take the pill, if only as a precaution.

'Mad Mina' (Dolle Mina), first feminist movement in the Netherlands, showing their slogan 'Masters of our own belly' © Nationaal Archief

According to one story, apocryphal but probably not completely plucked out of thin air, the seed of feminism in the Netherlands was planted at the Maagdenhuis occupation, when the boys were all sitting around deliberating and speechifying while their girlfriends campaigning with them were sent downstairs to make coffee and sandwiches. Women did not get a look-in when it came to the content. Their function was the same as it always had been: in the kitchen and in bed.

From the beginning there were two schools of feminism: equality feminism, which was largely socially oriented and aimed for equal treatment of the sexes in all areas, and difference feminism, with the slogan 'the personal is political'. In equality feminism the biological differences between the sexes were played down; in difference feminism, which tended to present women as weak, potential victims or, by contrast, as morally superior beings, those differences were emphasised. Both schools sought to liberate women and, not surprisingly, sex became the big point of contention.

Hedonism?

The sexual revolution was first and foremost a time of hedonism. People rapidly threw off their social and religiously inspired shackles. Sex could perfectly well take place recreationally before and outside marriage, and ultimately without the need for a relationship. Space opened up for acceptance of homosexuality, group sex, sadomasochism and swinger clubs – there was even support for paedophilia in the 1970s. An ideological injection of the Marxist philosophy popular at the time led to experimentation with communes, which dispensed with all private property including exclusive relationships. Jealousy and territorial behaviour were seen in such circles as bourgeois tendencies which inhibited true freedom.

It was difference feminists who applied the brakes on unlimited free sex, observing that the sexes still tended towards different points of departure despite the apparent freedom. Hedonism is all well and good, but women were exploited through pornography and prostitution, ran the risk of abuse and rape within relationships as well as outside them, suffered sexual harassment, judgement based on their appearance and date rape, and when they said no they were not taken seriously or were dismissed as prudish. In short, women were sidelined not only as victims of a male-dominated society, but also in their personal lives. The sexual revolution primarily served excessive male desires, while women's wishes were ignored.

The two feminist schools of thought persist today. On the one hand you have the statistical figure fetishists of the equality standard who are preoccupied with the percentage of women on boards of directors, girls opting to study the exact sciences, women breaking through the glass ceiling, statistics on media attention for women writers, artists and presenters, and income by gender, showing unequal pay and the double burden on working women. On the other hand the personal victimisation of women by badly behaved men continues to provide fodder for criticism. Take, for example, the sexist way in which hateful male trolls insult women on social media or the repeated sex scandals used to ruin famous politicians and senior executives.

On the Beach, Zandvoort
© Ed van der Elsken /
Nederlands Fotomuseum

Looking back nostalgically on light-hearted sex

The sexual revolution burnt out long ago. Its demise began with the manifestation of the AIDS virus in the mid-1980s. Even if gay people and heroin addicts ran the greatest risk of the disease, carefree promiscuity in general was a thing of the past. The era of free sex, with no fear of unwanted pregnancy, when the worst-case scenario was contracting an STD, easily tackled by antibiotics, had only lasted fifteen years. Funnily enough, that period coincided precisely with my years as a student and single adult. On entering the sex and relationship market I encountered a ready-made bed of limitless possibilities. I enjoyed all the freedom of no-strings sex and complicated relationships, and when the AIDS alarm sounded, I entered marriage.

Perhaps for that reason I have retained a weakness for the 1960s (which, as everyone knows, only really got going in the '70s). It is currently the done thing to refer to the 1960s as something of a black page in human history, a wild mess, during which everyone egocentrically chased after their own desires with excesses such as child porn, but I primarily remember the light-heartedness with which one could approach sex. The feminist victim philosophy, on the other hand, made it a highly charged issue. Sex emerged as something to watch out for and handle with care, with trauma always lurking around the corner. The best example is the rules of conduct for sexual encounters between students, as they are proclaimed at many American universities, forbidding male students from attempting sex with drunk female students and stipulating that they must ask for explicit consent before every intended act, from kissing to touching to removing clothes. These codes are supposed to prevent rape.

In my day, such regulations would have been utterly inconceivable. That is not to say that I only have positive, comfortable experiences to look back on. Of course things went wrong due to the complicated entanglement of sex with relationships and rivalry, which led to endless difficult conversations. But things went wrong with sex itself too. Some people behaved like egotistical boors, leaving a sour taste. Sometimes I went to bed with someone out of politeness or pity, simply because he so wanted to, or I had sex with someone to take revenge on someone else. All the wrong motives, and certainly in retrospect the wrong kinds of encounters, but no reason to feel tainted or abused. Sex just was not that important. Occasionally I look back nostalgically on that light-heartedness with regard to sexual matters, because the current social discourse is certainly on the heavy side. Particularly when it comes to teenagers, there are regular eruptions of moral panic instigated by media reports on sexting, grooming by paedophiles, 'loverboys' or sex slavery. Very unpleasant excesses, to be sure, but the average kid has nothing to do with all that. They have other things to fear, the most important being divorce.

The real victims

For my generation of twenty-somethings the 1960s barely had harmful consequences, but the baby boomers were not the only ones affected. Adults all over the place joined in, in their thirties and forties, often with the entire family. They

Après-Ski, Switzerland, 1967

© Ed van der Elsken / Nederlands Fotomuseum

Kralingen Pop Festival, Rotterdam, 1970 © Ed van der Elsken / Nederlands Fotomuseum

Young Family, Volendam, ca. 1970
© Ed van der Elsken / Nederlands Fotomuseum

started open relationships outside their families, experimented with swingers' clubs, alternative family arrangements, anti-authoritarian upbringing and communes. A great deal more went wrong with all this than with autonomous free sex among young people. These were the first families torn apart on a wide scale by divorce. In 1971, the requirement for the so-called 'great lie' (regarding unfaithfulness) was dropped from divorce law and while birth rates dropped divorce rates rose. On the wings of feminism and with self-determination with regard to their own reproduction, a substantial number of women opted to do without men altogether and intentionally embraced unmarried single motherhood.

The real victims of the sexual revolution were the children confronted with the chaos of parents preoccupied with self-exploration, without devoting sufficient attention to their progeny, as heartrendingly revealed by two films. In Ang Lee's *Ice Storm* (2004), a group of married couples, friends and neighbours become embroiled in machinations with car keys in a bowl during a party. Picking a key determines who will go to bed with whom. The children have their own problems, and do not dare to bother their parents with them; their loneliness and emotional neglect is hard to watch, and the end is catastrophic. The other film, Thomas Vinterberg's *Collectivät* (2016) is even more gruelling, if that is possible. The mother of a fourteen-year-old girl persuades her husband to start up a commune in a large house they have inherited. Tired of just sitting at the table with her spouse, she wants more excitement in her life. Housemates are sought out here and there. The husband later falls in love with a student and brings her to live with them too. The woman cannot bear this and has a breakdown, in response to which the daughter tells her it would better if she went to live somewhere else, 'because she doesn't fit in with the group'. The child is so consumed by the commune's ideology that 'everything should be possible' that she betrays her own mother.

For my children's generation (in their twenties), in practice sex and relationships do not look so different from when I was their age, except that gay people now have a rather easier time. The parent-child relationship is more intimate, based less on authority and more on negotiation, and all the freedom for which young people previously left home can now be enjoyed under the parental roof. Parents and adolescent children get on much better and are much more involved with one another than in the days of the youth revolt, something which contributes, at least in my view, to making young people rather tamer than in the riotous 1970s. Experiments with free sex and polyamory are now marginal phenomena, more likely to be practised furtively by parents than by their children. In mainstream society the ideal of the nuclear family is back with a vengeance.

The big difference with half a century ago lies in self-determination as a collectively embraced value. Personal freedom and women's emancipation have become definitively fixed in culture. The transition from a hierarchically structured society, in which the interests of the group prevailed above those of the individual, to a society which stands for individual rights and freedoms is seen historically as an irrevocable revolution.

The result is divorce. Family life is always riddled with individual interests and when the conflicts between partners become too great, there is a way out. For children divorce is almost always a hard knock, because their sense of security is undermined. On an individual level it spells loss, grief and fear. On a social level it means weakened academic performance, more criminal behaviour, more psychological problems, plus a greater chance of divorce later in life for those who themselves come from broken homes.

Acquired rights

The institution of marriage as a lifelong bond, as a secure foundation for children to grow up in and as cement between two families, has sustained serious damage. Forty percent of marriages end in divorce, and as many as half of second marriages. Divorce forms an enormous social and psychological cost. Nevertheless almost everyone strives for a monogamous relationship within which to share their lives. It is the price of freedom. Everyone is free to enter into a profound bond with another according to their own insight and without interference from anyone else, even with someone of the same gender, and at the same time equally free to end that bond if it fails to live up to expectations. The freedom to move on was won in the 1960s and however much collective weeping and wailing there is about skyrocketing divorce rates, no individual is prepared to trade in personal freedom in this. ∎

Translated by Anna Asbury

From Ice-Block Action to Peanut-Butter Floor

Belgian and Dutch Pop Art since the 1960s

[MARC HOLTHOF]

During a sit-in at the end of June 1968, the 'Antwerp Free Action Group' (VAGA) demanded that the historic Conscience Square in the centre of Antwerp should be declared a traffic-free zone. The demonstrators had even brought traffic signs with them saying 'Car-Free Zone'. To prevent any further action, the police ordered car drivers to pass through the square. But by doing so they seriously underestimated the activists' creativity. A truck carrying blocks of ice destined for a restaurant drove onto the square. Under the supervision of the artists Hugo Heyrman and Panamarenko, the blocks were stacked on the road. They froze together and formed an insurmountable barrier against traffic. The police was powerless.

The success of the action was celebrated exuberantly on the square with festivities for all: white balloons were handed out and turf laid. But it was not until 1972 that Antwerp city council finally yielded to the demand to make the square car-free. Nowadays you can hardly imagine that this historic square was once dominated by cars.

The *Ice-Block Action* is a celebrated event of Antwerp's alternative scene. It was part of a whole series of 'happenings' and forms of action that were popular in the second half of the 1960s. It may have been a coincidence, but with it Panamarenko repeated – less aesthetically, but in a socially much more effective way – a 'happening' that Allan Kaprow, the American guru of the genre, had carried out a year previously: he built a melting artwork – a wall of blocks of ice – entitled *Fluids*.

Playboy

As his pseudonym Panamarenko suggests, Henri Van Herwegen (Antwerp, 1940) had always been fascinated by American culture. For an exhibition at the Wide White Space gallery in Antwerp two years previously, in 1966, he and his mate Hugo Heyrman (Zwijndrecht, 1942) took inspiration from an issue of *Playboy* magazine devoted to the 'James Bond girls'. Panamarenko made two life-size female figures in felt and expanded polystyrene. One of them, called *Feltra*, now in the collection of the S.M.A.K. in Ghent, is based on a glamour

Above
Panamarenko/Hugo Heyrman,
Ice-Block Action, Antwerp, 1968
© Ensembles MHKA

Left
Panamarenko, *Molly Peters*, 1966.
Collection Agnes & Frits Becht.
Photo by Ernst van Deursen
© SABAM Belgium 2017

photo of Margaret Nolan from the film *Goldfinger*. The second figure, called *Molly Peters*, portrayed a British actress who appeared in *Thunderball*. For the young Panamarenko, these pieces – indisputably pop art – were only a stage in his work, a stepping stone to his later career as the utopian inventor of flying, sailing, driving and diving machines. He explained, 'I felt like sanding down one of those ladies in Playboy with my own hands!'

Figuration/defiguration

On 10 July 1964, as chair of the 'Society for the Museum of Contemporary Art' in Ghent, Karel Geirlandt opened the exhibition 'Figuration / Defiguration – The Human Figure since Picasso'. In this exhibition, the work of such American pop artists as Andy Warhol, James Rosenquist, Robert Rauschenberg, and Roy Lichtenstein, and the Englishmen David Hockney and Allen Jones, could be seen in Belgium for the first time. Only one Belgian 'pop' artist was represented: Paul Van Hoeydonck.

In the catalogue of the exhibition, the leading Paris critic Pierre Restany attributed the success of this new and provocative art to the crisis and deterioration of the abstract art that had dominated the post-war art scene. The German painter Sigmar Polke even declared that this post-war abstract art was complicit in suppressing Germany's recent past. As a reaction against this 'conventionalised' abstract art, realistic and figurative trends arose which aimed to reconnect with everyday life or to intervene in it directly - as Panamarenko and Heyrman had done in their happenings.

Raoul De Keyser,
Tap and Hose, 1965
© SABAM Belgium 2017

The Dutch art world also discovered pop art. The 'American Pop Art' exhibition opened at the Stedelijk Museum in Amsterdam on 22 June 1964, and 'New Realists' one day later at the Gemeentemuseum in The Hague. 'American Pop Art' had previously been shown at the Moderna Museet in Stockholm. In addition to a large selection of work by Jim Dine and Claes Oldenburg, it also included pieces by George Segal, Andy Warhol, Roy Lichtenstein, James Rosenquist, and Tom Wesselmann.

The Gemeentemuseum in The Hague presented a much wider range, with three sorts of artists: traditional realists; artists of the 'Nouvelle Figuration', which included mainly French but also Dutch artists such as Woody van Amen, Hans van Eck, Jan Henderikse, and Wim T. Schippers; and lastly pop artists, including all the major Americans and Britons such as Richard Hamilton, R.B. Kitaj, David Hockney, and Allen Jones. Instead of a catalogue, there was a 44-page newspaper. In 1965, a modified version of this exhibition was mounted at the Palais des Beaux-Arts in Brussels under the title Pop Art, Nouveau Réalisme, etc.

The critics, more accustomed to the world of abstract art than the new art forms, were keen to ask rhetorical questions to point out the provocative nature of pop art. For example, in the introduction to his own exhibition, 'Figuration / Defiguration', Karel Geirlandt asked, 'Will this new fetishism have a longer lifespan than the Beatles?'[1] It's hard to imagine today but the Beatles were then seen as a fad that would soon pass!

There was also the ambiguous question 'does this belong in a museum?', which the otherwise enthusiastic critic of Het Vrije Volk raised with regard to the exhibition in The Hague.[2] And things became completely crazy when Wim T. Schippers – an artist who was himself very much influenced by pop art – wrote that 'there is little to be said about this meaningless art'.[3] It illustrates how hard it was for the advocates of pop art to persuade the conventional public opinion of the time that the genre was worthwhile. In the early 1960s, a clear difference between high art and low art still existed. Pop art was only the first skirmish in the struggle to demolish that ivory tower.

Moulage

The art historian Carl Jacobs based the catalogue for the 2015 Pop Art in Belgium! exhibition at the ING Art Center in Brussels on his PhD thesis.[4] He wrote that when he started his research he encountered a lot of incredulity: 'Pop in Belgium? What on earth could that be?', his colleagues wondered. Had there been any pop art in Belgium, and in what form? 'However, the story of pop art in Belgium turns out to be a more substantial chapter than one might at first think,' Jacobs wrote. And he brilliantly demonstrated that a series of well-known artists were profoundly influenced by pop art at the beginning of their careers before going their own way. The finest example is undoubtedly Marcel Broodthaers, an artist who is now associated more with conceptual art.

In 1963, the Sonnabend Gallery in Paris exhibited the white plaster casts of human figures in everyday poses made by the American pop artist George Segal. Several major Belgian collectors went to Paris and bought works, and the Belgian press hesitantly reported on the exhibition. For example, in the magazine *Beaux-Arts* there was a review by the poet and critic Marcel Broodthaers. And he too was equivocal. He wrote, 'Les personnages de Segal sont de vulgaires moulages d'êtres humains surpris dans un mouvement de la vie quotidienne... Ils ne sortent pas d'un atelier d'artiste, mais d'une fabrique.' And yet, having seen Segal's work in Paris, Broodthaers decided to start creating art himself: 'Il y a 18 mois j'ai vu à Paris une exposition de moulages, ceux de Segal: ce fut le point de départ, le choc qui m'entraîna à produire moi-même des œuvres.'[5] In early 1964, he submitted four works to the Prix de la Jeune Peinture Belge. And in April 1964 he opened his first solo exhibition at the Galerie Saint-Lambert in Brussels, with the provocative title, *Moi aussi je me suis demandé si je ne pouvais pas vendre quelque chose et réussir dans la vie....* (*I, too, wondered whether I could not sell something and succeed in life ...*).

Broodthaers's artistic career arose literally out of the shock of seeing pop art. He even claimed 'Je fais du Pop'[6] – and you might indeed call his 1966 *Grande casserole de moules* the Belgian equivalent of Warhol's 1962 *Campbell's Soup Cans*. But Broodthaers's oeuvre transcended the influence of pop art in order to create his very own poetic world in which what had so fascinated him in Segal's work – the cast, making moulds of reality – continued to play a leading part alongside the legacy of René Magritte and conceptual art.

The death of a pop star

In 2015, Tate Modern in London held the exhibition *The World Goes Pop*. This worldwide survey of pop art included work by just one Belgian artist. Not Marcel Broodthaers, not forerunners as Paul Van Hoeydonck, Vic Gentils or Pol Mara, but Evelyne Axell, who until a few years ago was as good as unknown.

Evelyne Axell was only thirty-seven when she died in a car accident in Zwijnaarde in 1972: she got out to take over the wheel from her drunken friend and was knocked down. She had been an actress for seven years and then an artist for another seven – partly thanks to her husband, the director Jean Antoine (who made several films about pop art, including *Dieu est-il Pop?* in 1964), and to René Magritte, from whom she received a few lessons. Axell's work was forgotten for thirty years after her death, but is now again the focus of great interest. She was one of the few women in the very male world of pop art. Nowadays, with her erotically charged works on perspex, she is the prime representative of Belgian pop art. And because of her untimely death she never had the opportunity to evolve away from it.

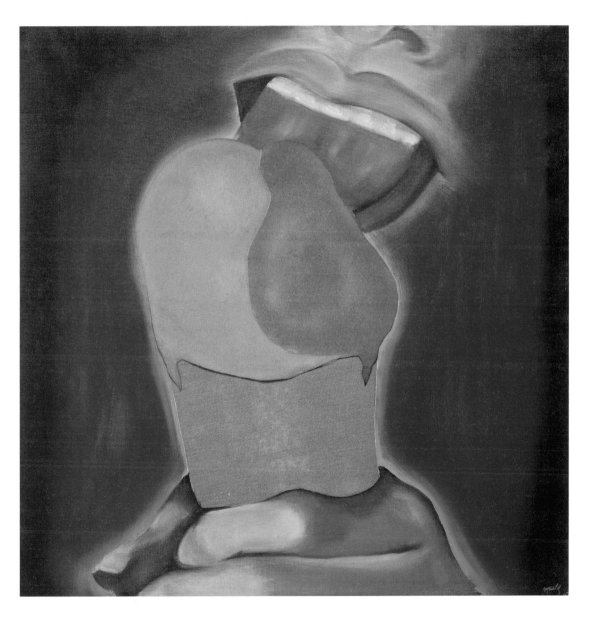

Evelyne Axell, *Ice Cream 2*, 1967. Private Collection. Photo by Paul Louis © SABAM Belgium 2017

Guillaume Bijl, *Giantess* (Festive Sculpture Series), Europaplein,
Amsterdam, 2014 © Guillaume Bijl

Confrontation with ordinariness

In a 1966 book on this phenomenon, the critic Geert Bekaert wrote that 'Pop art shows us the mythology of the ordinary'.[7] Pop art rediscovered the ordinary at the very same moment as the consumer society had gone into overdrive. That explains why the influence of pop art was not limited to the artists already mentioned.

However, in the careers of most Belgian and Dutch artists, pop art was no more than an episode, a stop along the way. This was the case for the Pan-amarenko-Heyrman duo and for Broodthaers. Carl Jacobs demonstrates that it was also true of Jef Geys and even of Roger Raveel and Raoul de Keyser, artists you would not normally associate with pop art. You find the same phenomenon in the Netherlands: Daan van Golden was very closely associated with pop art for a time, but then went his own way. Jan Cremer pursued his 'pop art made in Holland' (with lots of cows), but remained best known as the author of controversial bestsellers. The multifaceted oeuvre of Joep van Lieshout is also indebted to pop art, even though he turns the genre inside out and uses it against himself: in his work, the ordinary becomes strange.

The influence of pop art can still be felt in the younger generations. It would also be hard to imagine the work of Van Lieshout, Leo Copers, Wim Delvoye, Guillaume Bijl, Ria Pacquée, Hugo Roelandt or Anne-Mie Van Kerckhoven without the influence of pop art. They repeatedly use everyday images, objects and situations in their work. The happening, in many forms and guises, also crops up in quite a few of these artists' work. This is the case in Ria Pacquée's public performances as a 'madame' and Hugo Roelandt's 'post-performances' with toy cars, model helicopters and windscreen wipers.[8] The ordinary is again and again confronted with itself.

Wim Delvoye, *Wim Shop*, Bozar, 2010

© Wim Delvoye

It is also the main theme in the unclassifiable oeuvre of Wim T. Schippers, which ranges from Fluxus-like actions (emptying a bottle of lemonade into the sea), through notorious television programmes in deliberately bad taste (the shows including Fred Haché, Barend Servet and Sjef Van Oekel) to a play such as *Going to the Dogs* (performed by sheepdogs). Schippers 'could have been acknowledged as one of the most important artists of the second half of the twentieth century, but because he prefers to wander winding paths that seem to lead nowhere, his work still arouses irritation' – as the Boijmans Van Beuningen Museum warned in 2011 on the occasion of its controversial purchase of his 1962 work *Pindakaasvloer (Peanut-Butter Floor)*.

Yet what could be more ordinary – in the Netherlands – than peanut butter? Sjarel Ex, the director of the museum, called the 1,100 litres of topping spread over an area of 4 by 14 metres in one of the museum's rooms 'a brazen, unrivalled work'.

Wim T. Schippers, *Peanut-Butter Platform*
© Museum Boijmans Van Beuningen, Rotterdam, 2011 (1962).

Translated by Gregory Ball

NOTES

1   Karel Geirlandt, introduction to the exhibition *Figuratie/Defiguratie*, catalogue, Ghent, 1964, p.X.

2   Paul Van der Put, 'Nieuwe Realisten: Carnavalesk en gruwelijk tijdsbeeld', *Het Vrije Volk*, 27 June 1964.

3   Wim T. Schippers, 'Onvolwassen "kunst" in het Haagse gemeentemuseum', *Trouw*, 10 July 1964.

4   Carl Jacobs, 'Pop art in Belgium, een/un coup de foudre'. ING Art Center, Brussels, 15 October 2015 - 14 February 2016.

5   'Marcel Broodthaers par Marcel Broodthaers', *Beaux-Arts* 1086, 1965, p.5.

6   On the invite to the exhibition *Objets de / Voorwerpen van Broodthaers* at Galerie Aujourd'hui in Brussels, April 1965.

7   Geert Bekaert, 'Pop, het wezen van de kunst'. Leuven, Davidsfonds, 1966.

8   See Marc Holthof, 'Hugo Roelandt – Let's expand the sky', Occasional Papers, 2016.

Church Bells Are Still Ringing. But the Minarets?

Secularisation in Flanders

[PATRICK LOOBUYCK]

During the past few decades, the framework of shared values and beliefs in Flemish society has changed fundamentally. People of my generation (I was born in 1974) or younger, can hardly imagine the extent to which social and personal life until the beginning of the 1970s was still steeped in religion. Virtually everybody was a church-going Catholic and non-believers had much to fight against. God was everywhere and the church enjoyed wide influence and power.

Parishes made up the social fabric. They created tightly knit communities and fostered the development of all kinds of social activity. Sunday was a special day with its own dress code and rituals. Sacraments were holy; priests were counsellors. Confession was therapeutically liberating for an all too pervasive sense of guilt.

The best students became priests or Jesuits. Flanders enthusiastically sent its sons and daughters out as missionaries. Catholic priests wore the cassock; nuns graced schools and all kinds of other institutions with their often ostentatious wimples. Preaching instilled respect and sometimes even fear in people, and bishops could give powerful political advice quite shamelessly. Flanders had long been a Catholic state and anyone who did not attend a Catholic school could forget about going to heaven. In any case, the secular state schools were intended for 'a different kind of public' from the Catholic schools.

Until the end of the 1960s, the contraceptive pill was not freely available. Those who did not want too many children therefore had to rely on periodic abstinence. Making love freely and for pleasure, abortion, euthanasia, and homosexuality were taboo subjects. God was omniscient, so swearing was prohibited – even in the toilet hung signs to remind you. Moreover, beyond blasphemy, swearing symbolised self-gratification and the harbouring of deviant or exciting thoughts.

Flemish society was marked by ideological fault lines and civil society was compartmentalised along these lines. The many organisations still with a 'C' (Christian) or a 'K' (Catholic) in their name bear witness to this 'pillarisation' of society. The press, nursing, social services, education, trades unions, workers' movements, the health service, development aid, youth movements, sports clubs and brass bands were all subjected to the logic of pillarisation. Daily life

Ida Claes (Sister Amata),
Sister of Love of Jesus and
Maria

was organised on the basis of vertical pluralism without horizontal connections. You were born, went to school, were professionally and socially active, were insured and syndicated, were nursed and died all within the same 'pillar'. Individuals and families were given a clear ideological label which determined their social and professional opportunities. There was scarcely any contact with other ideological groups. Those living in local authority housing would not be given social housing run by the church. Not only was there no contact, there was also a form of polarisation. Liberals and socialists were long regarded by the church as allies of Satan, while atheists saw the power of the church's institutions and organisations as the chief obstacle to any kind of freedom. It is in this context that, in the Netherlands as well as in Flanders, organisations such as the Humanistisch Verbond [Humanist Association] emerged in the mid-twentieth century. They fought for the interests and equal treatment of non-believers and on the basis of humanist values such as freedom of enquiry, freedom of opinion, the separation of church and state, and self-determination, they struggled to free all sections of society from the domination of clerical power.

Secularisation

The society described above no longer exists. Secularisation, the process by which God and his commandments cease to impact on society, has in a short space of time redrawn the ideological landscape. Participation in the church and religious involvement have diminished drastically; the doctrinal authority of the church, even among believers and churchgoers, has shrunk; belief in God and a life after death is declining and in general religion is playing a much more modest role at the personal and social level than ever before.

Church festivals like Christmas, Easter and Whitsun have become *Catho-lay* festivals: everybody has a holiday and visits family and friends, but do not ask them what is actually being celebrated or commemorated. The old cultural frame of reference is vanishing completely, and young people often no longer even appear to recognise icons of the Madonna and Child.

Since Flanders was previously almost uniformly Catholic, secularisation can be seen as a shrinking process for the Roman Catholic Church. The statistics for church attendance may not tell the whole story but they are nevertheless striking and revealing. The percentage of those who attend church regularly has dropped to under 5% and their average age is above sixty-five. Weekly, let alone daily, church activity, which until a few decades ago punctuated so many people's lives, is as good as dead. Church buildings now lie empty and are being sold and diverted to other uses.

Whereas in the late 1960s virtually all children were baptised, the figure has now dropped to about half. The percentage of church weddings has declined even more. In 1967, 92% of all marriages in Flanders were celebrated in church. In 2016, that number had dropped to under 25%. In consequence,

Emile Claus, *First Communion*, 1893

we can expect the number of infant baptisms in the near future to fall sharply. Parents who are not married in church are less likely to have their children baptised or receive religious education; all sociological and psychological research shows how important parents are for the continuation of a religious tradition. The number of people who do not participate at all in church activities or are involved with the church in any way will continue to rise. The end of secularisation is not yet in sight.

In addition, the numbers in holy and religious orders are reaching rock bottom. Monasteries and abbeys have been turned into old people's homes or are standing empty. The Catholic Church in Belgium is entitled to more than 7,000 priests, paid for by the state, yet fewer than half that number has been appointed. The priesthood is faced with extinction and these days seldom seen as a vocation. There is therefore not only a problem of an aging priesthood, but also the threat of an absolute shortage of staff. Priests are working increasingly long hours and are being given more and more functions and parishes. The parish structure has been reformed; seminaries have been regrouped; priests are being imported and lay parish assistants are being appointed. But this still does not solve the problem of how the Flemish church can survive without priests.

When asked, about half the Flemish population still identifies as Catholic or Christian. But seen in the light of actual church practice, most of these people are 'cultural Christians'. They find Christian values important, recognise the value of certain parts of the Christian tradition; opt for a Catholic school and may even allow their children to receive their first communion but for the rest, they have little or nothing to do with the church and its religious activities and beliefs. Increasingly, one hears the complaint from priests and 'genuine' believers that rituals are being eroded because people no longer participate from religious conviction and have almost no sense of the religious. For instance, people may still want to get married in church but only on condition that the priest promises not to talk too much about God.

Flanders or Rome?

Even those who have not turned their back on the church often find themselves at odds with it. The Second Vatican Council's (1962-65) more conciliatory approach has been undermined by the church's rigid approach towards sexuality (e.g. *Humanae Vitae* 1968; *Veritatis Splendor* 1993) and the position of women in the church. This means that even those who have stayed with the church (sometimes described as 'terrain Catholics') live out their faith as if there were no Pope in a kind of concealed schism. Certainly in the case of sexuality, few Flemish Catholics, priests, theologians or teachers of Catholicism now accept the official position. Even the faithful no longer attempt to defend the view that contraception and homosexual activity are intrinsically evil, that sexuality outside marriage is a sin and that divorce is forbidden. A good number of priests have a 'forbidden' partner, but bishops overlook this so long as it remains 'hidden'. And in response to the convening of an Extraordinary Synod on the Family in October 2014, Johan Bonny the Bishop of Antwerp wrote a memorable working paper that called for greater openness and far-reaching reform in the sphere of ethics.

Graduation at Sint-Barbacollege s.j., Ghent, 1964: the Jesuits are still wearing a soutane

Research carried out in 2013 and 2014 confirmed that practising and non-practising Catholics are steadily losing confidence in the church. Nearly four out of five Catholics in Flanders said that they were ashamed or disappointed in the Catholic Church; almost sixty percent were of the opinion that the church had become irrelevant as an institution; and seventeen percent were thinking of leaving the church. There could be a connection here to the scandals of child abuse, involving even a bishop, which have come to light in the past few years.

In liturgical matters too, the faithful do not always find inspiration in the traditional church rituals. In recent decades, there have been various initiatives in liturgical experiment and the creation of new Christian communities. While some communities flourish, others soon disappear, and the Catholic Church tends not to support or recognise them.

Young people in Flanders

The education system in Flanders is unusual. About 70% of pupils attend state-funded Catholic schools. As these schools are fully subsidised by the government, in principle, anyone is welcome to attend, though the study of Roman Catholicism is obligatory. The majority of pupils in these schools are not religious and do not attend church, but half of all Muslim children in Flanders also attend Catholic schools. The secular state schools, on the other hand, are obliged to offer classes in any recognised belief system if there is demand. In secondary education, half of all pupils follow a course in non-confessional ethics organised by the government-recognised Union of Humanistic Freethinkers (UVV). About a quarter of all pupils in secular state schools study Catholicism; a fifth study Islam. Through immigration and demographic developments, the percentage of Muslim pupils has increased considerably. But in spite of secularisation, the balance of numbers between the courses in Catholicism and in non-confessional ethics has remained fairly stable. Rituals which were previously linked almost automatically to Catholic religious education, however, are steadily losing their attraction. The practice of confirmation (usually at the age of twelve) has declined by 30% in the last ten years and over a third of children in Catholic education no longer receive their first communion.

Indeed, surveys among young people have shown that the fastest growing group has no allegiance to any particular set of beliefs. Secularisation has not led to an increase of membership of the humanistic freethinkers organisations among young people. On the contrary, that group is also in decline. Young people are thinking outside the box. A third of them claim to be ideologically indifferent and not to follow any traditional set of religious or non-religious beliefs. Less and less do they look for meaning and orientation in their lives in what we would traditionally think of as religion or ideology. That does not mean they are nihilists; rather that they find meaning socially, materially and individually without much ideological dependency.

Will God return?

Whether one welcomes it or not, what is certain is that the role of religion in Flemish society has never been so small, and that hardly anywhere outside Western Europe has religion been sidelined to such an extent. Nevertheless, religion has not disappeared. In particular, the presence of Islam (and to a lesser extent evangelical churches) has contributed to the fact that religion remains visible and religious diversity is a topic of social debate. About 6% of the population of Flanders is Muslim. In cities such as Brussels, Ghent and Antwerp this percentage is considerably higher and in certain schools and neighbourhoods there are large Muslim majorities. It is, of course, true that because of immigration there is more religious activity in Flanders than if there had been no immigration. But that does not mean that the process of secularisation is being reversed. On the contrary, it simply shows that elsewhere – where the immigrants come from – secularisation has not manifested itself in the same way as here. Furthermore, it is still unclear how the traditional beliefs and

Graduation at Sint-Barbacollege s.j., Ghent, 1965: the Jesuits are wearing trousers for the first time

practices of Islam will survive here. In reaction against the pressure of Western secularisation, some have chosen to emphasise religion as an identity marker. The relative success of Salafism is an example. There is however also another larger group which is being secularised. The first signs of 'de-mosqueing' and a more relaxed attitude to religious rules are already observable.

Neither is the greater interest shown by the media for religion and religious issues in Flanders an expression of de-secularisation. Television programmes about religion sometimes do quite well and there is a great deal of information and discussion of religion on the radio and in the press. But far from signifying a religious revival, the focus is on particular religious phenomena, preferably when they are extraordinary or shocking, or at least presented as such.

It sounds paradoxical but it is precisely because Flanders is so deeply secularised that the presence of religion is attracting greater interest and is the subject of debate. Secularisation makes the presence of religion not only more noticeable but also more problematic. A few decades ago, for example, the current debate about wearing clothing with religious significance in public (e.g. the hijab, crucifix or turban) would have been unthinkable. Religion was everywhere and until the mid-1960s, the sight of priests and nuns in their religious attire on the street or in schools was commonplace. Now it is conspicuous,

Courtyard of the boarding school The Holy Sepulchre, Bilzen, 1992
© Annie van Gemert

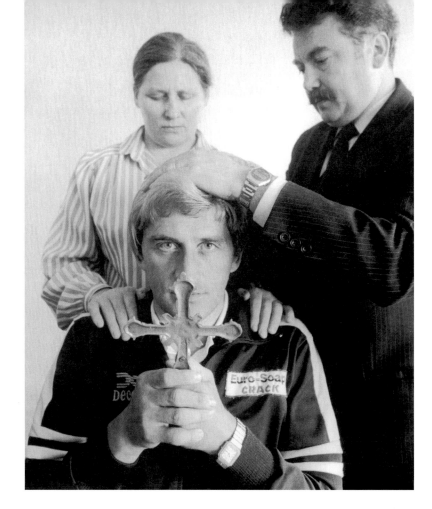

Translated by Chris Emery

sometimes even suspicious, when Muslim men grow their beards and women piously wear a headscarf. And whereas church bells may still be rung everywhere and at all times in Flanders, minarets (if they are allowed to exist at all) are enjoined not to make too much 'noise'.

So long as society was permeated by religion, the public expression of religiosity was hardly noticed, let alone the subject of public debate. Secularisation and religious diversity have changed all that. Just at a time when secularisation in Flanders has reached its peak and society hardly knows how to deal with domestic religious expression in public places, large numbers of immigrants have arrived with a strong and visible religious identity. Furthermore, their religiosity has had little experience of secularism and on some issues is fundamentally at odds with the assumptions of secular society. In that context it is therefore to be expected that Flanders should be debating the head scarf and religious dress, the preparation of kosher and halal food, the authority of sharia law, the interpretation of sacred texts, creationism, praying on the work floor, freedom of expression, homosexuality, animal slaughter without stunning, tensions between science and faith, freedom of religion, and equality between men and women. Religion is a subject of debate in spite of and because of secularisation – not because secularisation is in retreat. ■

A Feverish Decade

The Religious Heritage of the 1960s in the Netherlands

For a long time the Netherlands was one of the most Catholic countries in the world. That may well come as a surprise. If there is one religious denomination with which the Netherlands is invariably associated it is Calvinism. Art (from Rembrandt to Mondrian), literature (from Multatuli via Wolkers to Maarten 't Hart), morals (windows without curtains, allowing a full view of a sinless interior), business (diligence, thrift and a spirit of commerce), and sobriety, which needs no explanation: rightly or wrongly, everything is considered to breathe the spirit of Calvin's *Institutes of the Christian Religion* and the Authorized Version of the *Bible*. It seems it was only thanks to the latter that Dutch developed into a real cultural language in the first place. In the eyes of Europeans from further south, even Dutch Catholics think and behave like Calvinists in disguise.

Nonetheless, until the 1960s more than half of the Dutch population was Catholic. Admittedly, the majority of them lived in the southern provinces 'below the rivers', which had in the past long been governed by the central government like some sort of colony, where the inhabitants had little say. But further north, too, overwhelmingly Protestant areas had significant Catholic communities, from Rotterdam, which relied mainly on immigration from Catholic Brabant for its labourers, to the fishing village of Volendam, north of the capital, which always competed boldly with the very Protestant island of Marken opposite.

After the Protestants seized power in Amsterdam (the Alteration), in 1578, Catholic masses were officially banned, it is true, but the authorities turned a blind eye to the many conventicles. Only when the last impediments to the restoration of the Catholic hierarchy were removed, in the constitution of 1848, and the new constitution actually came into force, five years later, was it clear how strongly the Roman Catholic Church had withstood oppression. Although the last anti-papist articles were only removed from the constitution in the 1980s, the newly won freedom led, in the second half of the nineteenth and the first half of the twentieth century, to a Catholic triumphalism that got itself noticed in both urban and rural areas with large neo-Gothic people's churches.

This was the era of the 'rich Roman Catholic life', to which the weekly *De katholieke illustratie* bore witness in its column, *Uit het rijke Roomsche Leven*, with its colourful and lavish (and for those days revolutionary) pages of photos.

It was the era of large families, which were seen by the Protestants, with their considerably fewer children, as a major demographic threat; the abundant processions that were allowed only on the streets of the southern provinces; the thousands of silently praying men who, with their *Stille Omgang* through Amsterdam's red light district, commemorated the Miracle of the Host in clandestine protest against the ban on processions; the avuncular priests and nuns of which every family had a few; the exuberant social life along strictly confessional lines; and the immense passion for missionary work, which led the Netherlands to send its excess of priests, nuns and monks all over the world to spread faith, healthcare and literacy.

Numerically the proportion of Catholics in the Netherlands was never more than a good fifty percent, but the country exceeded every other nation in religious fervour. The fact that Dutch tulips decorate the papal blessing *Urbi et orbi* (*'Bedankt voor de bloemen'* – Thanks for the flowers – said Pope Wojtyla in shaky Dutch which became a much-copied pronunciation), has its origins in an adoration of the Holy See that stretches far back for generations. No less than one third of the Zouave army that unsuccessfully defended the Papal States against Garibaldi's nationalist troops in the 1860s consisted of Dutchmen. They gathered in Oudenbosch, in Brabant, where a small museum still keeps their memory alive.

Aggiornamento

There is hardly any of that vitality and confident triumphalism anymore though. Catholic social life has disappeared or been integrated into neutral organisations. The Dutch Catholic trade union NKV merged in 1976 with the 'red' NVV

Trappist Abbey, Zundert, the Netherlands, 1995
© Annie van Gemert

Dominicanen, Maastricht: a bookshop made in heaven

to form the neutral Federation of Dutch Trade Unions (FNV). Architect Pierre Cuypers's neo-Gothic churches have been demolished or changed into carpet shops or apartment complexes. Only a few parish churches continue to eke out an existence with a flock that has shrunk to a few dozen almost exclusively elderly parishioners and a pastor who must serve a handful of other churches, too, due to the shortage of priests. Instead of sending missionaries out to faraway countries overseas, the Archdiocese of the Netherlands now imports priests from other parts of the world, because it can no longer even meet the shrinking demand with its own recruits.

From Rome's most faithful and enthusiastic church to the wasteland of a mission area; seldom has the Catholic secularisation process been as disconcertingly fast and wholescale as in the Netherlands. In retrospect, the archdiocese looks like a balloon that was blown up to grotesque proportions and that has now deflated spectacularly after the tiniest of pinpricks. It leaves a memory of a bizarre extravagance that filled every minute of people's entire lives, but whose remains have disappeared now on the scrap heap of lost faith.

Common wisdom has it that the catalyst of all this is to be found in the Second Vatican Council (1962-1965). It promised to bring the church 'up to date' (aggiornamento), but in fact it seems only to have revealed how hopelessly outdated the Catholic world had become. Emblematic of this was the documentary book about the years 1925-1935, which the journalist, writer and poet Michel van der Plas published in 1963 under the same title as the aforementioned column in De katholieke illustratie, Uit het rijke Roomsche Leven (From the Rich Catholic Life). Drawing on a large number of written sources, Van der Plas showed how stifling and small-minded that life had been. Quotes from the back cover left readers in no doubt about the way Catholics used to think about themselves: 'Roman Catholic is top', 'The best novels are no good', 'God wanted the class system' and 'A red Catholic is a dead Catholic'.

While the council continued in Rome, the book became a bestseller, with more than ten reprints in a short space of time. However, there was no tension or contradiction between the two – or at least not yet. During the council years and the period shortly afterwards, Catholic religious fervour did not suffer in the slightest from the exposure of what meanwhile is felt to have been old-fashioned bigotry. Both the main highlights of Vatican II and the funeral service of the much-loved Pope John XXIII, who had convened it, were watched by huge numbers of viewers on Dutch television. Indeed the Pope's death that same year, 1963, plunged even some non-Catholic Dutch people into mourning.

Meanwhile, on the fringes of the council, progressive theologians, exegetes and liturgists played an important role as advisors and experts, so revolutionary that they gradually acquired a public face too. The Flemish-Dutch theologian Edward Schillebeeckx, along with men like the Swiss Hans Küng, the German Karl Rahner and the Frenchman Yves Congar, formed the vanguard of what had previously been called *la nouvelle théologie*. In open dialogue with philosophy (from existentialism to Marxism), inspired by a reading of the Bible in which its Jewish roots were expressly recognised, and eager to modernise liturgy to meet contemporary demands, they prepared the ground for the modernisation decisions that were taken at the council.

For the first time, Catholic theology, which until then had had little to say to lay people, went public both in writing and via radio and television, which had just become a mass medium. Edward Schillebeeckx, still wrapped in his Dominican habit in those days, became so popular that he was interviewed on the socialist television channel VARA, in the late 1960s, by the public's favourite journalist Mies Bouwman in her talk show *Mies en Scène*, every broadcast of which invariably became the talk of the day throughout the country.

A second Reformation

For the average Catholic, theology became a much-discussed phenomenon in the 1960s. Finally, Bible exegesis was something to get worked up about. Traditionally it had been something of a secret that was carefully kept out of sight of the faithful. Matters of faith were for the clergy and Rome; theories about them (to the extent that there were any) belonged in the seminaries. Even the fierce modernist struggles around the turn of the previous century had not put an end to the ignorance of lay people. On the contrary, the tensions aroused by them (like the later worker-priest movement in France) had once again convinced the doctrinal authorities that there would be no end to it if 'the people' were taught more than devotion and obedience.

Thanks to the Second Vatican Council, Catholic theologians and biblical scholars emerged from their isolation – and found a large and receptive audience in the Netherlands. Catholic schools organised evenings at which their views were explained to the parents. On the radio and television there was a busy schedule of debates and educational programmes. It was a period when family parties in Catholic circles invariably ended in fierce theological debate – about the vernacular liturgy, clerical celibacy, the real presence of Christ in the Eucharist, the expectation of a hereafter and, yes, the existence of God.

Looking back at Dutch Catholicism in the 1960s, we can see a sort of second reformation happening. The Bible, which until then Catholics had only been allowed to read in a much-abbreviated form, was suddenly available to them uncensored and immediately raised questions. In the liturgy, not only did the priest turn his face to the people, he also turned what had previously been a sermon mainly about piety into an important moment of education and explanation. The suddenly comprehensible language of prayers and hymns gave rise both to doubts and to the need for further clarification: what did all the dogmas that were stressed in it actually mean? Some were of the opinion that the clergy would understand their flock a lot better if they had an ordinary family life, like the Protestant clergy. And was the 'pillarised' isolation, in which the Catholic part of the population had been a nation in itself, inward-looking and self-absorbed, still of this time?

By no means everyone was convinced of the need for a far-reaching modernisation and many began to have doubts when the *aggiornamento*, which had initially been greeted enthusiastically in the Netherlands, began to show some revolutionary traits. In the early days, however, these appeared to be just the growing pains of a new fervour, which did indeed break through in many places in the Catholic Church. The new freedom with which matters of faith could be discussed and the hitherto unheard of extent to which a thrilling understanding of it could be gained during those discussions and instructional evenings did, it is true, lead to division and disunity. But most of all it led to the realisation that the church had begun a new life, possibly even a resurrection from what was increasingly being seen as a glorious but in the meantime dead-end path.

In fact there had been signs as early as the Second World War that Catholic isolation, triumphalist but ever more oppressive as it was, would eventually become unsustainable. Whether the experience of resisting the German occupation had contributed to this or not is a moot point. Even the underground resistance was divided up and organised along confessional and ideological lines. But the mutual dislike and closed mentality of pillarisation no longer fitted with the assumption that everything would be different after the war. The breakthrough concept, in which socialists and Christian movements sought rapprochement, gained ground.

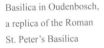

Basilica in Oudenbosch, a replica of the Roman St. Peter's Basilica

The Parrot, conventicle ('Schuilkerk'),
Kalverstraat, Amsterdam

The Episcopal Charge

It was still too early for that though. In 1954, in the notorious 'Episcopal Charge' (Mandement), the Dutch bishops whistled the faithful back into the corner of the strictly Catholic world and its organisations. Catholics were strongly advised against membership of the Dutch Labour Party and membership of socialist trade unions was prohibited. As we have seen, it was only a stay of execution. A little more than twenty years later, the two trade unions merged into one central union. From the very start the 'Mandement' was lagging behind the facts. The prohibition on listening to the socialist VARA radio was cheerfully and massively ignored. In the 1960s, the bishops had little choice but to go along with the unstoppable developments amongst churchgoers themselves.

In the meantime they were probably of the same mind. The role of Bernard Alfrink was typical: as Coadjutor Archbishop in 1954, he had participated in issuing the Mandement. In the 1960s, as Archbishop of the Netherlands, he turned out to be a careful but responsive church leader who, together with the other bishops, convened a Pastoral Council in 1966, where lay voices had a very important role to play.

For the most progressive Catholics Alfrink and even the Pastoral Council were still much too timid in their desire to reform. For the conservatives, who gradually began to assert themselves more and more, even Vatican II was verging on the unacceptable. But in the midst of all the turbulence of the period the intensive dialogue between the leaders of the church and the lay people at the Pastoral Council counted internationally as a shining and promising example of what the church could signify in the future. Bishops like Bekkers (he too had a memorable conversation on TV with Mies Bouwman), Bluyssen and, to a certain extent, Alfrink too enjoyed popularity and prestige in the Netherlands both inside and outside the Catholic Church.

But it did not last. In the 1970s the Vatican intervened hard and, with the appointment of new, considerably more conservative bishops, forced a change of direction intended to bring Dutch Catholics back on the track of their traditional loyalty to Rome. The Vatican did have some cause for concern. The most radical parishes (which now called themselves *ecclesia* or, in the style of the Protestants, 'congregations') had de facto left the Archdiocese. Where devotion to the Pope had once been unsurpassed anywhere in the world, there was now sharp criticism of the ultraconservative, yes even perverse ecclesiastical and power structure for which the clergy were blamed. Little by little the modernisation of the Catholic Church in the Netherlands seemed to have turned into a genuine second Reformation.

Rome's severity had the opposite effect though. More and more congregations and *ecclesias* that had been in the vanguard of the modernisation movement cut their ties with the church, and their loss was not compensated by a stampede to more conservative parishes. The anachronism of denominational organisations in every conceivable area rapidly disappeared and left behind a church that could only offer people something in the strictly religious field. In as far as a social life still existed in the face of an increasingly noticeable tendency towards individualisation, it operated in a society in which religious and ideological denominations acted less and less as dividing lines.

When Pope John Paul II first visited the Netherlands, in 1985, his reception was cool. The majority of the once large and enthusiastic Catholic section of the population showed itself indifferent; a progressive minority showered him with criticism and reproaches. They were the last heirs of the enthusiasm that had raised Dutch Catholics to great heights in the 1960s. In a sense the religious experience was greater than ever during those years; at least it was proof of a 'rich Roman Catholic life', which had paled in colour, it is true, but not in devotion.

Nostalgia

It lasted no more than ten years. Since then the Catholic Church has survived on the fringes of Dutch society. Developments in the 1960s were not the cause. At most they accelerated a process that would only start a few decades later in the mainstream Protestant churches and has since assumed even more dramatic forms. By the start of the twenty-first century, the Netherlands was a secularised country.

We should not be fooled by appearances though. Migrant churches and both fundamentalist and revivalist Protestantism are flourishing sources of 'modern' religiosity. The Catholic Church may be languishing, but the typically Catholic domain of rituals, liturgical sensuality and sensitivity to mystique have clearly made their way into both explicitly religious and quasi-religious movements and celebrations, and obviously meet a deep-seated need. Whilst church organisational structures disappear, the legacy of religious *forms* enjoys increasing, eclectic popularity – varying from atheist liturgical services to service companies like 'rent-a-priest', which aim to give important moments in life a fitting cachet. Even the traditionally scientifically rational Humanist Federation now offers secular wedding and funeral rituals, in which it blatantly borrows from church traditions.

So, the religious heritage of the 1960s in the Netherlands is in several respects ambiguous. It was not the increasing secularisation that characterised it, but a modernist resistance to the disintegration that was already making

Group of victorious Zouaves. Reenactment during or after the Italian Campaign in 1859

Translated by Lindsay Edwards

itself felt beneath the surface in the by then outdated traditional forms of devotion. The resulting feverish modernisation and reflection led in subsequent decades to a backlash that appears, however, in its turn, to be equally temporary. The traditional churches will not recover quickly and definitely not in their pre-1960s forms. But religion is by no means finished – certainly not in a country where it has traditionally been deeply cherished by both Protestants and Catholics.

Even the recently arrived Islamic faith will presumably not be able to avoid this dynamic eventually. For the time being it manifests itself in a fundamentalism that is not so very different from pre-war Catholicism and Calvinism, at least in its stricter forms. The reproach is often made that Islam 'has not yet gone through the Enlightenment'. But more to the point perhaps is the realisation that it has not yet experienced the 1960s. At the moment, that heritage, so much broader and more relevant than the eighteenth-century demand for the (dogmatically acknowledged) existence of God, is probably far more important for a lively religious culture.

It is a risky heritage with an uncertain outcome. It is still possible that it will make extremely short shrift of religion. But that is unlikely. If the 1960s were proof of anything religious, it was of a burning religious enthusiasm, not indifference. It is precisely the latter from which we seem to be suffering at the moment. The heritage of the 1960s is perhaps mainly evident in a gnawing nostalgia for a time when there really was something ideological at stake. ■

From Ownership to Usage

The 1960s' Legacy of the Sharing Economy

[TOM CHRISTIAENS]

Ownership is old hat. Swapping, giving and sharing goods and services is the new way of trading. That, in essence, sums up the sharing economy – a movement that has been growing strongly in Belgium and the Netherlands, too, in recent years and which is gnawing away at the roots of capitalism. *Sharing is caring* is the credo of its proponents. Their voices sound like an echo from the idealistic 1960s. But is it really the case that the sharing economy owes its legacy to the 'Golden Sixties'? Well yes, and no.

It is Friday evening in the city of Kortrijk in West Flanders. The ground floor of an old textile factory has been transformed into a creative 'factory of the future', with machines taking pride of place. Students, designers, artists and other kindred spirits are engaged in all kinds of activity in the BUDA::lab. While one waits patiently for the 3D printer to churn out a model, another is using a laser cutter to finish off a panel for his bike. Someone else is sitting at a computer, designing a valve.

BUDA::lab is a FabLab, or *fabrication laboratory*, a public 'makerspace' where anyone can make things in return for a small fee. There are computer-aided prototyping machines which can transform your ideas into tangible products. And any FabLab that is worth its salt will have an electronics section, a 3D printer, a film cutter, a CNC milling machine and a laser cutter.

The BUDA::lab in Kortrijk attracts people from a variety of sectors and disciplines. They come together in one of the many workshops to learn new skills, inspire and challenge each other to make objects together. The result is a 'community of makers'. Reference is made to the Holstee Manifesto: *'Life is about the people you meet, and the things you create with them. So go out and start creating.'*

BUDA::lab is one of sixty FabLabs that have been founded across Flanders and the Netherlands in the last few years. They are part of a global network of more than six hundred.

FabLabs are an excellent example of what in recent years has come to be known as the sharing economy, with at its heart the maxim that ownership is no longer important; what matters is what you have access to. The people making things in a FabLab don't own the machines, but they have easy access to them and can use them to the full. The logic behind this is that there is no

point in everyone buying costly equipment if it is easier and cheaper to share it. The makers are also encouraged to share designs and ideas openly within their own network and with other FabLabs. As a result, they are often fertile breeding grounds for innovation.

Community, access, sharing, using: these are notions which perfectly describe the sharing economy. It is given form in a wide range of initiatives which are enjoying growing support in all corners of the Low Countries, from small-scale endeavours to projects with national coverage.

All shapes and sizes

The best-known form of the sharing economy is the sharing, swapping, lending or donating of usable goods. Initiatives can be found in the smallest municipalities in which goods change owner through informal services that are provided both off-line and online, often free of charge or for a small fee. People can give things away at a *geefplein* ('giving event'), go to an *instrumentheek* to borrow tools cheaply, have faulty appliances repaired at a *Repair Café*, and fashionistas can swap rarely-worn apparel for hip clothing at a *swishing* event.

One highly popular initiative is *Peerby*, which began in Amsterdam in 2011 but is now used by tens of thousands of people in the Netherlands, Belgium, Germany and the UK. The *Peerby* mobile app or website can be used to borrow and hire things such as power drills, ladders or a wood chipper from people in the neighbourhood. It is a demand-driven process: you post a request online and your neighbours tell you whether they are willing to lend it to you. This kills three birds with one stone: borrowing means it costs less, you get to know the

BUDA::lab

people in your neighbourhood better and the planet benefits, because fewer products have to be made, meaning fewer CO_2 emissions.

Peerby is a social forerunner in the sharing economy, because it arose as a result of the desire to contribute to the environment or to community life. The examples in Flanders and the Netherlands are the *Repair Cafés* and the *Thuisafgehaald* initiative, in which people cook extra portions when preparing a meal and offer them to their neighbours for a small charge.

Some sharing initiatives have developed for financial reasons, to save money. This applies for expensive products, for example; and it is not just things that people don't have in their own homes that are shared *en masse*, such as scissor lifts or cherry pickers, but also cars or rooms for tourists.

The idea of shared mobility is also gaining ground. There are platforms today for sharing transport and related items, from cars, bicycles and boats to parking spaces, taxi rides and journeys, with examples such as *Uber*, *Cambio*, *Snappcar*, *WeGo*, *MyWheels*, *Samenrijden*, *Taxistop*, *Eventpool*, *Eurostop*, *Toogethr* and *Greeters*.

Space can also be shared, for example a home (*Oppas Taxistop*, *Huizenruil*, *Cohousing*, *Samenhuizen*, *Allesthuis*), holiday accommodation (*Airbnb*, *Couchsurfing*), workplace (sewing cafes) or office space (*Bar d'Office*, *Deelstoel*), or even a vegetable plot (*Tuindelen*, *Samentuinen*).

Initiatives such as shared gardening, food teams and food-sharing (*Shareyourmeal*, *Thuisafgehaald*) focus on shared food production. The emphasis here is on a 'fairer' relationship between producer and consumer, whilst minimising the ecological footprint. There are frequent examples involving regional and seasonal produce supplied by a local farmer.

And sharing need not always involve tangible objects; people can also share knowledge and skills, care, odd jobs and even time via informal networks (*Oudermatch*, *WeHelpen*, *Croqqer*, *Klusup*, *Konnektid*, *Timebank*).

A very well-known example is LETS, or *Local Exchange Trading System*, which started in Canada in 1982 and went on to gain a firm footing worldwide. As its name suggests, it is a local exchange system in which people do odd jobs for each other with no money changing hands. LETS networks use tax-free forms of credit, with original names such as *Noppes* in Amsterdam or *Stropkes* in Ghent. LETS members can earn credits by cutting hair, for example, which they can spend later, perhaps on a cake baked by another member of the same LETS group. There are more than eighty LETS groups in the Netherlands and over forty in Flanders.

Another phenomenon worthy of note is crowdfunding, in which people come together to contribute to a particular cause – though in this case there need not be a social purpose. There are for example group purchase initiatives where individuals can invest in a sustainable project together with like-minded others, such as the purchase of cheap (green) electricity, condensing boilers or solar panels.

Sharing for financial gain

The sharing economy began as a social experiment by private individuals, but has moved beyond this as businesses have also embraced the principles of sharing as a way of making money. The sharing economy has become a new business model. That is not without logic, because what business manager would not support a model that is based on making better use of spare goods and services by sharing them?

While most individual initiatives are focused on private individuals, more and more platforms are appearing which integrate these individualistic ideas into business-to-business models. Take *Floow2*, for example, the first – and globally active – sharing marketplace for businesses, which allows them to share surplus materials and infrastructure and the underutilised skills and knowledge of their staff. Businesses from the most diverse sectors, from the construction industry to the care sector, advertise online what space, goods, services and staff they are temporarily not using and are willing to share with other businesses. There is almost no limit to what can be hired, from cement

Peerby

mixers to commercial vehicles, meeting rooms to parking places and printing facilities to nothing short of an MRI scanner, a communications advisor or a designer. It is called 'asset sharing'. The initiators of *Floow2* are convinced that businesses can generate increased turnover via their platform whilst saving costs.

The best-known businesses targeting private individuals are undoubtedly *Uber* and *Airbnb*. The *Uber* taxi app connects people looking for transport to private drivers, allowing the latter to make better use of their vehicle and earn money from it. The digital *Airbnb* marketplace enables private individuals to rent out rooms to third parties. *Uber* and *Airbnb* are today worth billions. And that goes very much against the grain for the traditional market players. Professional taxi and hotel companies, for example, are heavily critical, claiming that they distort the market with unfair competition. They accuse *Uber* and *Airbnb* of pretending to be pioneers of the sharing economy, whilst their disruptive character, scale and structure means that in practice they are really commercial service platforms which abuse the original sharing principles for financial gain.

New economic reality

Debates such as these, which are going on across the world, show that the sharing economy is causing a major shake-up in traditional market thinking. It embodies a new economic reality, in which power is slowly but surely shifting from the supply side to the demand side and where access to goods and services is becoming more important than owning them. It is both an economic and a social model, based on collaboration on an equal footing among citizens and between citizens and businesses.

Most sharing initiatives operate on the principle of the 'resource-based economy', in which the economy and trading practices are driven by efficiency, sustainability and human need rather than by profit or endless growth. The sharing economy pokes its tongue at capitalism, with its overconsumption, waste of raw materials and frequent creation of artificial demand.

The sharing economy thus offers considerable added value for society. Sharing by people and businesses can save money. The different forms of shared use lead to greater social cohesion and personal interaction. And the environment also benefits because fewer goods have to be produced.

The figures do not lie. In 2014, the Flemish sharing initiatives *Velt*, *Voedselteams*, *Autopia*, *Taxistop*, *Netwerk Bewust Verbruiken* and *Bond Beter Leefmilieu* produced a joint memorandum on the sharing economy in Flanders to draw the attention of the Flemish government to the importance of this new economic model. The memorandum quantified a clear added value from the sharing economy. If one fifth of the underutilised homes in Flanders were to be shared with other occupants, this would remove the need for an additional 300,000 residential units by 2030. And if half the residents of a town engaged in car-sharing, this would lead to a fivefold reduction in the number of cars on the roads. While if everyone had their faulty appliances repaired in a Repair Café, the mountain of electronic waste would shrink by 70%.

Not surprisingly, therefore, businesses are increasingly heeding the message that they need to embrace the principles of the sharing economy rather than fighting them. Otherwise they will fall hopelessly behind and be in danger of being forced out of the market by new sharing initiatives. The sharing economy is penetrating all sectors of the market, and most traditional businesses are looking for ways to deal with the competition. For example, what strategy will the hospitality industry pursue in order to fend off competition from the likes of *Airbnb*, *Campr*, *Chef aan Huis* or *Thuisafgehaald*? And what about the Flemish and Dutch governments? Their slow, piecemeal development of an appropriate legislative framework for the sharing economy is in stark contrast to the speed with which sharing initiatives are impacting on the economic system. No figures are currently available for Flanders or the Netherlands, but according to American studies, the global turnover of the sharing economy was estimated at 26 billion dollars in 2013.

If even the European Union is actively supporting the sharing economy, the only conclusion can be that this is no longer a marginal activity reserved for thrifty citizens and economic adventurers.

Not a new phenomenon

The sharing economy, then, is blowing a breath of fresh air through our economic system. But it is not a new phenomenon. Borrowing, sharing and swapping have always been with us, and were especially common in the Low Countries in the pre-industrial period, when society was not yet organised by the market and the state.

In the Middle Ages, for example, there was the phenomenon of *naoberschap*, or 'neighbourliness'. When the Dutch regions of Drenthe, Twente and Achterhoek were predominantly populated by farmers, residents largely had to rely on each other, following the social norm of *naoberplicht* ('help thy neighbour'). Members of these close-knit communities not only shared the joys and sorrows of life, but also their time, material and knowledge. It was driven by pure need. This form of community help was a matter of survival, because they could not place any reliance on good public amenities in their villages. The agricultural regions of Flanders also have a long tradition of looking after and helping one another whenever possible.

These kinds of informal economic interaction fell out of use with the onset of the Industrial Revolution and the arrival of the nation-state. Henceforth, the market and the state regulated economic life. Giving, sharing and borrowing were confined to the personal sphere. People were still happy to water their neighbours' plants when they were away on holiday, but that was about it.

Today, these forgotten forms of interaction are back in favour and are in fact being used on a wider scale. In reality, today's sharing economy is a reintroduction of those old customs and market traditions, only now the success of sharing initiatives is hugely supported by digital technology. More on that later.

Legacy of the 1960s

When today's young people in Flanders and the Netherlands share cars, homes and goods for financial and ecological reasons, they are also paying homage to the 1960s and '70s. Several sharing initiatives can be traced back directly to experiments that began during these tumultuous decades, which changed society in Belgium and the Netherlands forever.

The social criticism that we hear today from proponents of the sharing economy is very reminiscent of the 1960s and '70s: society needs to change; we cannot carry on polluting the environment; overconsumption and the exhaustion of raw materials has to stop; we must once again strive for sustainability and form communities and move away from stifling hierarchical and bureaucratic systems. Not a week goes by without a campaign somewhere in Flanders or the Netherlands against the growth of capitalism at the expense of

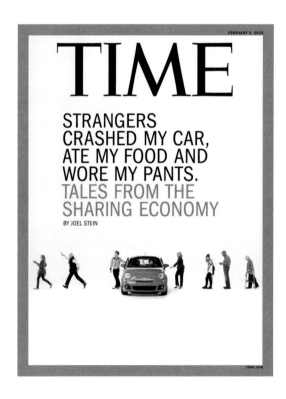

people, work and the environment. Young people especially are less and less convinced by the mantra of eternal economic growth if it is no longer able to guarantee prosperity and well-being.

This discontent and note of warning about the way things are going were also very prominent in the 1960s and '70s. For the first time, there was a generation which had the (free) time to ask fundamental questions about whether society was moving in the right direction. Their political and ideological motivation was fired by the ideas for alternatives to capitalism formulated by thinkers such as Herbert Marcuse and Karl Polayni. Those theories are being dusted off once again, but the actions of the proponents of the sharing economy are today driven more by pragmatism and rationalism than by principle.

That was not so in the 1960s. Social criticism led among other things to the formation of the *Provo* youth movement in the Netherlands in 1965. Inspired by the slogan 'Better long-haired than short-sighted', the Provos spread out from Amsterdam looking for alternatives to make life, living and working more pleasant.

Free love, ecology and the environment, emancipation, democratisation, artistic innovation, questioning authority and consumerism: the field of action of the Provos was a wide one. The movement subjected new social questions to scrutiny and often came up with innovative responses which they publicised through entertaining campaigns and in the form of 'White Plans'.

Long before it became a trend, the Provos embraced the principles of sharing, with calls for individual access to collective products and services. The bicycle and car sharing that we know today, for example, can be traced back to the 'White Bicycles' and 'White Cars' initiated by the Provos. More than half a century after its invention, the shared bicycle that can be used by everyone either free or for a small charge is now commonplace. There are today more than 700,000 of them in more than 600 cities throughout the world, offering a viable and environmentally friendly alternative to inner-city transport. The Provos can also claim credit for the success story of car sharing, which is now common in many countries.

The Provo movement was thus far ahead of its time with the sharing economy. And that applies not just for mobility: as a means of combating housing shortage, today's 'co-housing' initiative for sharing homes is motivated by the same need as the Provo, squatter and commune self-housing movements of the 1960s and '70s, including in Flanders. In 1966, the youth movement published a 'White Housing Plan', exhorting anyone looking for somewhere to live to occupy empty dwellings, and the door posts of empty homes were painted white to indicate their accommodation potential to anyone without a roof. The Royal Palace on Amsterdam's Dam Square, which at the time stood empty, was hailed as the symbol of the housing shortage.

There was no powerful movement in Flanders comparable to the Dutch Provos to shake up public attitudes and repopularise the concept of sharing. It would be the 1970s before meaningful experiments took place there.

Digital technology makes the difference

Despite the shared belief that the economy and society need to be organised differently, today's sharing initiatives are by no means simply copies of the experiments from the 1960s.

According to Rogier De Langhe, a specialist in economics and philosophy at Ghent University, the present-day sharing economy differs fundamentally from its predecessor in the use of digital technology, with the Internet and digital natives – the generation who have grown up with modern technology and who use it intuitively. This factor was non-existent in the 1960s. The technology allows people to organise themselves easily, even at global level, facilitate sharing and lower costs. Without the Internet, initiatives such as *Airbnb* and *Uber* could never have become so popular so quickly with so many people.

Giving event

Translated by Julian Ross

What is often forgotten in analyses of the sharing economy, De Langhe argues, is that digital natives are also a crisis generation. They reached the age of 18 in the year 2000, and almost immediately on reaching adulthood were confronted with 9/11 and what was widely regarded as the unjust war in Iraq. They have gone through many crises – financial, economic and institutional – since then.

'Everyone has a sense that something isn't right', De Langhe argues. 'We have a sort of Frankenstein feeling. We have created a system that we can no longer control. Not a single policymaker, economist or politician can give us confidence that things will turn out all right. Since the banking crisis, even senior bankers today admit that they have no idea which way things are going. It is logical then that citizens react with their own initiatives in which they no longer want to be dependent on governments and the business establishment.'

The context in the 1960s was not exactly the same. The 1960s generation experienced the biggest economic boom in our history; it is no coincidence that this decade is known as the Golden Sixties. Almost everyone was able to buy their own home and go on holiday. Saving energy and conserving space were not yet an issue. Taking action against the economic status quo was not a necessity, but more a matter of principle. Things are rather different today, with visible problems such as climate change, scarcity of raw materials, unemployment and economic crisis. More and more experts are acknowledging that we are today paying the price for the prosperity of the 1960s, marked by their unbridled production and consumption.

The sharing economy is an attempt to come up with a sustainable alternative, so that we do not make the same mistakes again. ■

'Beneath the Paving Stones the Beach!'

A Small Anthology from and about the Sixties

An Extract from *Message to the Rat King*

By Harry Mulisch

Hystericisation by TV

If anyone says that all those Amsterdam riots don't represent anything 'brand new', but are an expression of normal generational conflict, one may ask them how it was that twenty years ago young people did not bat an eyelid during the police action of the Dutch government against the Indonesian freedom fighters, whereas now the Amsterdam monument of the colonial general Van Heutsz is regularly defaced. Those who say that all those Amsterdam riots are 'a passing phenomenon', are of course right; but only because what they are directed at will pass. Flooding Amsterdam with riot police – like Vietnam with Americans – can only put an end to *these kinds* of riots. Those who say that it must be simply tackled firmly and eradicated root and branch, can be referred for information to the dismissed chief commissioner of police, the mayor with nervous exhaustion, the Internal Affairs minister drowning in derision and the politically undermined prime minister.

If something is to be eradicated root and branch – I can summarise in this way the core of what I am saying – it is this 'root-and-branch eradication'.

Anybody who has grown up in the 'affluent society', the white fatherland of the haves, thinks differently about things than his parents, who come from an earlier time and *acquired* it all – and if what is more he lives in a capital, he will when the opportunity arises make it clear that he has a different opinion. Affluence, or what passes for it, is natural for him. A car is for getting about in, or for having fun with, apart from that it doesn't represent a thing. When he realises that that same car represents a *triumph* for his parents, he shrugs his shoulders and thinks they are suckers, which they are. This young man plays with things. For him things really are *things*, not symbols. For him a car is a car, not a CAR; for him television is television, not TV. When a programme bores him, he turns it off – an action that gives his parents the holy terrors. Screeching and falling over each other they rush to the set to turn the TV on again.

The young man strolls into the street.

Harry Mulisch at a demonstration against the Vietnam war, Rokin, Amsterdam, 1967
© Ed van der Elsken / Nederlands Fotomuseum

This is the way the rift between young and old has come about in the last ten years, and this rift is deeper than previous generational differences. In addition, it has become clear in the past five years that both groups have undergone radical changes, which have driven them even further apart. Let us first examine the change in the older section of the Dutch population. (The idem 'people' does not exist: that is what the fascists tried to make of it.)

Probably because they were cut adrift from their children, the older generation were hystericized step by step. That dispensed with the myth of 'Dutch sobriety' in particular, and in general again with the belief that 'national character' existed. If half a million people are murdered in Indonesia, as recently (little attention was paid to it in the press, they were after all not so much people as communists: imagine the consternation if conversely the communists had murdered even a fraction of that number of people), the ex-colonial can of course say that this is 'un-Indonesian', but in reality it has been shown that the Indonesians were never 'Indonesian', at most that they were forced for a century or so to behave like arse-licking lackeys. Neither has it now been shown that mass murder is 'Indonesian'. Apart from that of course all kinds of things have been shown, but we are not talking about them now. The Dutch 'national character' neither is nor was sober, because there are no national characters, since there are no characters. What does exist in the older section of the Dutch public is a hysterical condition.

From *Message to the Rat King* (Bericht aan de rattenkoning)
De Bezige Bij, Amsterdam, 1966

Translated by Paul Vincent

An Extract from *Gangrene*

By Jef Geeraerts

GOD IN HEAVEN, here it is already 1967 and what I'm about to tell took place at the very start of the heathen holy age, in the year 1955, the year of the basalt virgin, ha, she had just turned thirteen and her nipples still jutted up and out and in warm lands such things don't last long, but all four of those goddamned months slid by in a daze of artful oriental pleasure even though, miracle of miracles, all we lay on was a cot, but then of course a cot's narrow and leaves you no choice but to be intimate, enormously intimate, and thus, although we played full many a game, we did not sleep together (in the ordinary euphemistic hypocritical sense of the word) and later - with others of her race - it naturally happened that frequently no sleeping at all was done (but then in the utterly literal sense of the word), and the place where this came to pass was called Bodedemoke, which is to say Little Bodede (population: 47), a cluster of slanting huts in the shadow of the impenetrable, nearly two-hundred-feet-high rim of the forest, an unwilling virgin through which I had to make my way for six miles with the help of three hundred somewhat less than wildly enthusiastic blacks whom I did my casual best to keep hard at work, and I had, luckily, an iron trunk full of hooks with me so that on days when I did not hunt or when it poured I lay on: my cot, naked, tense, unsure. Occasionally, when the wind suddenly sprang up, I rushed outside, sweating with terror, and gazed up at that black wall of lianas, dead limbs, leaves, mushrooms, snakes, spiders, all hooked up to something high, nearly two hundred feet high, above me and just waiting to fall and crush me as the whole thing came down in a storm while I lay by my woman as snug as a boa, and I smoked my way through entire days, drugged, amorphous, no man, and read and let myself be borne along by the sluggish hours of eating, sleeping, feeling evening coming on and thus starting to think of what games we would play when it was night. She was called Marie-Jeanne and she was very dear, playful as an antelope, and young and beautiful, oh so beautiful, and she laughed a lot and talked more and her teeth were like a flock of sheep that are evenly shorn and up from the washing and she bound her hair in pigtails that stuck straight out like the antennae of a weather satellite and she had thick curls on her Venus-mound and firm pubic lips and cool snug buttocks under her thin cotton dress and after the first long, slow, all-embracing, world-enveloping kiss, a single greedy suck, her clitoris was a drop of quicksilver trying to elude the top of my mid-dle finger and after three nights she, young as she was, was a skilled partner in practices which would astonish and delight most so-called experienced, older women, and her father, a cultured quiet carpenter (named not Joseph but Cyprien) rejoiced in this relationship and instead of working on the road, as was his duty, went off hunting for his new-found son-in-law as well as for himself on occasion, and my boy Mohongu - a sly scoundrel if ever there was one - also profited from this liaison since he too promptly found himself a girl and Marie-Jeanne and Mar-tha got along remarkably well, a singular event since the Budja proverb says that no two women are ever truly fond of each other and proverbs never lie, and only rarely did the two young ladies have to be pulled apart; it never came to anything vicious or bloody, though there are always countless reasons for one woman's lighting into another, and daily the piercing screams of jealous women going at each other with their manioc scrapers echo through the Budja villages while the men watch grinning or urge the fighters on by shouting and clapping, and in the evening or around nine when the village, lit here and there by a still-glowing heap of ashes, lay still in the night, reabsorbed into the forest and its deafening sea of crickets, Marie-Jeanne, that warm weasel, slipped into the hut and I sprang out of bed and barely had time to flip my cigarette away before she embraced me pas-sionately and 'bési,' she said, and we kissed expertly while I pulled down the pant-ies which, among other things, I had bought for her, and she smelled very nice, like kittens, like ground almonds and sugar, and she washed herself with expensive soap and I had also bought her a set of bathtowels, wine-red with a black ivy design, in which she often paraded through the village, and while, at the start and still standing, I had to finger her off, she gave me precise instructions because she was very demanding, and 'elengi, elengi, elengi,' she said, time and again, which in all languages means delight, and when she came her knees buckled and her arms gripped me like branches and I had to lay the whimpering bundle in under the flung-open mosquito net on my cot, and while I undressed she lay staring up at me with wide eyes and when at last I lay beside her she bent over and skilfully began to lick my scrotum and to suck the tip of my penis, the Lybian slave of the Roman conqueror, and when, sometimes after an hour's pleasure and pain, I came, she came too, in shuddering waves, and afterward she was generally thirsty and I brought her white wine and she let me drink from her glass and tenderly, almost ashamedly, she asked me to do the same for her, and one night I knelt there, my hands on her buttocks, kissing, eating raw oysters, when suddenly I felt her whole body stiffen, she was no longer breathing, and I stopped and by the yellow gleam of the lantern I saw rising up steeply above me an Egyptian sculpture in dark-red basalt, cold, polished (and breathlessly I looked: the sources of Greece lie here, the Nile is the vein, I thought, and with ancient, sacred gestures I began to worship my origin), and as she – wormed close up against me, breathing like a glistening beast, clutching my penis, her weapon, in one hand - fell asleep, I lay relaxed, content-

edly gazing at her, from time to time stroking her skin, which was fine as polished walnut, or sniffing her like a hound, and I was, at times overwhelmed by the thought that some day she would be, old and as wrinkled as all the other shapeless, snivelling, fat women in the world and then it was as if the hand of a corpse gripped my penis and would not let go and I felt cold and had to drink whisky in order to think again as unconcernedly and superficially as usual (as always, out in the sun, dreaming of fresh conquests) and to be able to fall asleep, to shudder or pant through strange dreams and in the morning, shortly before five, when the sun was just up, she woke me by pinching my nose shut and Mohongu could tell by our talk that we were awake and with downcast eyes he brought in first a kettle of hot water, then a cup of strong coffee to prevent the day from getting off to a bad start, wished me a ritual good-morning, and vanished, and then I was soaped from head to foot by my slave, carefully rinsed, dried off and powdered, and after that she left without a word so that I could breakfast all by myself as befits a man, and every two weeks I covered the hundred miles that lay between me and headquarters in Yandongi and each time I left I had to swear on an infallible charm - a bunch of leaves - that I would not sleep with my wife and if I broke my oath I would suffer an agonizing death, and I didn't either, which is to say, didn't sleep with my wife who was, moreover, very pregnant and in that state the act of procreation is spoiled by something unspeakably morbid, the all-too-obvious association between the powerful jet of sperm and the soft fontanel of the infant's skull made me gag (Marie-Jeanne explained her own unshakeable conviction thus: white women *bazali na masoko na maimai*, a particularly cutting insult which, euphemistically translated, means that they ought to wash themselves a bit more carefully in certain places, after which she would spit on the ground, a sign of the utmost contempt) and oh, after roughly a hundred and twenty days of almost unbearable joy, the hour of departure arrived and Marie-Jeanne too had undergone various important changes, for now she wore lots of nail polish, used lipstick and mascara, wore minuscule panties, Maidenform bras, expensive sandals, blouses, flowery sarongs, sunglasses, and her movements were liquid and languid and her eyes slanted and around her mouth hovered the great inner calm of La Gioconda, that eternal wanton, and as a farewell present I gave her a shiny bike with drum brakes, gears, two lights, and ribbons all over the spokes and our farewell was formal and a bit breathtaking: my darling promptly jumped on the saddle of her brand-new bike and, dinging the bell, rode waving and shrieking with glee down the hill.

From *Gangrene* (Gangreen 1 – Black Venus, Manteau, Antwerpen, 1968),
The Viking Press New York, 1974

Translated by Jon Swan

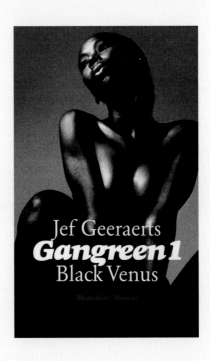

Poems from *Breach IV*

By Leonard Nolens

11

Field preachers were turned on by hammers
And sickles and jerked us off with their mouths.
And dockers sang themselves hoarse in the choking tearjerker
Of a pair of hands embracing the whole world.
Priests cursed the church into factories
And worked there on conveyor belts too.

We were the cowards. Only later did we see the daring
Of our lonely gangway, no Trotsky whisks us away
Through the rotten trick of international horseplay.
Only our morning bodies had the impact
Of natural slogans. We were rhetorically silent.
We had no power but the force of our inertia.

We formed a huge throng of the absent
In the public forum. We never signed
Another's manifestos, we hid
Our singular signal under a bushel.
We measured our future by the daily suicide
Of Chamfort and Jos de Haes, we reached out to each other

Over the grave of our children's children.
We studied the active pride of boredom
And swore by a conspiracy of the aloof.
We would not be appeased, we were not being fucked over
By a shit storm of luxury, we remained dirt poor,
Like these poems, a scattering of ashes in letters.

16

I'll just write with your permission we,
I can't say it differently.
We were not simply born after May '45.
We were not simply born.
We were not simply.
We were simply not.

We played a pioneering part in a mouth without men.
We got worked up in a tongue with no mouth.
We spread like viruses all over the screen.
The word made flesh became an open secret
Behind the locks and bolts of many tabernacles.
We hanged ourselves in poems deprived of their poet.

We were not simply. We were simply not.
We had no close family, that's why we were relations.
We did not swim round in a letter of Darwin's.
We did not pick a heart from the heart of the stone
Rolled up the mountain by my father.
We did not roll out of our mother, a mould for life.

We had no mirrors indoors
And let our self-image lose itself in papers and pubs.
We became troublemakers on the neighbourhood committee,
Lyricism of bohemia and filth from the street.
There we bought our bonds back from ourselves.
Many sentences together produced no emotion.

I'll just write with your permission we,
I can't say it differently.
We were the silent ones after May '45
We were the silent ones of May '68.
We were not simply.
We were simply not.

17

We were few.
We were some.
We were a few.
We were others.

We played no part in a riot
Of European proportions.
We did not take to the streets.
We did not take our place.

We put up a tent of books and canvas,
We mugged up a modernity in libraries.
We timed in sheet music the staggering effect
Of silence – the echo still sounds.

We carved our sculptures from study and stone.
They are still standing here in rows.
They are going to read themselves aloud.
They found their partners in crime only later.

We were not a poetic theme by Mao.
We thought, we'll make our own poem.
We thought, we'll make history here
On the sly.

From *Bres IV*, a cycle in: *Derwisj*,
Querido, Amsterdam, 2003

Translated by Paul Vincent

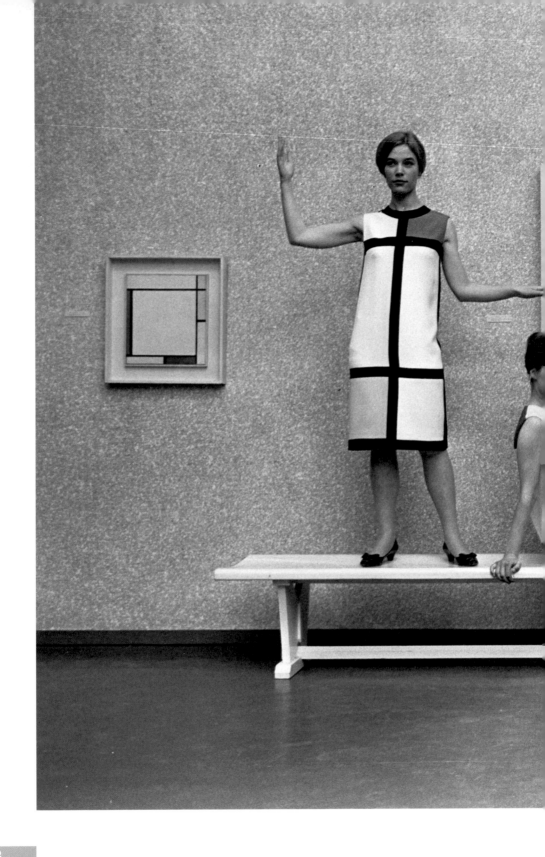

The Importance of De Stijl

An International Unity in Life, Art and Culture (1917-2017)

This year, the Netherlands is celebrating the centenary of De Stijl, the avant-garde movement that grew up around the *De Stijl* magazine that Theo van Doesburg launched in Leiden in 1917 together with Piet Mondrian, Bart van der Leck, Vilmos Huszár and J.J.P. Oud. Like Rembrandt and Van Gogh, De Stijl belongs in the canon of Dutch history. De Stijl is also the most important Dutch contribution to the modern art of the twentieth century. It has gained a permanent position for itself in surveys of modern art, architecture and design, with several members who are well known by the general public, including Mondrian, Van Doesburg, Van der Leck and Gerrit Rietveld. Their work confirms De Stijl's effort to employ artistic ideas in a range of disciplines and to arrive at a form of *Gesamtkunstwerk*. Van Doesburg was the main driving force behind the group and took responsibility for editing the magazine from the very start. He worked to build up a broad network so as to establish an international art movement, and had contacts with Dadaism, Constructivism, the Bauhaus and other avant-garde movements. His death in 1931 signalled the end of the magazine, and the final issue, which appeared in 1932, was dedicated to him. The body of ideas lived on, however, both in the work of the artists linked to De Stijl and in the views of later generations. De Stijl is therefore not only considered an important historical movement, but has continued significance. After all, the multidisciplinary orientation and the aim of using art in society in concrete ways are once again topical notions, making De Stijl a relevant point of reference even for today's art and design world.

Nieuwe Beelding

In around 1917, Mondrian's work evolved towards a radical form of painting pared down to just horizontal and vertical lines, rectangular areas, primary colours and the non-colours white, black and grey. This abstract visual idiom is a direct expression of the universal harmony that cannot be seen in the visible reality around us. In the first issue of *De Stijl* (October 1917), Mondrian called this painting the 'nieuwe beelding' and later also used the term 'neo-plasticism'. From the moment *De Stijl* was founded, Van Doesburg wanted to

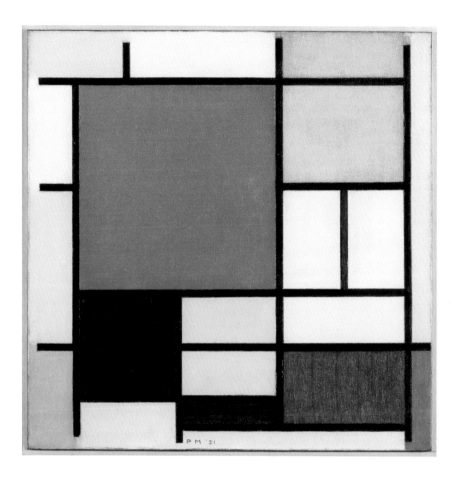

demonstrate that this new concept of art could bring the various disciplines together. In the first issue of the magazine, Bart van der Leck and Anthony Kok wrote about the place of modern painting in architecture and the interior, and J.J.P. Oud argued that the image of the modern city would be defined by building blocks with flat roofs, strong emphatic rhythm and modern materials.[1] In this first issue, Vilmos Huszár applied the new concepts to the typography and Van Doesburg wrote about the way Oud's design for a 'housing complex for a beach boulevard', *Huizencomplex Strandboulevard* (1917), expressed the ideas of neo-plasticism in architecture. The first manifesto of De Stijl, which appeared in the magazine in November 1918, aimed for 'an international unity in Life, Art and Culture' and called upon progressive artists abroad to help give shape to it.

Furniture also fitted into this unity. Van Doesburg initially considered the chair made of uncoloured slats that Gerrit Rietveld designed around 1918 and which, in a later version, became world-famous as the *Red Blue Chair*, as an example of sculpture in the new interior. In a later issue of *De Stijl* (1920), Van Doesburg made a distinction between the work of a sculptor and that of a furniture-maker: the former expressed harmony on the basis of relationships of volume, and the latter on the basis of open relationships of space. Rietveld's slat construction was functionally distilled and stands free and clear in the

Piet Mondrian,
Composition with Large Red Plane, Yellow, Black, Grey and Blue, 1921,
oil on canvas, 59.5 × 59.5 cm.
Collection Gemeentemuseum Den Haag

room. In a note on a children's chair of his that appeared in *De Stijl* (1919), Rietveld wrote that he was seeking 'the clear image of the thing itself, with no inessentials'. He restricted himself to standardised parts in keeping with machine production, even though he made his furniture in his own workshop. In the article entitled 'Schilderkunst van Giorgio de Chirico en een stoel van Rietveld' (Painting by Giorgio de Chirico and a Chair by Rietveld, *De Stijl*, 1920), an enthusiastic Van Doesburg referred to a high armchair by Rietveld as a 'slender space creature' and identified a 'dumb eloquence like that of a machine' in the chair. Van Doesburg used innovative typography and syntax to express the individuality of this piece of furniture *and* of the modern era.

Dada barks

These modern times also found an outlet in Dadaism, an avant-garde movement with which Van Doesburg and even Mondrian felt a kinship for a shorter or longer period. In Mondrian's case, this was expressed in a quest for what neo-plasticism might look like in the field of literature. His article entitled 'De groote boulevards' (The Grand Boulevards), published in *De Nieuwe Amsterdammer* on 27 March 1920, was an experiment in which he did not describe the bustle on the boulevards of Paris in words, but showed it in concrete terms in the phrasing as a moving mass of sounds, images and ideas. Like his painting, language too could become 'plastic'. Mondrian continued to reflect on literature as neo-plasticism and in this regard referred to himself as 'Piet-Dada' in a letter to Van Doesburg in June 1920. In the meantime, he had joined Van Doesburg and the Dutch poet Anthony Kok in putting his name to the second Manifesto of De Stijl (*De Stijl*, April 1920). This manifesto was a call to express in literature the depth and intensity of the collective experiences of their time by merging form and content. Their intention was, using sound poems, sound images for letters, and expressive typography, to give a literary construction to the 'manifold occurrences around and through us'. It was Van Doesburg in particular who, as from 1920, embraced Dadaism under the pseudonym I.K. Bonset, and in addition used the name Aldo Camini for the novel *Caminoscopie, 'n antiphilosofische levensbeschouwing zonder draad of systeem*, chapters from which appeared in De Stijl. Van Doesburg called I.K. Bonset 'the only real Dutch Dadaist' and for a long time left the art world in the dark about the fact that I.K. Bonset was the alter ego of the Van Doesburg whom people knew as the neoplasticist artist. Under the pseudonym I.K. Bonset, Van Doesburg published poems in *De Stijl* that referred to nothing and expressed no individual feelings, but which derived meaning from their image and sound. There was a lot of room for contributions by Dadaists in the magazine. De Stijl and Dadaism felt akin because both these art movements were opposed to a naturalist representation of reality and because they believed that abstract art was able to give shape to a new and modern culture. Van Doesburg invited both constructivist and Dadaist artists to the Konstruktivistische Internationale in Weimar on 25 September 1922. He was working enthusiastically on an international network and was in touch with Francis Picabia, Tristan Tzara, Kurt Schwitters, Hans Arp and other Dadaists. He initiated a notable Dutch Dada tour that started with a Dada evening in the 'Haagse Kunstkring' (The Hague Art Circle) on the Binnenhof on 10th January 1923. Van Doesburg gave a lecture entitled 'What is Dada?', and when he paused briefly during the talk the German Dadaist Kurt Schwitters made various sounds including barking from his seat in the midst of the audience. Schwitters also read Dadaist poetry, Nelly Van Moorsel played eccentric music and Vilmos Huszár put on a shadow play with a mechanical puppet. In 1922, Van Doesburg launched the largely Dadaist magazine *Mécano*, which he published in parallel with *De Stijl*, but only four issues appeared before it closed down in 1923.

Z' Z' Z' Z'
i _ _
Z' Z' Z'
i _ _
Z' Z'
i _ _
Z
a

p' p'
P P P P P P P P

I.K. Bonset, 'Letterklankbeelden' (*Lettersoundimages*), in *De Stijl* 4, 7 July 1921, p. 105

The importance of De Stijl lies largely in the way it communicated. Its principles were disseminated and promoted in its magazine and the international avant-garde was invited to cooperate, which among other things led to contributions by foreign artists appearing in *De Stijl*. Contacts with progressive artistic circles in other countries, including Belgium, France, Germany, Italy and Switzerland, also involved the exchange of ideas and/or influence. In Belgium alone, De Stijl influenced artists, architects and designers, mainly in the 1920s. Such people as Jozef Peeters and Victor Servranckx opted for an abstract geometric idiom and spoke of community art and 'pure plastic vision'. Peeters was the main driving force behind the founding of the 'Kring Moderne Kunst' (Modern Art Circle) in Antwerp (1918); he was in touch with Van Doesburg, who, in 1920, addressed his lecture 'Klassiek, barok, modern' (Classical, Baroque, Modern) to the group. In Antwerp, they were aware of the impact this might have. Van Doesburg's lecture in Brussels one month later also had an effect. According to Pierre Bourgeois, among other things it prompted the founding of the group of artists associated with the *7 Arts* magazine in 1922, which included Victor and Pierre Bourgeois, Karel Maes, Jozef Peeters, Victor Servranckx, Marcel Baugniet and Pierre Louis Flouquet. Georges Vantongerloo, who stayed in the Netherlands during the war years, abandoned his impressionist work in late 1917 and, partly under the influence of De Stijl, developed his own variant of abstract art. In 1918, his sculpture and painting resulted in compositions of horizontal and vertical planes in which the primary colours – red, yellow and blue – were joined by black, grey and white. However, from the very beginning Vantongerloo formulated his own personal version of abstract art, one in which he used his own colour theories and complex mathematical calculations.

The Belgian interest in the vision propagated by De Stijl is also apparent in numerous examples of architecture in the 1920s, including Huib Hoste's Kapelleveld garden district (1923) in Sint-Lambrechts-Woluwe and Sint-Pieters-Woluwe, and his De Beir house in Knokke (1924). The term 'cubist' was often heard as an ironic comment on architecture and design that involved rigid lines. Members of De Stijl used the term in a positive sense, to emphasise the link with major innovations in art. It was also an *epitheton ornans* among Bel-

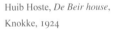

Huib Hoste, *De Beir house*, Knokke, 1924

gian artists. In 1923, Victor Bourgeois, who among other things imposed rigid lines on the Cité Moderne garden district in Sint-Agatha-Berchem (1922-25) and invited Pierre-Louis Flouquet and Karel Maes to design stained-glass windows and furniture for this district, had the street where he had built a block of flats renamed as 'Kubismestraat'. Louis Herman De Koninck remembered that the public mockingly called the house he had built for himself in 1924 'le trou du cubisme' (the cubist hole).

In Flanders, De Stijl was considered a revolutionary movement that deserved appreciation and support, but not blind allegiance. Huib Hoste, who published an article on modern architecture in *De Stijl* in 1918, in which he claimed that modern materials 'are most logically to be used horizontally or vertically', was later accused of treachery by Van Doesburg because he had also expressed a positive opinion on the pure visual effect of fluid lines in *De Nieuwe Amsterdammer*. Jozef Peeters called it premature to view Mondrian's 'horizontal-vertical image' as the climax of contemporary cultural development. In his article under the title 'Gemeenschapskunst' (1921), he denied that neo-plasticism was *the* universal art form. In his own 'community art' he made room for 'any geometrical constructional principle whatsoever', which also included the circle and the triangle. Victor Servranckx also distanced himself sufficiently from what he considered too prescriptive in De Stijl. In the first half of the 1920s he showed that he had been influenced, but formulated clear criticism of the 'too academic system' that 'threatens to impoverish us'. Servranckx left room for other geometric forms, which were also allowed to overlap.

Bauhaus

At the end of 1920, Van Doesburg travelled to Germany and was intrigued by the abstract films of Viking Eggeling and Hans Richter. Here too the influence of Van Doesburg and De Stijl was noticeable. In the publication that accompanied the recent exhibition *Theo van Doesburg. A New Expression of Life, Art and Technology* at BOZAR in Brussels (2015), this influence was summarised as follows: 'Van Doesburg was not only important for the promotion of abstract films, but also for their continued development. In Klein Kölzig, where Richter worked, his temporary presence was one of the elements that persuaded this film-maker to limit his visual vocabulary to straight lines, squares and rectangles.' Richter's film *Rhythmus 21* (1921-24) illustrates this very fully.

In Germany, Van Doesburg also influenced teachers and students at the Bauhaus in Weimar. He organised a course to promote the principles of De Stijl in both theoretical and practical terms. At that time, the thinking at the Bauhaus was mainly in terms of individual expression and craftsmanship, whereas Van Doesburg advocated a modern art founded on a rational attitude and was interested in technology and machine production. This helped influence the change of course that took place at the Bauhaus between 1922 and 1923 and which Walter Gropius summarised in 1923 in the motto 'Art and Technology, A New Unity'. The impact of the ideas of De Stijl on the Bauhaus was sometimes abundantly clear, as for example in the architectural designs by Herbert Bayer, with their coloured planes. And the 'slatted chair' that Marcel Breuer made as a student in the furniture workshop in 1922-24 was directly influenced by De

Stijl, more particularly by Rietveld's furniture. Publications in the Bauhausbücher series included not only Mondrian's *Neue Gestaltung: Neoplastizismus* (1925), but also Van Doesburg's *Grundbegriffe der neuen gestaltenden Kunst* (1925) and Oud's *Holländische Architektur* (1926).

Functional and economical

The Rietveld Schröder House (1924) in Utrecht, now open to the public and a World Heritage site, is an icon of the views of De Stijl. Gerrit Rietveld designed it in close cooperation with the client and occupant, Truus Schröder. The house is a three-dimensional composition built up using horizontal and vertical relationships. The structure of the architecture, the interior and the furniture are defined by straight lines, and this makes the house a unified experience. On the first floor with its open-plan and main living areas, rigid planes create variable spatial relationships instead of immobile masses. The Rietveld Schröder House is a flexible environment and the occupants' handling of it is conscious and based on practical needs: they can move a straight wall, fold out a table top, lengthen a rectangular bench. Colour is not decorative, but an organic element of the architecture. This house gives

Marcel Breuer/Tischlerei Bauhaus Weimar, *Lath chair*, 1924. Bauhaus-Archiv/Museum für Gestaltung

The Rietveld Schröder House, 1924, Prins Hendriklaan 50, Utrecht.
Photo by Ernst Moritz

concrete form to the ideas of De Stijl as listed by Van Doesburg in 'De nieuwe architectuur' (1924), a piece that appeared in *De Stijl* in a slightly modified form as the manifesto 'Tot een beeldende architectuur' (Towards a plastic architecture) (1924). This new architecture – elementary, economical, functional – used an open floor-plan divided by rectangular planes and no longer separated indoor and outdoor spaces. The division is not symmetrical or in accordance with fixed patterns, but is in keeping with the functional requirements of a dynamic outlook on life. Such architectural elements as function, plane, mass, time, space, light, colour and material are at the same time visual elements of the composition. Since time had also become an element of architecture, Van Doesburg used the terms 'four-dimensional' and 'time-space image aspects'. The unity of time and space (where a coloured space is experienced as a sequence of colour planes, as 'the direct expression of the time and space relationships of the new architecture') contributes to a dynamic experience of space. Point 11 in the manifesto states that

'The new architecture is *anti-cubist*, meaning it does not endeavour to contain the various functional spatial cells in one single closed cube, but *casts the functional spatial cells* (e.g. canopy planes, balcony volumes, etc.) *outwards, away* from the middle point of the cube, whereby the height, breadth and depth, plus time, become an entirely new item of plastic expression in the open spaces. This makes the architecture look more or less as if it were floating (insofar as this is constructionally possible – a task for the engineers!), and as if, in a manner of speaking, it contravenes nature's law of gravity.'

Van Doesburg had previously already visualised this dynamic vision of architecture in his *Contra-Constructies*, such as in the architectonic sketches for the *Maison Particulière* (1923) that he had done with Cornelis van Eesteren.

Tributes to De Stijl

The ideas behind the artistic movement lived on after the demise of the magazine *De Stijl*. For example, in the 1930s and later, the influence of De Stijl was visible in designs for interiors and household textiles, such as the tablecloths and tea towels with blue and red stripes woven in by the Dutch textile designer Kitty van der Mijll Dekker (around 1935-40), and in the efficiency of the Bruynzeel modular kitchen by Dutch designer Piet Zwart in 1938. In addition, De Stijl continued to be a frame of reference as soon as red, yellow and blue rectangles were used in a rigidly geometrical design. The architecture and design of the 1950s and 1960s regularly played with striking areas of colour. Walls, doors and windows were divided up like a grid in which coloured panels created accents. Patterns of intense red, yellow and blue were popular: 'the primary colours that have previously been appropriated by De Stijl'. A series of photos entitled *RedYellowBlue – Salon van horizontalen en verticalen* (2009-10) by the Belgian artist Annemie Augustijns is a tribute to this late-modernist architecture and an explicit reference to Mondrian's painting. This reference is equally obvious in the renowned Mondrian dresses that Yves Saint Laurent designed in 1965. This French fashion designer found that Mondrian's pared-down art summarised the spirit of the 1960s. The rigid design in lines and planes is also a cliché, but precisely for this reason is extremely effective. It crops up in the most diverse products and situations.

Still, many of the tributes to De Stijl are part of an artistic or design approach. Dan Flavin's two-part light installation – *Untitled (to Piet Mondrian through his preferred colours, red, yellow and blue)* and *Untitled (to Piet Mondrian who lacked green) 2* – which the American artist created specifically for the Stedelijk Museum in Amsterdam in 1986, and which was reinstalled in 2011 and later purchased, links Mondrian's art to the new views on art advocated by minimal art and related movements. In *Counter-Compositions* (2006-08), the Dutch artist Germaine Kruip took Van Doesburg and De Stijl as her basis and through art tried to make the beauty in reality visible. She also quoted Mondrian in her exhibition at De Vleeshal in 2006: 'Art is only a substitute as long as beauty is absent from life. As life gains in balance, art will gradually disappear' (vleeshal.nl). Even young artists who have grown up with multimedia and digital art play with the memory of Mondrian and Van Doesburg. *Odette* (2008), a temporary installation by the Belgian artists Boy & Erik Stappaerts and Nick Ervinck in the rotunda of the Royal Arcades in Ostend was an explicit reference to the *Aubette* amusement complex in Strasbourg (1928). In the *ciné-dancing* on the first floor of this complex, Van Doesburg gave shape to his dynamic vision of colour in space, just as, from 1924, he had injected movement into his painting by introducing diagonals into his *Contra-Composities*. Stappaerts's and Ervinck's installation used square building blocks to create a cheerful discotheque cum meeting-place. At the same time, its geometric decoration looked like a pattern of colour pixels in a digital model. It looks as if Mondrian and Van Doesburg had turned up in the hybrid space of a real-virtual world. The exhibition and publication entitled The *Bauhaus #itsalldesign* (Vitra Design Museum, 2015-16) also explicitly makes the link between the twenty-first century and the modernism of the twentieth. Rietveld's 1919 *Buffetkast* is exhibited there, or at least the version of it that the Rotterdam-based Italian-Japanese design firm Studio Minale-Maeda made of it in 2010, using Lego bricks. In this *Lego Buffet*, Rietveld's production on the basis of standard components is made playful and accessible to a broad public. And a human touch seems to be given to the

Studio
Minale-Maeda,
Lego Buffet,
2010

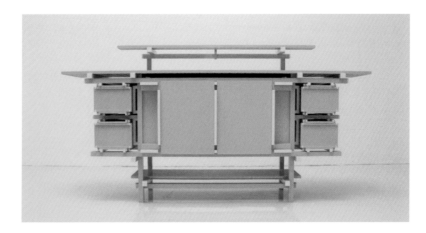

Annemie Augustijns,
Red Yellow Blue/Salon van horizontalen en verticalen, 2009.
© Annemie Augustijns

Translated by Gregory Ball

standardisation found in the industrial processes that made such a mark on the twentieth century (minale-maeda.com). It takes no great step to reach a situation where one makes one's furniture oneself: in an open design context such as the one 'opendesk' creates, the user downloads designs and has the material cut out locally or 3D-printed using computer-guided machines (opendesk. cc). De Stijl and Bauhaus are in this instance fundamental points of reference in a reflection on the place of design, designer, production and user in the twenty-first century. So it is also possible for *The Bauhaus #itsalldesign* to state that

'Although the historical context was very different, the topics that were discussed by Bauhaus members are, a hundred years later, as current as they were then: humans versus machines, individual versus society, authorship versus the collective, unique products versus mass production. In order to address these changes, designers return to the origins of industrial design, to movements such as the Bauhaus or De Stijl, with ironic comments or critical reflection. At the same time, they test the transferability of tried and tested methods such as the manifesto, which was used to spread new ideas at the beginning of the twentieth century.' ■

NOTES

1   Oud, 'Het monumentale stadsbeeld' (The Monumental Townscape), translated by Hans L.C. Jaffé in Hans L.C. Jaffé, *De Stijl*, New York: H.N. Abrams, 1971.

FURTHER READING

Avant-garde in België 1917-1929 (exhibition catalogue). Brussels: Gemeentekrediet, 1992

Fabre, Gladys, Doris Wintgens Hötte and Michael White (eds.), *Van Doesburg and the International Avant-Garde*. Constructing a New World. London: Tate Publishing, 2009

Janssen, Hans and Michael White, *Het verhaal van De Stijl. Van Mondriaan tot Van Doesburg*. Antwerp-The Hague: Ludion-Gemeentemuseum, 2011

Fabre, Gladys, *Theo van Doesburg. A New Expression of Life, Art and Technology*. Brussels: Bozar Books & Mercatorfonds / Yale University Press, 2016

The Indo Author Tjalie Robinson

Pioneer of a Multiracial Identity in the American Sixties

[JEROEN DEWULF]

When President Barack Obama decided to identify himself as 'Black, African American or Negro' in the 2010 census form, he confirmed the enduring legacy of the United States' one-drop rule. Having a white mother and a black father, he could have made a different choice, such as checking both the 'White' and the 'Black' box or defining himself as 'multiracial' in the box 'Some Other Race'. Obama's decision to identify himself exclusively as black provoked both satisfaction and disappointment. While groups associated with the civil rights movement greeted his decision with joy and interpreted Obama's self-identification as a reflection of solidarity with the country's traditionally underprivileged black community, organizations that represent multiracial America perceived his decision as a lost opportunity to finally overcome the country's racial divide by moving from a static to a fluid definition of race.

While myriads of multiracial societies have developed throughout American history, from the mulatto castes of New Orleans to the Punjabi-Mexican families in California and the Chinese-Irish ones in New York, it is generally assumed that the conscious framing of a mixed-racial American identity is a recent phenomenon that started in the late 1970s with groups such as iPride, Biracial Family Network and Interracial Family Circle who in 1989 jointly created AMEA, the Association of MultiEthnic Americans. It is not well known that such organizations were preceded by the *Tong Tong* group for more than a decade. Founded in California in 1962 by the Dutch Eurasian 'Indo' writer Tjalie Robinson, *The American Tong Tong* was probably the first magazine in the United States to consciously advocate a multiracial identity.

Indo emigration to the United States

Following Sukarno's unilateral declaration of Indonesian independence in August 1945, some 300,000 people with European status, including some 180,000 Eurasians, repatriated to the Netherlands. In a country that was still recovering from the destruction of the Second World War, there was little enthusiasm for the arrival of tens of thousands of destitute 'colonials'. Many doubted whether people who had grown up in Southeast Asia would be able to adapt

Jan Boon
(a.k.a. Tjalie Robinson),
1929

themselves to Dutch society. These reservations were particularly strong in relation to Eurasians. The Dutch government reacted to these concerns with a twofold policy. On the one hand, it imposed measures to enforce assimilation into Dutch society: repatriates were spread all over the country and pressured to adopt Dutch habits. On the other hand, the government urged repatriates to consider renewed emigration.

In its efforts to boost emigration to the United States, the government made a promotional film about life in sunny California with the unmistakable message that repatriates from the Indies would feel more at home in California than in the chilly Netherlands. The film, strategically entitled *Een plaatsje in de zon* (A Cozy Place in the Sun, 1961), did not miss its aim. Some 25,000 Dutch citizens with roots in the Indies – most of them Eurasians – emigrated to America and the large majority effectively settled in California, where the mild climate allowed for a similar lifestyle to that in the Indies. Among them was Jan Boon (1911-1974), better known under his alias Tjalie Robinson.

Tjalie Robinson as intellectual leader

Boon was born in 1911 in Nijmegen, when his Dutch father, a sergeant major in the colonial KNIL army, and Eurasian (British-Javanese) mother were on holiday in the Netherlands. He spent his youth in Cimahi (on West Java) and Batavia, the later Jakarta. Unlike most other Eurasians with a European status, Boon decided to stay in Indonesia after its independence. In those early 1950s, he started the columns *Piekerans van een straatslijper* (Ruminations of a Flâneur) that would make him famous under the Eurasian *nom de plume* Tjalie (a corruption of 'Charlie') Robinson (his mother's maiden name). He wrote his 'ruminations' from the perspective of the *anak Betawie*, the Indo, who, with a mixture of irony and melancholy, witnessed how the (colonial) Batavia was changing into (the postcolonial) Jakarta. Robinson's columns were a statement of belonging, which was reflected in the frequent use of Petjo, a typically Eurasian mixture of Dutch and Malay.

Jan Boon with his mother, 1933

The inner conflict of being torn between Indonesia and the Netherlands, two cultures that for Robinson could only exist interconnected, is also a characteristic of his short stories, written under the pseudonym Vincent Mahieu. The pen name refers to Auguste Mahieu, founder of the Komedie Stamboel, a late nineteenth-century form of popular theatre that combined Western and Asian traditions. Mahieu's short stories represent the first genuine Eurasian voice in Dutch fiction and focus on topics such as motorbike racing, guitar playing, boxing, and above all hunting. Both titles of the anthologies in which these stories were later published, *Tjies* (1958) and *Tjoek* (1960), refer to guns used for hunting. In accordance with the tradition of oral literature, Robinson defined his stories as 'tales', and adapted his language to the way stories were told in the Eurasian community: with short sentences, plenty of suspense, and full of expressions in Petjo.

Unlike most other Indo-Europeans, Robinson originally believed that there would still be a future for him in the Indonesian Republic. Soon, however, the political situation in Sukarno's Indonesia moved in a direction that excluded the survival of a Dutch-oriented culture and he repatriated to the Netherlands in 1954. Despite his repatriation, Robinson refused to accept that there would be no place for people like him who identified with both Dutch and Indonesian culture in the postcolonial world order. While most Dutch authors with roots in the Indies tended to recall their country of birth with the assumption that they wrote about an epoch that was irrevocably in the past, Robinson distanced himself from those who wanted to reduce Indonesia to *tempo dulu* (sweet old colonial times). He believed that 350 years of shared history had created a special bond between two cultures that should continue to develop.

In 1957, Robinson became editor-in-chief of *Onze Brug* (Our Bridge), a small magazine made by and for repatriates from the Indies. While *Onze Brug* had been characterized by a nostalgic perspective of the former colony, Robinson changed its editorial policy. He decided to use it as a platform for the elaboration of a Eurasian identity, which was reflected in its new name *Tong Tong*: a hollow trunk that is beaten to call the attention of the community. Having started with only 400 subscribers, *Tong Tong* quickly achieved a circulation of over 11,000 copies. Instead of deploring Indonesia's independence as the end of an era, Robinson considered it as the beginning of a new phase of Indo identity. He believed that the end of the East Indies liberated Indos from their slavish imitation of Dutch culture and would catalyse them to recognize their cultural and ethnic singularity.

After a visit to California's Indo community in 1961, Robinson decided to apply for immigration to the United States and eventually settled in Whittier, California. Together with his wife Lilian Ducelle, he founded *The American Tong Tong* as a supplement to *Tong Tong*, which was followed in 1963 by the foundation of the Indo community centre De Soos in nearby Pasadena.

Framing a Eurasian identity in America

The Indo community was not totally unknown to American scholars. In the 1930s, they had figured prominently in American sociological studies. This interest related to the work of Robert Park, whose perspective on multiracial people was ambivalent. Although his ground-breaking article 'Human Migration and the Marginal Man' (1928) carried the stereotypical image of 'mixed bloods' as 'spiritually instable', 'intensified self-conscious' and 'restless' people that dated back to nineteenth-century racialist theories, Park also considered them to be cultural innovators. In a later article, 'Race Relations and Certain Frontiers' (1934), Park focused specifically on the Eurasian community in the Dutch East Indies, which triggered the interest of Everett Stonequist. Stonequist's theory in *The Marginal Man* (1937) came close to Park's insights, but his perspective on multiracial people had a stronger negative bias. Stonequist perceived mixed-racial people as a problem both to society as well as to themselves by relating them to inferiority complexes, hypersensitivity, spiritual distress and a general malaise. Not surprisingly, his chapter on 'the Indo-Europeans of Java' recycled the stereotypical image of Eurasians as people who 'live useless discontented lives'. In 1963, a popular version of Park's and Stonequist's theories appeared. Under the title *Almost White*, Brewton Berry again put the spotlight on 'Indo-Europeans in Indonesia' as 'pathetic folk of mixed ancestry who never know quite where they belong ... raceless people, neither fish nor fowl.'

Robinson's identity concept was strongly influenced by these sociological studies. In 1961, he still referred to himself as a 'marginal man ... a child of two races and cultures, living on the border between the imperial-colonial era and a new era.' By 1971, however, Robinson had distanced himself from theories of marginality and claimed that 'where there is no margin, there is no marginality ... he is NEVER MARGINAL who manages to achieve his proper identity.' In his attempt to rescue the Eurasian community with roots in the East Indies from either a deplorable existence in the ethnic margin or disappearance through assimilation, Robinson used a strategy he copied from the civil rights movement: transforming shame into pride. While the abbreviation 'Indo' for 'Indo-European' had been a term of abuse during the colonial era, Robinson adopted it as a *nom de gueux* and propagated 'Indo pride'.

As early as 1958, Robinson established a connection between Indos and the black community in America. He argued that, just as black people had to develop a proper identity in the diaspora after the end of slavery, Indo people had to do the same at the end of colonialism. 'Despite hanging parties ... one finds a strong, creative, indestructible form of black culture in America', he argued, and linked this to his own community that 'can also create such a culture if only we are conscious of our proper values, proud of our own heritage and confident about our own future.' Robinson interpreted the strength of the civil rights movement as a sign that American society offered opportunities for self-development that did not exist in the Netherlands. In an open letter, Robinson encouraged all Indos to consider immigration to America: 'In Indonesia, they still want to make every Indo into an Indonesian, in the Netherlands every Indo has to become a perfect Dutchman. In the United States, they think that such assimilation is ridiculous.'

To those who were already living in the United States, Robinson made an appeal to resist the assumption that one had to forget about one's origin in order to become a successful American. Instead of the word 'Americanization', he used the expression 'to become Yankee' in reference to assimilation in American society according to the melting-pot theory. This choice can be

Jan Boon, 1933

Jan Boon with children and his wife Lilian Ducelle at the Pasar Malam
in The Hague, in the 1950s

explained by the influence of Nathan Glazer and Daniel Moynihan's work *Be-yond the Melting Pot* (1963) on Robinson. Glazer and Moynihan had distanced themselves from the notion that the mixture of peoples in American society was soon to blend into a homogeneous end product. Rather, they claimed that 'the point about the melting pot ... is that it did not happen.' Robinson real-ized how Glazer and Moynihan stood at the beginning of a transformation of American society, where the concept of diversity was about to replace the melting-pot theory. Hence, 'Americanization' was no longer an adequate term to describe assimilation into American society. From Robinson's perspective, 'Americanization' now represented the opposite: to enrich American diversity with one's own identity. He therefore insisted that being a self-conscious Indo would make one more American, not less. Consequently, he highlighted Eura-sian cultural achievements that had been traditionally neglected by scholars: *stamboel* theatre, *bangsawan* opera, *kroncong* music and the *Petjo* language. He proudly included the *Tong Tong* magazine in this list as 'proof that the Eurasian is not indolent nor marginal, but capable of conquering a valuable place among other peoples with his own force.'

In Robinson's construction of a unique Eurasian identity for people with roots in the former Indies, hybridity and homelessness became distinctive fea-tures. He presented a self-confident transnational existence in the diaspora as a compelling alternative to an inglorious assimilation in Indonesia or the Neth-erlands. In a reply to Berry's disparaging remarks about Eurasians, he wrote:

'I did not care that people wanted to call me "neither fish nor fowl," and wanted to label me either Indonesian or Dutch. ... I compared our Indo identity to that of the turtle that is "neither fish nor fowl," and praised this animal as a unique, land- and sea-lover ... that cuts through oceans from continent to continent.'

Robinson linked his multiracial identity concept to a world without discrimination and predicted that 'we are the people of the future – heralds of an era free of racial and nationalistic discrimination.' He distanced himself, however, from those who believed that the disappearance of identity markers was the best way to overcome discrimination. In his article 'Negervraagstuk' (The Black Problem, 1964), Robinson defended the importance of cultural differences and argued that in order to overcome discrimination one should learn to respect cultural difference rather than try to abolish it. He rejected the assumption that there was a 'black problem', but rather identified a 'white, European problem' as the real challenge for the future: 'People assume there is a "black problem" only because black people were able to preserve their identity despite millions of attempts to prevent this. The real problem is the "European problem," that of a strange kind of people, who ... assume that they need to tell other people what to do.'

Jan Boon at his worktable, 1960

Contrary to what Robinson had expected, his project was much less success-ful in America than in the Netherlands, where pressure to assimilate had the opposite effect. Almost all major cultural events of today's thriving Indo com-munity in the Netherlands — including the magazine *Moesson* and the annual *Tong Tong Fair* in The Hague, the world's largest Eurasian fair — were founded by Robinson.

This was different in America, where Robinson had set the ambitious goal of 1,000 subscribers for *The American Tong Tong* but only reached 300. Time and again he complained that Indos in America were more interested in money than in culture. Another problem was language. Robinson was well aware of the fact that in order to become successful in American society, members of his com-munity had to become fluent in English. Accordingly, he made *The American Tong Tong* a bilingual (Dutch-English) magazine, which reflected his wish for integration without assimilation. At the same time, however, it was clear to him that 'precisely because we are aware of our heritage, we should not abandon our original language.' Yet he did not anticipate that first-generation Indos in

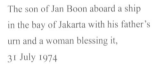

The son of Jan Boon aboard a ship in the bay of Jakarta with his father's urn and a woman blessing it, 31 July 1974

America would massively switch to English as the language of communication with their children. When Robinson realized that most second-generation Indos were unable to read anything of his work, as they did not know Dutch, let alone Petjo, he did not have an answer.

Robinson cancelled *The American Tong Tong* in February 1965, only two and a half years after its creation. By then, his enthusiasm about America had considerably diluted after several attempts to become an entrepreneur had failed. Even more worrying for Robinson were problems with *Tong Tong* in the Netherlands, where many had interpreted his emigration to America as a form of betrayal and had turned their back on the *Tong Tong* group. In 1966, Robinson returned to the Netherlands, where he died eight years later.

With Robinson leaving America, the local Indo community lost its intellectual leader. In 1988, De Soos was dissolved after a last play with the appropriate title *En toen al* (And that was it). None of Robinson's ambitious projects in the United States succeeded. Robinson's only concrete legacy is the magazine *De Indo*. What had originally been a club magazine for *Soos*-members survives in the present as a modestly printed monthly publication by an enthusiastic group of volunteers with news from and about Indos in the diaspora.

Robinson's ambition to pass Indo culture and identity over to the next generation was largely abandoned by Indos in America. One rarely finds second- or third-generation Indos at their *kumpulans* (social gatherings). The main concern of these groups is to save Indo heritage from oblivion rather than reviving or reinventing it in cooperation with younger generations. First-generation Indos in America therefore generally perceive themselves as a dying community, or, as one of them said in an interview with Greta Kwik in 1989, as 'the last of the Mohicans'. What remains is Robinson's written legacy with a fascinating wealth of ideas about identity issues that only long after his death achieved prominence in Dutch and American society. ∎

FURTHER READING

Brewton Berry, *Almost White*. New York: Macmillan, 1963

Nathan Glazer and Daniel P. Moynihan, *Beyond the Melting Pot*. Cambridge MA: Harvard University Press, 1963

Greta Kwik, *The Indos in Southern California*. New York: AMS Press, 1989

Tjalie Robinson, *Piekerans van een straatslijper*. The Hague: Tong Tong, 1976

Tjalie Robinson, 'Ut benne net mense', *Tong Tong* (30.10.1958); 'In de marge', *Tong Tong* (15.03.1961); 'Voor en over Emigranten', Tong Tong (15.04.1961); 'Op weg naar succes', *The American Tong Tong* (15.08.1962); 'In welke taal?' *The American Tong Tong* (30.09.1962); 'Amerika. Theorie en Werkelijkheid', *The American Tong Tong* (30.10.1963); 'Negervraagstuk', *Tong Tong* (15.08.1964); 'Memo van Maria', *Tong Tong* (01.06.1970); 'Nostalgie, Marginaliteit en Heimwee', *Tong Tong* (15.06.1971); 'Vindt u eigen weg!' Tong Tong (15.05.1972)

Robert E. Park, 'Human Migration and the Marginal Man' (1928), in *Theories of Ethnicity: A Classical Reader*, ed. Werner Sollors. New York: New York University Press, 1996, 152-282

Robert E. Park, 'Race Relations and Certain Frontiers'. In *Race and Culture Contacts*, edited by E.B. Reuter. New York: Mc. Graw-Hill, 1934, 57-85

Everett V. Stonequist, *The Marginal Man: A Study in Personality and Culture Conflict* New York: Russell & Russell, 1937

The Secret of the Royal Concertgebouw Orchestra

[JUDITH VAN DER WEL]

In the concert hall of the Sydney Opera House, the audience grows silent. The musicians of the Royal Concertgebouw Orchestra concentrate. Everyone in the hall looks expectantly at the door where chief conductor Mariss Jansons is about to appear. Silence. For a few very long minutes, the door remains closed. A murmuring goes through the hall. Why doesn't he come? The audience starts to talk louder. Then, finally, the door opens and Jansons appears. His face is ashen. Bent and unsteadily, he makes his way between the orchestra members. Concertmaster Vesko Eschkenazy gives him a hand and helps him onto the podium. The musicians exchange worried looks. They know that Jansons suffers from serious heart problems and that once, years ago in Oslo, he even collapsed on the podium. The story goes that despite lying unconscious on the floor, he kept beating time with his baton. Jansons survived, but his own father had died on stage, just like the former chief conductor of the Concertgebouw orchestra, Eduard van Beinum. Why is Jansons here? He can hardly stand up.

The concertmaster moves to the edge of his chair and turns towards the orchestra so everyone can see him well. The other orchestra members move closer together. With Jansons's first gesture, the double bass and cello players emit their first growling sounds. The musicians look at their conductor, but even more than on other occasions they follow each other's directions. Anxiously, they manage to bring Stravinsky's *Firebird* to a proper conclusion. While an assistant conductor takes over for the second half of the concert, Jansons is immediately transported to hospital. He leaves the Sydney Opera House, which, in honour of the orchestra's 125th anniversary, is bathed in an orange glow. The year is 2013.

It's not for every conductor that an audience will hold its communal breath. And the Sydney Opera House does not light up in a special colour for every orchestra that has an anniversary. But the Royal Concertgebouw Orchestra isn't just any orchestra. In 2008, it was voted the best orchestra in the world by the British magazine *Gramophone*. Who the best conductor was had not been asked, but according to many newspapers it was Mariss Jansons. He was the only principal conductor with two orchestras in the top six: München's Bayerische Rundfunk and Amsterdam's Concertgebouw Orchestra. In 2015, in a new poll, the international critics of the classical music site bachtrack.com named

Concertgebouw Orchestra
in Amsterdam.
Photo by Anne Dokter

the Concertgebouw Orchestra the second best orchestra in the world. The Berliner Philharmoniker came in first. This time, conductors were also rated. Mariss Jansons was number three on the list of best conductors; number one was Riccardo Chailly, who had been chief conductor of the Concertgebouw Orchestra from 1988 to 2004.

Although such lists are somewhat arbitrary and are disliked by many musicians 'because music is not a competition', they do show that the Royal Concertgebouw is one of the top orchestras in the world. But what accounts for the excellence of this Amsterdam orchestra? How do these 120 musicians with diverse backgrounds and characters unite their sound into one orchestra? Do they owe their success to Jansons or can they do without him? What is their secret?

A fine from the conductor

When the Concertgebouw Orchestra was founded in 1888, no one would have guessed that this symphony orchestra would become so successful. Most members had been plucked from provincial orchestras and ensembles, where the music sounded pretty good but never great. Yet its first chief conductor immediately set the bar high. Willem Kes was an experienced musician who had studied in Leipzig, Brussels and Berlin and had seen and listened to famous orchestras and conductors. He approached the music with a precision the members of the orchestra were not accustomed to. They were shocked when the conductor called the players who had not been up to par during rehearsal to his office to go through the composition note by note. They were just as indignant when he started handing out fines to musicians who were late or missed a rehearsal. Kes was no more accommodating to his listeners. They could no longer walk around, drink tea or chat during a concert. The conductor demanded absolute silence in the hall. In this way, Kes taught the orchestra an important lesson: a good orchestra needs discipline and attention to detail to make the music sound as beautiful as possible.

Today this speaks for itself. In 2013, I travelled for a year with the Royal Concertgebouw Orchestra on its world tour in celebration of its 125th anniversary and wrote a book about it, *Stemmen* (Voices, Querido/Van Halewyck, 2015). During the tour, I saw how the whole rhythm of the orchestra members was directed at giving good concerts. The musicians took a nap before each concert, restrained from drinking too much alcohol and went to the gym to stay fit. Every day, I heard musicians playing in their hotel rooms to improve their performance even more. Some of them even practised in the departure hall of the airport. Not because they had to, but because, as a violist said to me, 'It hurts when the music doesn't get its due'. A faultless concert was to them not necessarily a satisfying concert. As first solo oboist, Alexei Ogrintchouk said, 'I want to share my vision of the music as completely as possible with the audience, not missing the tiniest detail.'

Not everyone has the passion, imagination and technique to express the richness of a composition. The musicians of the Concertgebouw Orchestra have all passed rigorous auditions. For someone to be accepted is like a dream come true. The velvet sound of the string players is known all over the world, just like the refined solos of the wind section and the ingenious rhythms of the percussionists. The acoustics of the Concertgebouw add to the uniqueness of

Strings. Photo by Anne Dokter

Bernard Haitink
conducts Mahler.
Photo by Ronald Knapp

this sound. 'When you are in the Concertgebouw you start playing differently',
says cellist Daniël Esser. 'You can't escape it. The acoustics of the Concertgebouw are like a Madonna on a Raphael painting holding the orchestra in her
arms.' Those acoustics unite the musicians and serve also as a benchmark, for
every week the orchestra has another guest conductor leading it with a new
programme. Even when the orchestra goes on tour, the musicians remember how the music sounded in the Main Hall. This very resonance also has its
challenges, as the musicians can sometimes hardly hear each other on stage.
But that is exactly why they have become even better listeners to each other's
specific sound.

The love with which musicians talk about the Concertgebouw Orchestra is
not a given in the orchestra world. When first solo trombonist Jörgen van Rijen played in a French orchestra, he noticed that its members were not very
motivated. This was due to the orchestra's organization model. In France, the
Minister of Culture or the mayor chooses the conductor. In the Concertgebouw
Orchestra, the orchestra members also vote when a chief conductor or a new
colleague is chosen. On top of that, they have a say in the choice of music and
the work provisions for the orchestra. According to Van Rijen this makes an
enormous difference. 'When orchestra members feel that their opinion doesn't
make any difference, they think: as long as I play my notes I will get my salary.'
So participation is essential for a good orchestra. It's no coincidence that the
three best orchestras in the world, the Berliner and Wiener Philharmoniker
and the Concertgebouw Orchestra all have a good system of participation.

Principals and tuttis

In spite of this participation, in every orchestra there is tension between the
individual and the collective. To get accepted in the Concertgebouw Orchestra
a musician has to be almost as good as a soloist. But in an orchestra there is

Mariss Jansons.
Photo by Anne Dokter

less room for that. All 120 members of the Concertgebouw Orchestra have, after all, their own musical ideas, but if they were to sound all at the same time it would be a cacophony.

That's why there is a strict hierarchy in an orchestra. It does not only have a conductor, but each instrumental section also has a principal. The principal of the cellists, for example, shows the other cellists, the tuttis, with his gestures when he starts playing faster and louder. At the same time, he has eye contact with the principals of the other sections to coordinate his timing. A principal will also play solos regularly. At such a moment, he may give his own interpretation. But the rest of the time he does his best to blend his own timbre with that of the orchestra.

The principal of the first violins has a special position: he is the concertmaster. He can mediate between the orchestra and the conductor. When an ill Mariss Jansons stood on the podium in Sydney, concertmaster Vesko Eschkenazy partly took over his duties. He shifted to face the orchestra more directly to let them know: if the maestro is unclear or becomes unwell, I'm here. At the same time, the other principals kept an even closer eye on each other. That way an orchestra still functions quite well without a conductor.

But the conductor isn't there for nothing, of course. It is up to him to blend the sound of all those different personalities in the orchestra into one. He has studied the score, listened to earlier renditions and arrived at his own vision of the music. His fingers dictate the tempo and volume, single out musical lines and phrases and guard the tension arc of the composition as a whole.

The Royal Concertgebouw Orchestra has had very few, but very good chief conductors. After 128 years of existence, the orchestra has only just come to its seventh chief conductor. It's the Italian Daniele Gatti who will be leading the orchestra from September 2016 on. Shortly after the concert in Sydney, Mariss Jansons decided that he would have to step down because of his health. By then he had been chief conductor for eleven years. If Gatti follows in his and in his predecessors' footsteps, he is at the beginning of a long career with the Concertgebouw Orchestra. Willem Mengelberg even made it to fifty years as chief conductor.

Unfortunately, the relationship between an orchestra and its conductor is not always a bed of roses. Kes, as I mentioned earlier, was feared because of his strict, pedantic approach. Mengelberg, who was indeed a very great musician, nevertheless brought his own 'chocolate club' into existence by passing advantages ('chocolates') to his protégés in exchange for their howls of derision when tearing down another musician. His successor, Eduard van Beinum, on the other hand, was so meek, that he appeared one day at the door of the then still very young Bernard Haitink and sobbed: 'They say that I'm no good at tuning up.'

Recently, Haitink himself got into conflict with the management of the Concertgebouw Orchestra. In March 2014 in an interview with the Dutch newspaper *Het Parool*, he said that he never wanted to conduct the Concertgebouw Orchestra again, as he had felt 'totally neglected' during the 125th anniversary celebrations. Still, Haitink *had* conducted a Bruckner symphony that year, but apparently that had not been enough. The management of the Concertgebouw Orchestra was 'perplexed'. Executive director Jan Raes indicated that, over the years, in order to make Haitink's appearances possible, they had stretched the flexibility of other leading conductors 'to the limits of what was acceptable'. He also said that he respected Haitink greatly and that there would always be an extended hand. It now appears that Haitink has accepted this hand. After the management of the Concertgebouw Orchestra apologized once more for 'unnecessarily hurting his feelings', he promised that he would conduct the Concertgebouw Orchestra again. A great relief to all. Haitink is one of the greatest still living Dutch conductors and was chief conductor of the Concertgebouw Orchestra for no less than twenty-seven years. It's not for nothing that he is also its honorary conductor.

Haitink's magic

Bernard Haitink was only thirty-two when he landed on the podium of the Concertgebouw. His predecessor, Eduard van Beinum, had unexpectedly died of a heart attack during a rehearsal. After his death, the management appointed two conductors: the seasoned old hand, Eugen Jochum, and the emerging talent, Bernard Haitink. After two years, Haitink was promoted to chief conductor.

But a lot of repertory was still new to him and the orchestra wasn't making it easy for him either. 'Mr. Haitink', a cellist once derisively said when he made a remark: 'you could have been my son.' Later Haitink would say that he aged twice as fast during those years.

In the late 1960s, early 1970s, Haitink began to grow. He started performing the big cycles of, among others, Bruckner and Mahler and recorded them for Philips, with whom he had meanwhile signed a recording contract. Those recordings struck a chord. The Christmas matinees in the 1980s, where he performed Mahler symphonies, also added to his popularity in Europe.

In 1978, the orchestra appointed a permanent conductor alongside Haitink: the Russian conductor Kirill Kondrashin. Haitink had to take a deep breath, especially when he saw that the orchestra appreciated Kondrashin's meticulous approach. But Haitink had his own strength. 'He gave the musicians space', cellist Daniël Esser says. 'Out of that freedom something could arise and the orchestra would then surpass itself. Haitink was a master in atmosphere, which especially enhanced French music.'

The idea that Haitink would never again lead the Concertgebouw Orchestra was therefore painful for the musicians. Especially when Mariss Jansons – as meticulous as Kondrashin – was its conductor, some orchestra members missed Haitink's free approach. But Haitink would also have missed the orchestra. After all, not many orchestras have such a special sound or rise as singularly to the occasion when a conductor gives it the freedom. Moreover, Haitink had built up a history and connection with the musicians. Fortunately, he was magnanimous enough to accept the extended hand.

Breathing together

This story also reveals one of the Concertgebouw Orchestra's secrets, for the Concertgebouw Orchestra has many secrets. The acoustics of the Concertgebouw have already been mentioned as have the rigorous auditions for new orchestra members. The orchestra has always had exceptional chief conduc-

Cellists in
New York.
Photo by
Anne Dokter.

Trumpeter Wim van Hasselt
practising in Durban,
South Africa.
Photo by Anne Dokter

Timpanist
Marinus Komst
in New York.
Photo by Anne Dokter

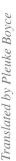

tors and, from an early age, participatory bodies, which increase musicians' feeling of belonging and motivate them even more to outshine themselves. The variation in guest conductors, programmes and tours also kept the orchestra sharp and inspired.

But the biggest secret of the orchestra is revealed during hardship. When the orchestra has to help Mariss Jansons to the finish line of *The Firebird*. When an orchestra member fears his playing level is slipping and asks a colleague for advice. When musicians sharing a music stand do not get along, but still cooperate. Or when management and Haitink genuflect to each other to restore their relationship. In each case people let go of their ego because of the orchestra. Of course, that is not easy, but most of the time their love of the music and bond with the orchestra turn out to be triumphant.

'In a good orchestra all personalities blend because they all have the same goal', top violinist Leonidas Kavakos said when he was a soloist with the Concertgebouw Orchestra. 'An orchestra member can't just play what he wants, however good he may be. Musicians have to listen to each other, look at each other, they have to breathe and play together. That happens in the Royal Concertgebouw Orchestra and that's exactly what the world of today needs.' ■

Translated by Pleuke Boyce

Manneken Pis
or The Subversion of a Water Pipe

[GEERT VAN ISTENDAEL]

As you arrive in Brussels you see the town hall tower from afar. From afar you see the Basilica of the Sacred Heart, its copper-green dome, the spheres of the Atomium, which have been cleaned up again. The Palais de Justice, with its golden dome and worn-out mantle of scaffolding, are visible from all around.

But the most famous monument in Brussels is one you only see when you stand right in front of it. A little chap in bronze. A *menneke*, as we locals say; *manneken* to the outside world. You do not need to search for it either; just follow the stream of tourists around the Grand Place. Be ready to turn down narrow alleyways. Do not be surprised if you see it before you reach your destination. Rows, regiments, cohorts, legions of mannekens adorn the shop windows along the path to the one true manneken. Manneken bottle stoppers, manneken corkscrews, mannekens painted onto jugs, tankards, mugs and cups of various sizes, manneken beermats, manneken fridge magnets and lots, lots more. I suspect that somewhere in China, in a small town with a couple of million residents, the entire population manufactures mannekens in all conceivable shapes and sizes from morning until night, to the delight of foreign visitors, many of them also Chinese, who grace the capital of Europe with their presence, and to the benefit of the local tradespeople.

Everyone in Brussels is fake

Did I just write 'the one true manneken'?

Nonsense! Firstly, it's not unique. A little further on you will find Jeanneke Pis, then outside Brussels in Zelzate there is Mietje Stroel. Genuine mannekens can be found in Geraardsbergen, Poitiers, Colmar, Osaka, Botafogo near Rio de Janeiro, and Cuernavaca in Mexico. In Lacaune, in the Tarn, France, the fountain is named 'dels Pissaïres', and boasts four gentlemen. There is even one in Algeria. The United States, however, will not grant him entry. A waffle maker from Orlando, Florida, thought his Belgian product would sell better if he erected a manneken in front of his shop. Passers-by, however, were shocked and complained; yes, that's how it goes in the United States. The waffle maker was obliged to remove the statue. I await with considerable

The oldest known picture
of the fountain, early 18ᵀᴴ
century © City of Brussels
Museum

anticipation the moment when some sensible soul on Facebook might start a
campaign against the manneken for its political incorrectness.

Secondly, it is not the genuine article. Brussels' oldest citizen is not an original, but that is no problem around here. We have pretty flexible ideas about
who counts as a true local. The solution we have found is obvious: everyone
does. The reason is equally obvious: more or less everyone in our city is fake.

In the course of history the statue has been stolen and damaged a number of times. In 1965 vandals broke it in two, leaving only the feet and ankles
standing. The culprits were never found, but the remains of the statue were
recovered, restored and put on show in the Broodhuis, the Museum of the City

of Brussels. The Compagnie des Bronzes of Ransfortstraat in Molenbeek was commissioned to make two new casts, which resemble the original like peas in a pod, and one of which has adorned the fountain ever since. The Compagnie closed its doors in 1979, having cast countless statues, including Jan Breydel and Pieter de Coninck in Bruges, the craftsmen on the Kleine Zavel square and the Brabo fountain in Antwerp. The site now houses the Museum of Industry and Work, and the street may see the occasional passing jihadist from time to time.

Gushing fountains

In fact this is really a tale of water pipes. The earliest documents tell us that around 1450 a 'menneke pist' (little man urinates) on the corner of Stoofstraat and Eikstraat. That menneke was a stone statue.

Battle of Ransbeek, now Neder-Over-Heembeek (middle 12ᵗʰ century). The people of Brussels had brought the duke along in his cradle, which they hung on the branch of a tree (see on the left). The infant stood up and pissed over the edge of his hanging bed, right onto the helmets of the advancing enemy © City of Brussels Museum

Around a century earlier, Brussels' leaders had had three underground pipes made to feed the city's fountains. To avoid confusion among pedants, by city I do not mean the area covered today; only its pentagonal core, the area situated within what is currently called the small ring, which largely follows the line where the second city wall once stood.

Most housewives hauled buckets and pitchers daily to the nearest public fountain to supply their families. Those fountains were monumental. The greatest number were found in the neighbourhood of the Nedermerct, today's Grand Place. Brussels is a hilly city. The water was piped from high to low points via reservoirs and associated buildings. One of those, beautifully named 'De Grote Pollepel' (the big ladle), was situated halfway up a slope, where the Ravenstein Gallery is now. When the gallery was built De Grote Pollepel was moved to the park behind Egmont Palace, but the ladle only catches rainwater now. Egmont Park is not well known, as it is only accessible from three narrow alleys, one on Wolstraat, one on Waterloolaan and one on Grote Hertstraat.

The pissing child was far from the only fountain. On today's Priemstraat, for example, the Juliaenekensborre spouted drinking water; on the Grand Place itself there was a spectacular model with as many as five basins; there was even a fountain with three women apparently spouting water by pinching their nipples. Sadly nothing remains of these. That does not mean, though, that the Lower Town is now otherwise devoid of fountains. Look for De Spuwer, for instance, behind the town hall, or take a peek at the courtyard of the town hall, where the Maas and Scheldt fountains flow.

Manneken Pis embedded by the Belgian Socialist Party in the elections of 1929
© City of Brussels Museum

Pissing on the helmets of the enemy

The peeing child would inevitably become the hero of many a tale. The stories even refer to times long before the first statue existed. In the eighth century, the father of a baby was said to have threatened the virtue of a beautiful noblewoman, later known as Saint Gudula. She chased her assailant away with a double curse: 'Your only son will never grow again and will continue to urinate for eternity!'

Other stories mention a child urinating against a witch's door and immediately turning to stone or a little chap suffering a call of nature during a procession of crusaders and finding himself unable to stop, or a little guy who, when Brussels was under siege, pissed on the burning fuse of a keg of gunpowder.

Perhaps the best story is as follows. Around the middle of the twelfth century, a new duke took office in Brabant at the tender age of two. In those days, parents were in the habit of dying at inconvenient moments. The arch-enemies of the child duke saw their chance and attacked Brussels with all their might. There was a confrontation in Ransbeek, now Neder-Over-Heembeek, the northernmost corner of Brussels. The people of Brussels, however, had brought the duke along in his cradle, which they hung on the branch of a tree. The infant stood up, stark naked, and pissed over the edge of his hanging bed, right onto the helmets of the advancing enemy. Panic broke out. The people of Brussels made mincemeat of their besiegers.

There was indeed a Duke of Brabant, Godfried III, who bore the nickname 'dux in cunis', the duke in the cradle. But cradle or not, the historical truth is of minor significance in this kind of story. In my view this tale is the most uniquely Brussels of them all. Episodes such as the one with Saint Gudula or the witch can be found in countless variants all over the world, but a naked child chasing away soldiers by pissing on their helmets is something completely different.

The child wins against brute force. Now it might be argued that the motif of the weakling who is laughed down by everyone and wins against the mighty, the cruel, the bully or the giant, can equally be found in a great many languages and cultures. David and Goliath, Tom Thumb, the Brave Little Tailor; who does not know such stories? But this is about a single deed, or, to put it better, a single stream. The mighty are effortlessly humiliated, in the most natural manner humanly conceivable. David slung a stone. There is nothing natural about that. That is a story of guile and aggression. The stone is slung to kill the giant enemy or at least to injure him. The naked duke did nothing of the sort. Someone pissing is not committing an act of aggression. On the contrary, he makes himself quite vulnerable in the moment. Nevertheless he chases away men armed to the teeth, simply because the need arises, and it is a need we all share. There is something irreverent, something anarchistic, subversive, but also extremely human, about it. And thus something particularly characteristic of Brussels.

Arresting the oldest citizen of Brussels, 1846 © City of Brussels Museum

SOUVENIR DE BRUXELLES.

Histoire et origine de Manneken Pis, suivie de l'historique de la Place des Martyrs, de l'Eglise de Ste Gudule et de l'Hôtel-de-Ville, un volume orné de 4 figures coloriées Prix 1 Franc. Le même en anglais, Prix 1 Fr.

ARRESTATION DU PLUS ANCIEN BOURGEOIS DE BRUXELLES,

Pour contravention à l'Ordonnance de Police sur les Pissoirs.

Ceremony for the official presentation of
the costume of the Welsh Guard, 29 July 1945
© City of Brussels Museum

Smiling down at passers-by

We know that in the seventeenth century the people of Brussels were devoted to their manneken, and in his current form too.

In 1619 the city council in any case considered it worth the trouble and expense of commissioning a famous sculptor, Hieronymus Duquesnoy, to provide a new bronze statue for the fountain on Stoofstraat. Duquesnoy was one of the best, if not the very best, at his craft in the Spanish Netherlands and did not disappoint his commissioners. He produced a lively little chap, just over half a metre tall. The boy holds his winkle in his left hand, his little head bowed slightly to the left, smiling down at passers-by. He stands tall, the most base of figures elevated.

We jump ahead in history to 1695. On 13 August of that year, the army of the French King Louis XIV began to fire upon the city of Brussels from Scheut. Two days later the entire city centre was ablaze. One third of the built-up area was razed to the ground. There were very few victims, as the residents managed to flee to Koudenberg, where the governor's palace was located. But first they evacuated their manneken to a safe place, such was the importance they attributed to the little statue. It was clearly held in higher regard than the other city fountains.

Just a couple of days after the barbaric bombardment the manneken returned triumphant to the smouldering ruins. A long satirical poem emerged in which the French are cursed for failing to let him get on with his wet work in peace and because their fireballs drove away his admirers.

Manneken Pis dressed up as Elvis Presley
© City of Brussels Museum

Manneken Pis dressed up as Lawrence of Arabia
© City of Brussels Museum

Admirers

Over the ensuing centuries, their ranks swelled. In 1698 the governor of the Spanish Netherlands, Maximilian Emmanuel of Bavaria, presented the manneken with his first suit of clothing: Bavarian blue, with a hat far too big for the bronze child's head. It was the beginning of a wardrobe which has now expanded to more than eight hundred items. Manneken Pis can dress up as Elvis Presley and Mozart, as a spaceman or a street sweeper, as Nelson Mandela, Obelix or an Anderlecht footballer; he has every conceivable costume, or so it would appear to the visitor, because for a good long time he has really just worn skilfully cut pieces of cloth, attached by Velcro.

Over time the manneken has gained all kinds of symbolic meanings. Mention was made of fertility and even Jesus Christ. Only one such meaning remains today. Manneken Pis is the symbol of Brussels, both the city and the region. The rest is fodder for history. The symbol of Brussels is a naked little lad pissing in public. People have been reported for less.

Government attempts at curbing public urination are not just a recent phenomenon. In Brussels they were trying to stamp it out more than a century and a half ago. There is a satirical drawing from 1846 which depicts a police officer up a ladder which he has placed against the railing in front of Manneken Pis. 'Arrestation du plus ancien bourgeois de Bruxelles,' the caption states.

Manneken Pis stands for the lightly satirical attitude with which the people of Brussels greet any form of authority. The little street child is as unconquerable as he is small. He may appear to be hidden away in a corner of an unprepossessing side street, but the entire world comes to see him.

He once stood in the capital of the Duchy of Brabant, initially only pissing on the heads of the people of Brussels, and perhaps by extension those of Brabant. He then stood in the capital of the Kingdom of Belgium and pissed on the heads of all Belgians. Now he stands in the capital of the European Union and pisses on the heads of half a billion Europeans. He remains the same, but his domain grows, so in relative terms, according to mathematical law, he becomes smaller. His irony grows proportionally and has now reached gigantic dimensions. He does not need to do anything other than engage in the double offence of standing naked where he has always stood and pissing in public. Mighty Europe is rendered impotent. The richest empire in the history of humanity is forced to put up with a pissing toddler as the prevailing symbol of its proud capital.

Many of the tourists parading past the fountain appear perplexed. Isn't he a bit small? Look what a ridiculous little corner he's standing in. For it is not only his public indecency which is subversive. He is an anti-monument par excellence. His half-metre stature satirises, lightly, perhaps, but no less mercilessly, the disingenuous glorification of all statues depicting scoundrels, whether they are crowned or not.

Such statues are always displayed on prominent squares or broad streets. The Place Bellecour in Lyon, adorned by an equestrian statue of Louis XIV, or Unter den Linden in Berlin with Frederick the Great, are shining examples. Our manneken does not even come up to the buttocks of a bronze horse like that. Those are just two examples out of dozens and dozens. In the centre of Skopje there is a statue of Alexander the Great twenty-eight times the size of our manneken, along with one of his father Philip twenty-six times larger. If Macedonia ever enters the Union the capital of Europe might perhaps send them two copies of the manneken to piss on their pedestals.

A little resistance to Europe's conceitedness

In all the self-mockery of Brussels, the anarchy (and of course the disagreeable tendency of the people of Brussels towards indifference), combined with the labyrinthine Belgian state structure, we have failed to note the explosiveness of it all and it has blown up in our faces. Brussels is not a failed city, nor Belgium a failed state – far from it – but it is high time we set our house in order. It is an urgent task of social responsibility and civilisation. But however necessary it may be, that work cannot be allowed to crush our sense of small-scale resistance, as stubborn as it is carefree. That is more precious than ever, especially now that cold technocracy, lacking any sense of harmless fun, penetrates ever deeper into our daily lives. A pissing toddler in a corner of the European capital – I cannot imagine a better remedy for Europe's conceitedness. ■

Translated by Anna Asbury

Characters in Search of an Author

Maria Stahlie's Engagement

'"Hey, you there!"'
The first sentence of the extremely witty and poignant story *Galeislaven* (Galley Slaves) from the 2004 collection of the same name by Maria Stahlie (the pseudonym of Madelien Tolhuisen, 1955). It continues as follows: 'Even before I opened my eyes I knew who was rousing me so abruptly from my afternoon nap. I also realised immediately that she had not come alone.' That first-person narrator is the writer Maria Stahlie, who here features in one of her own stories. She is just having a nice snooze and her characters come and shake her awake. To work, you! Incidentally you can also interpret this cry as an appeal from Stahlie to the reader, not only of this story, but of her whole work. Hey, you there, the reader of this book, pay attention, wake up, I've got something to tell you.

Formulating dreams

So it is no accident that this exhortation forms the first sentence of Stahlie's bulky Collected Stories. The character Maud Labeur (note the meaning of the name: labeur = hard graft) addresses her writer. Hey, Stahlie, get to work. 'Having a snooze in the middle of the day then... what about us then?' That Maud has a right to speak, as the Stahlie-watcher knows; she occurs in many novels and stories. For example as a young, hypochondriac woman in *De Sterfzonde* (The Deadly Sin, 1991), as a little harridan in the story 'Understanding Thought' and as a woman obsessively in love in *Het beest met de twee ruggen* (The Beast with Two Backs, 1994). In 'Galley Slaves' she is accompanied by other Stahlie characters, at the bedside: Maud as a ten-year-old girl, Miriam, her twin sister Nadine, Lucien, plus the grown-up Maud, who has just woken the writer with a cry. They want to get back to work, be characters again, where are the stories, they want to be involved again. And then there follows a new subtle witty aside: '"And I want to be called Debbie," said little Maud. She looked at me with open aggression. "She's already called Maud Labeur..." She nodded towards her forty-year-old namesake.'

Maria Stahlie
© Bob Bronshoff

Characters in search of a story, precisely when the writer is having a nice nap. The nice thing about this scene is that the 'I', the writer Maria Stahlie, if you read back carefully, was not sleeping at all, she saw the characters before she opened her eyes. Her novel characters were already with her, she was dreaming of them. They appeared to her as if in a dream. In this ambiguous scene, Stahlie formulates a starting point for her literary agenda: reality is a dream in which many worlds may appear to you and which you as a writer can flesh out as you see fit. All you need is a bunch of characters. And so she has created again and again in her expanding oeuvre characters who want to set out into the world and fathom it. In the hope of being able to change, and perhaps even to save, themselves and others. The work of this extremely ingenious writer consists in formulating these 'dreams'. What else is literature but a dream about reality? In her novels she introduces her characters into a world that at first sight slightly resembles ours, she always gives that world a realistic setting, and then brings that setting into sharp focus. She charges it with electricity, might be a better way of putting it. And then it all begins.

Further on in this basic story the 'I' (that is, Stahlie) states that she wants to transport her characters step by step from their realistic world, not to reality but 'to regions where mythical forces define reality, to regions where excessive behaviour is a necessity.' Then she writes this: '(...) Don't you understand that I do that so that all of us, you, the reader and I... can wind up in the same dream! What could be more intimate, radical, more far-reaching than sharing a dream?' This is her writing programme, a programme that she has been presenting to us since 1987 in fifteen novels and story collections.

For that matter, the characters make all kinds of demands on their writer: they do not want to strive for fine and noble goals, they want anarchy, they don't mind being the victim of incest, or an SS officer, if need be they will accept some autobiographical role, provided the aim is not to make the world a better place. Here too Stahlie is formulating an aspect of her view of literature. She does not want to become engaged with what happens to be in fashion, no political engagement then. She wants disruptions, experiences, enchantments, transformations, the wide ocean of literature. Only then will she be better able to plumb human desire. And that is the crux of her work. In the novel *Egidius* (2014) it is expressed as follows: '(...) painters in the Golden Age were convinced in every fibre of their being that there was no better chance of penetrating the fire hidden in the human spirit than through a composition produced by the fire itself.' That is, getting closer to the fire via a story, a composition, via literature. In the story *Stoomcursus* (Crash Course) it is put thus: 'As if literary problems were not made of flesh and blood, as if a composition could not be flesh and blood! Oh, to make a composition, a rich and full and playful plot that is impossible to unravel.' In an interview she states that 'every passion has its origin in the imagination. Love, rage... it is no more and no less than what a person gets into their head.' And what a person gets into their head constitutes Stahlie's work as a novelist.

The first sentences of her novels and stories are always striking, she immediately focuses her 'dreamed' worlds with challenging introductions. In this way, like a fisherman, she draws the reader into her (narrative) net:

- 'Merciless physicians make merciless wounds.'
  Het beest met de twee ruggen (The Beast with Two Backs, 1994)
- 'Downstairs in the stone hallway the telephone started ringing for the second time within half an hour.'
  Sint-Juttemis (Saint Never, 2005)
- 'It was because of the flame that counting down the days had been not only solemn but also exciting.'
  Egidius (2014)
- '"Françoise, I beg you: come back!"'
  Boogschutters (Archers, 2008)
- 'Everything comes to an end, including living in the place where you were born.' The story *Verstand van denken* (Understanding Thought) from the collection *Verleden hemel toekomst* (Past Heaven Future, 1998)
- 'Here's hoping for the best: after all, the story has to begin somewhere. Johan has just gone to the kitchen to pour us a glass of orange juice.'
  The story *Van alle verhalen op aarde* (Of All the Stories on Earth) from the collection *In de geest van de Monadini's* (In the Spirit of the Monadinis, 1989)

Of course this is a classic writer's trick: involving the reader in the story with a bang, but Stahlie gives it a twist of her own, she takes us, readers, out of our everyday mode ('"Hey, you there"') and promises us a new world, one that is ready to explode.

'It was on the third morning after I had been pulled out of the path of an approaching bus by an unknown woman, that I looked in the mirror and officially established that I was not myself.'
The story *Uit de best denkbare wereld* (The Best Conceivable World) from the collection *Zondagskinderen* (Sunday's Children, 1999)

Note particularly here the witty compelling tone that characterises all her writing. In this way she gets us where she wants us: in a world where the characters are propelled by rampant ambitions, by ardent longings, by half-magic dreams, by involvement, by attempted rescues of themselves and others, by unlimited astonishment and curiosity and mainly by constant attempts to change oneself. All her sentences, constructions and 'full and playful and inextricable plots' are focused on this. Something must happen, and quickly. Stahlie's engagement is characterised by a desire for transformation. In 2011, Peter Sloterdijk wrote a particularly penetrating book under the title *You Must Change Your Life*, which can serve as a background model for Stahlie's original oeuvre. All the main characters in her work want to change their life, preferably through interminable and constant rationalisations about it. What went wrong and what can be improved? What should I do? Occasionally by acting energetically, to the point of murderousness. Everything always has to change in the lives in her work. Sitting still is not an option, come on, come on, do something. Hey, you there. In *Honderd deuren* (A Hundred Doors) she has one of her heroes formulate it yet again:

'Every human being must work out for themselves if they must go in search of that one door. Very occasionally someone walks into it by accident. Once eye to eye with the hundredth door one great question still remains: can you go through it or must you leave it closed for ever.'

The characters come invariably from the upper middle class, they have no money worries, they are not mentally disturbed, do not suffer from illnesses or self-pity, they are white, hetero, they are art connoisseurs, academics, adolescents, landlords, schoolchildren, trainee doctors, high-school pupils, or simply wives. They are as 'normal' as can be and live a more or less domestic life. Subsequently she exposes all her characters, who are like test subjects, to big problems and starts gnawing away at their normality, until everything collapses. In inner monologues, letters, diaries, or fiery reports, they give an account of this. Stahlie's work relies on digressions and manipulative language. She lets her characters rationalise to their heart's content, lets them contradict themselves, dig holes for themselves, be incredible, talk nonsense and in any case never resign themselves to the unchangeable and unavoidable. She can't stand quests for vanished treasures, stories of misery from petits-bourgeois who are tormenting each other, existential problems of gloomy artists, or sob stories about failed marriages, racism and discrimination. Those are for fashionable writers who want to get on *The World Goes On* (about the most popular show on Dutch television). There is always an oddly optimistic tone implicit in her work, even when drama approaches or is irrevocable. As a reader, you feel you are on an emotional roller-coaster. A striking feature is the regularly recurring anecdote about two characters who force each other to choose. What would you prefer to do if you commit suicide? Hang yourself or jump off the bridge? 'You must choose, you must... you must.' What would you prefer to be: an alcoholic, or a junkie? 'You must choose, you *must*.. you *must*.' In *Sint-Juttemis* (Saint Never), an absolute high point in her work, she puts it as follows: 'You had to leave all your certainties behind you, give up all control and plunge blindly into the inhospitable, hostile area.'

Pure urge to write

In her case all this is written in a bright, hurriedly advancing, electrifying, often witty and laconic style, which is unique in the Dutch language area. A tone that says: we are going ahead and won't let ourselves be ground down. Complete with digressions, details and odd associations. Sometimes her sentences meander on and on along the deep valleys and high summits of rationalisation, at other times she writes reportage-like accounts of colourful experiences that have sprung only from the writer's imagination. As in *De lijfarts* (The Personal Physician, 2004):

> 'I redirected my eyes towards the grass, towards the people, and it struck me that the park had a lot to offer in inclement weather and wind, snowed on, covered in ice, sodden with rain, under low, ink-black clouds and also beset by the great shadows of high, white clouds, but that neither of those two spectacles was a match for the way the park looked on a sun-drenched, summer Saturday like this: everywhere there were men and women sitting and lying, in groups or alone, on benches or on the grass, reading or just looking around them, sunning themselves or eating, in thin, colourful clothes or partially unclothed and everyone had time off from their work, time off school, and no one had to hurry, not even the inevitable solitary figure who was trying out his bungalow tent, not wanting any surprises when he went on holiday with his family the following week. Among all these sitting and lying people the children ran, played ball, climbed, pestered, yelled and crawled, the two to twelve-year-olds who could never sit still for very long at a time. The difference between this prospect and the prospect I had had two months before from my living quarters at the time in the interior of America, is almost too crazy for words. At that time I had no balcony but two narrow high windows and if I stood on a chair I could look outside, at the bare field where Pig lived in his battered caravan, amid discarded refrigerators, the carcass of a small horse, four burnt-out cars and a growing number of non-identifiable rusting parts.'

Typical Stahlie: full of the urge to write, full of enchantment. Wanting to see everything in an intoxication of writing, wanting to describe everything. She uses a style and a tone that does not shy away from either irony or pathos and often creates magic from the combination of the two. '(...) I was in search of real understanding... had to confront everything... my God, Christophe, my God! I dropped the box containing the incontinence bandage and opened the tailboard' (*Sint-Juttemis*). This is Stahlie's world in a nutshell.

She often takes family relationships as the initial setting, quite simply because she and her readers are familiar with them. A woman falls in love with her husband's son from a previous marriage, a woman hears that she originally had a twin brother who died at birth, a woman tries to beat her twin sister at everything, a woman hears that the former boyfriend of her youth, now a famous film star, has been committed to an asylum, a growing boy tries to maintain his high ideals about love and life. She then takes all the time in the world to develop these settings with great precision, she is curious about the motives and backgrounds of her characters and writes about them with great flair and in great detail. Stahlie practises the art of expansive writing: in her work one detail evokes another. She assumes that her readers are as curious as herself. How did her hero(ine) come to be as he/she is? She is always on the side of her characters, though she often makes them look before they leap. She sets them down in small, but delicate scenes which regularly set you giggling. All is welcome in her literature, even the children's games her heroes used to play. Take, for example, in *Egidius* the two sisters who, right at the beginning of the novel, are bored. One says to the other: 'Shall we play with elastic bands? It's only raining a bit...' This is graphic writing, you see the room and the girls in front of you, their longing for change. And you want to know more.

She describes at length contemporary morals and habits in such, for us, exotic areas as South Dakota (*De lijfarts* / The Personal Physician), Greece (*Honderd deuren* / A Hundred Doors), or Paris during a heat wave (*Sint-Juttemis* / Saint Never). You begin thinking along with her heroes and talking at them, at least that is always the feeling I have when I read her work. Should you do that, no, you're right, that's not on, yes, that really is the only solution, you've got to do something now, keep your spirits up, don't hesitate, it will all come right. And before you know it, you find those elegant, daft or ingenious ruminations of her heroines (they are almost always women) perfectly normal and you are totally caught up in the stories that tumble over each other. With her one story simply evokes another, she has to tell them all, she has to and she will, otherwise it won't be right. Precisely this magical view of writing, which boils down to desire to map and plumb the world via stories, gives her novels and stories a sphere of great necessity. They *must* be written. For Stahlie writing is an obsession, not a game or a pastime.

Stahlie does not shrink from banal starting points, and in interviews admits that chivalrously. For example, in an interview in the Flemish daily *De Standaard*, she discusses the fairly banal starting point of her novel *Het beest met de twee ruggen* (The Beast with Two Backs, 1994): an older woman falls in love with a boy of eighteen. 'The intention was to appropriate the subject, to impose my own questions and images on it, so that it would stimulate my imagination.' In the same interview, and for that matter in others too, she states that what mainly matters to her is the tone of the story. And she creates that tone by having some characters repeatedly return. I already mentioned a few above. But the same themes and situations also crop up. Twins populate many of her stories, voyeurism plays a role, disobedient children, there are often tennis balls in roof gutters, awkward adolescents are involved, parents often keep their distance and excel at not understanding, deceit and misunderstanding rule, strange rituals are regular features, magic is never far away. With these ingredients, Stahlie writes herself time after time into a world. Sometimes even longer scenes from one novel recur almost literally in another. The end of *Het beest met de twee ruggen* is roughly the same as *Egidius*. An admission of weakness? Big differences of opinion are possible. Stahlie does not usually work with neat endings, she can't be bothered to tie up all the loose ends, that is part of cheap airport literature. The stories and novels simply stop or she gives them a magic twist. For example in *Sint-Juttemis*. There she has Christophe, the film star who finally awakes from his coma, in a brilliant and very satisfying scene, simply fly away.

'We looked outside and saw Christophe flying away – it was more a kind of swimming flying – with arm movements that were very like the butterfly stroke with the occasional breaststroke movement from his legs. We watched him fly up at an angle, past the apartment of the lads across the road and after about fifty metres saw him (his heart was already at a bird's temperature, 42 degrees Celsius) turn westward in a smooth arc. We saw him fly – Liza, Sophia and I – we saw his swimming movements and much more besides... everything at once, interwoven, and yet as clear as glass.'

This is great writing. Note also in this extract the highly realistic details (for example, those 42 degrees Celsius in birds and the exact description of the swimming motion) which merge with the magic cores of her writing. As a writer you must simply want to show everything, 'everything at once, interwoven, and yet as clear as glass.' Like an enchantress.

The lame person saves the blind

The key word to her oeuvre, finally, is saving. This modest writer, who rarely appears in public and does not take part in 'literary life', has thus far created an extremely ambitious programme. She sends her characters into the world time after time to save others or themselves. They sacrifice themselves, they look out for others. To that end, they eschew no means at all. Lies, deceit and murder. Usually they are not capable of seeing that they themselves need saving. In her literature, the lame person tries to save the blind, that is the heart of the matter. In the last instance, Stahlie of course wants to save the world via her characters, although she will probably go on denying this. Nothing more and nothing less, as befits the tradition of romanticism to which Stahlie's work belongs.
'"Hey, you there."'
Wake up! Read this work. Be amazed. ■

Translated by Paul Vincent

A Victorian 'Arbiter Elegantiae'

The Paintings of Sir Lawrence Alma-Tadema

[LUC DEVOLDERE]

'(...) two drunken women embracing, over-coupled, over-perfumed, over-come, swooning, turned pale, eyes bulging, and died together, with hiccup-ping gurgles... A little further, a boy rose, laughed madly, punched the air and collapsed senseless in a heap of black violets, sinking as in a bed of velvet...'
Louis Couperus, *De berg van licht* (The Mountain of Light, 1905)

Not so long ago Dutch Prime Minister Mark Rutte compared the influx of refu-gees into Europe to the invasions by the barbarians that led to the fall of the Roman Empire. A persistent topos it seems. An equally persistent topos to ex-plain the collapse of the Imperium Romanum is that of the 'decadence' of the Romans. A tough combination: threatened from both inside and outside, the once so glorious imperium must almost inevitably fall.

The ingredients of that 'decadence' are a cocktail of dissoluteness, sexual excess, drunkenness and moral degeneration that led to the kind of physical exhaustion and moral vacuity that we can see in the monumental painting by Thomas Couture, *The Romans of the Decadence* (1847) in the Musée d'Orsay in Paris. The metaphorical setting is that of a feast, an orgy past its zenith, ex-hausted bodies, lust satiated, danced off their feet.

Compare this rather cliché painting with *The Roses of Heliogabalus* (1888) by Lourens Alma Tadema (Dronrijp, Friesland, 1836 - Wiesbaden, 1912), later known as Sir Lawrence Alma-Tadema.

Born in Syria, Heliogabalus had been Roman emperor for four years, be-tween 218 and 222 AD, when, not yet twenty, he was murdered by soldiers from the Praetorian Guard. He created a furore as high priest of the sun god, married several times in his short life, including with a man (whereby he was the 'woman'), prostituted himself and became legendary as the proverbial ec-centric, shamelessly perverse and decadent emperor. It was inevitable that Couperus would glorify the tormented, androgynous 'boy emperor' with unde-cided sexual identity in *De berg van licht* (The Mountain of Light, 1905).

Unconscious Rivals, 1893, oil on canvas, 45.1 x 62.8 cm

© Bristol Museums & Art Gallery, Bristol

A rose is a rose is a rose...

But let's take another look at Tadema's roses. The setting of the painting is again a feast, but there is something completely different going on here.

The painter must have been inspired by an anecdote from the emperor's gossipy biography (Historia Augusta, *Vita Elegabali*, 21), 'In a dining hall with a moveable ceiling he once buried his parasites under violets and other flowers, so that some actually suffocated because they were in no state to crawl out of the flowers.'

Heliogabalus was not the first to splash out on this technology. In his Domus Aurea, the megalomaniacal new palace that Nero had had erected after the fire of Rome, in 64 AD, he already had ceilings that could shower his guests with flowers and sprinklers that sprayed perfumes (Suetonius, *Vita Neronis*, 31, 1-2).

Couperus describes it like this: 'The roof turned, the cupola tipped, the caissons opened and rosettes ... There, in the four corners of the hall, suddenly and simultaneously, and in such a deluge that you could hear them rustling, it snowed flowers like colourful snow, fluttering in a flutter of petals (...).' And this is followed by page after sensual page, almost tumbling over each other, about the rain of scents and flowers that Heliogabalus (Antoninus in The Mountain of Light) poured out over his guests.

The Roses of Heliogabalus, 1888, oil on canvas, 132.1 x 213.9 cm © Colección Pérez Simón, Mexico. Photo by Arturo Piera

Tadema's canvas intrigues in a different way. Unmoved, the impassive protagonist Heliogabalus, reclining above left, with flaxen moustache and goatee beard, looks down on what he has wrought, the practical joke quietly turning into manslaughter. His victims, equally impassive, leaning languidly on cushions, seem to embrace their demise. Their death by drowning is reminiscent of Leopardi's verse from *L'Infinito*: 'E il naufragar m'è dolce in questo mare' ('... and shipwreck in this sea is sweet for me'). There is a pact between impassivity, overrefinement and perversion in this picture. We are far from the feast in Trimalchio, a scene from the picaresque novel *Satyricon*, by Petronius, one of Nero's courtiers who had fallen into disfavour. In the novel, the nouveau riche host astonishes his guests with the choicest foods, but his vanity and stupidity ruin the setting.

In Tadema's work you see at the most some fruit and a few goblets. The rose petals (the painter prefers them to the violets in the biography) flutter into the room like confetti and pile up at the bottom left. Like a wave spreading widely on the beach. Like swirling clouds, motionless yet nonetheless moving. A maenad, one of the followers of Dionysius, the god of intoxication and ecstasy, plays the double flute. A statue of Dionysius himself with faun and panther towers above the emperor's mother, who looks straight at us. On the right, a bearded man looks searchingly – judgementally? – at the emperor. In front of him, a reclining woman stares impassively at the spectator. She is not buried under the petals. Not yet?

Tadema worked long and meticulously on the large canvas. He even had roses shipped in from the French Riviera. For four months during the winter of 1887-1888, masses of them were sent weekly to the artist's studio in London. Months after the painting was completed the painter still found dried rose petals there.

In Victorian England flowers had all kinds of meanings. Deep red ones stood for romantic love, the pink ones we see on the canvas were an expression of a milder affection. In John Everett Millais's *Ophelia* (1852) we see the tragic heroine of *Hamlet* floating dead amidst flowers in a shallow stream. Even a century later swimming in rose petals still seems to have fascinated visual artists. Annie Leibovitz photographed a naked Bette Midler (New York, 1979), asleep among roses, and in the film *American Beauty* (1999) Kevin Spacey gazes at the girl next door, floating in a bath full of blood-red petals.

But I am still not tired of Tadema's roses. This canvas transcends the historic art of the Antwerp school where he learned his trade. Is it moralizing? Or just a style exercise? An impression? Or is it after all a unique depiction, a picture of a civilisation that knows it is doomed?

The king is dead. Long live the king

How different from *A Roman Emperor, 41 AD* – the only work by Tadema that depicts an historic fact, although the painter tries to condense a complex series of events and actions into one scene, and succeeds too. Leaving the theatre, Caligula is murdered by officers of the Praetorian Guard. At the palace, his uncle, the stuttering cripple Claudius, hides behind a curtain fearful for his life. A soldier sees his shoes protruding and greets him – as emperor. Tadema puts the two together in one picture. The dead Caligula ('little boot') lies, fallen backwards on top of another corpse, in the centre of the picture. His head is not visible, but he is recognisable by his green boots. On the left, voyeuristic women and cheering soldiers watch. Meanwhile a hooded figure has already taken advantage of the situation to steal from the palace.

On the right the soldier pulls the curtain back – his flamboyant red shoes have betrayed Claudius. But you can also read the guard's gesture and bow as recognition of the new emperor – who recoils in panic. An unheroic transfer of power indeed. It becomes even more complex if you zoom in to the bloodied bust of Emperor Augustus, rising above the dead Caligula. The founding father of the dynasty looks away. To the left of him hangs a truncated painting showing the Battle of Actium in 31 BC, where he defeated Anthony and Cleopatra and laid the foundations for his rule as emperor. So what does Tadema mean by this? That decline has already crept into the Julio-Claudian dynasty? Power is bestowed and removed for the first time by soldiers.

The picture continues to perplex. Does the title of the painting refer to the dead Caligula, a crazy pervert who does have something in common with Heliogabalus, or to the new Emperor Claudius? Whatever else, this 'historic picture' does not reveal its secrets.

Surprising perspective

A Coign of Vantage (1895) is Tadema's version of the three Graces, whose circular arrangement we recognise from, for example, Botticelli's *Primavera* and Rubens. In Tadema's painting, they have become frivolous, slightly bored, pre-Raphaelite young ladies, hippie girls in rustling dresses 'with flowers in [their] hair'. Tadema breaks the circle open and lets his three Graces harmonise subtly with each other on their exquisite belvedere (*A room with a view!*), gazing out nonchalantly over the sea round Capri. For that is where we see them, on the famous island in the Bay of Naples, at the villa of the art collector Axel Munthe. Tadema photographed the vantage point himself and changed the sphinx into a lioness. A Roman luxury galley passes heedlessly below. The luxuriously extended rear deck suggests that this might perhaps be Emperor Tiberius himself sailing in. In his later years, Tiberius withdrew to the island to indulge his paranoia and sexual excesses. Did the painting's Victorian buyer, who undoubtedly knew his Suetonius (Tiberius's biographer) – think of this? Look at the three rose petals on the marble balustrade. They must have fluttered out of the hair of the woman leaning over the balustrade and will be blown away by the wind in the blink of an eye. If you consider where the painter (photographer?) must have stood to portray these women, you realise just how surprising the chosen perspective is. The title is substantiated, and applies to many of Tadema's canvases: *A Coign of Vantage* is always a good place to observe and assess. Tadema avoids classical frontality; he likes decentring and goes for daring cut-offs. That was already true of *A Roman Emperor*. They are choices that work in a subtly disturbing and unsettling way – very different from the neo-classicist Winkelmann's ideal of 'noble simplicity and quiet grandeur'.

A Coign of Vantage, 1895, oil on canvas, 58.88 x 44.45 cm

© Collection Ann and Gordon Getty

Soft eroticism

Tadema did paint a few nudes. His most suggestive can be admired in the small but striking *Tepidarium* (1881). A flushed woman lies on an animal skin and silk cushions beside the tepid bath in a Roman bath complex, an ostrich feather fan just concealing her private parts. Only the bronze strigil situates the picture clearly in Antiquity – it was used to scrape oil from the body. A little later, Freud will almost certainly see it as a phallic symbol. The association with the pink, flushed cheeks and open lips is quickly made. Here lies a woman who has just pleasured herself? But the painter's subtlety evades this explicit interpretation. This Venus does not lie with her back to us looking at herself in the mirror, like Velasquez's. She reveals herself completely yet remains submerged in her individuality.

The Women of Amphissa (1887) shows a scene we find in Plutarch: a band of wandering maenads ends up in the Greek town of Amphissa. According to the myth and the rite, the maenads go into the mountains, singing and dancing themselves into a trance, whereupon they tear apart a wild animal and eat it raw. The transgression and sexual connotations are obvious.

In the morning the women wake befuddled and dishevelled in the town's market place. They are encircled by the local matrons and given food. Compassion. Seldom has the chasm between virtue and control and licentiousness and abandon been made more visible than in this juxtaposition of women in animal skins and flowing garments and their tight-laced congeners.

Tadema does not show the sexual act but suggests the befuddlement, the flushed languor after the erotic madness, the memory of the transgression,

Tepidarium, 1881, oil on canvas, 24.2 x 33 cm
© National Museums Liverpool, Lady Lever Art Gallery

The Women of Amphissa, 1887, oil on canvas, 121.8 x 182.8 cm

© Sterling and Francine Clark Art Institute, Williamstown

which was not publicly tolerated at that time and in that milieu. Its buyers must have recognised it, but they could hide behind the historic setting: a bathhouse in ancient Rome; an historic story from Plutarch. His eroticism is soft. It is no coincidence that his naked woman lies in the *tepidarium*, so she is lukewarm, and not in the hot *caldarium*.

Simply...marbellous

Tadema has gone into the history books as one of the finest painters of marble (*Punch* magazine referred to him as a 'marbellous artist') and the blue of the Mediterranean Sea and sky. On his honeymoon, in 1863, he had studied the interiors of Roman houses and their decoration in Pompeii and at the Museum of Naples, and he reproduced them perfectly in his depiction of an Antiquity that looked like an elegant, upper-class Victorian England, with ladies in their intimate environment gazing languorously in patrician *ennui* at some undefined point. His Antiquity was not that of the romantic, foliage draped ruins of Piranesi, but that of the archaeological discoveries. They influenced Hollywood cineastes' settings from D.W. Griffith's *Intolerance* (1916) and Cecil B. De Mille's *Cleopatra* (1934) to Ridley Scott's *Gladiator* (2000) and *Exodus* (2014).

In his archives, Tadema kept photos of objects and artefacts grouped per theme, but he did not hesitate to mix styles and objects from different periods on canvas if that suited the composition better. The details are therefore historically accurate but the composition is a deliberate construction. His treatment of history can probably best be compared with what Marguerite Yourcenar says about historical novels: 'Whatever one does, one always reconstructs a monument in one's own fashion. But it's already quite a lot to use only authentic stones.'

Meanwhile, we are aware that every period has its Antiquity, its idea of Antiquity, which says more about the period itself than about Antiquity. Ancient Rome in the time of Caesar and Octavianus in the British-American-Italian television series *Rome*, which was filmed in Cinecittà (2005-2007), is shown as a city of filthy, dark alleys where violence and sex are raw and explicit. It is a very long way from Tadema. A perfectionist and control freak, he was trained at the Academy of Art in Antwerp in the historic style of Henry Leys and Louis Jean de Taeye. In 1870 his career planning took him to London, where he found an environment and a public with plenty of purchasing power that he could readily supply. The right man at the right moment in the right place, who held up a mirror of themselves to his clientele: affluent Victorians with leisure, cultural aspirations and a desire to travel. After their grand tour in the South, he gave them back a vicarious Antiquity, with a glistening blue Mediterranean Sea and sky, and the memory of marble: a manageable, socially acceptable, readily available Antiquity.

Tadema's art was also a response to a tendency for escapism in the class that profited from the industrial age, a desire to escape the machines and the harsh trading to which they owed their luxury and their class identity. Add to that just socially acceptable erotic titillation, packaged in a pseudo mythical decor, and the morally admissible splendour and magnificence of another time and place. In short, Tadema's canvases could be seen as an upper-class version of what the butler saw. In the end, though, Tadema's appeal goes deeper. By transposing his own culture to a revered civilisation which, like his, derived its pride from property and the showy display of material wealth, the painter put Victorian England first in the succession to Rome.

Art or kitsch?

Having lost his first wife and a son by the age of thirty-three, Tadema subsequently married a young English artist. His chic residence in Regent's Park developed into a shrine and a mirror of his oeuvre. He entertained there with style, but no one was allowed to touch or move any object, however carelessly it seemed to have been put down. He was, as Tacitus Petronius described it, an *arbiter elegantiae*, someone who determined etiquette, fashion and life style and embodied them with refinement. Perhaps, in the end, he felt trapped by his phenomenal skill and commercial success. To a friend he admitted, sighing: 'I paint a piece of marble, and they want nothing but marble; a blue sky, and they want nothing but blue skies; an Agrippa, and they want nothing but Agrippas; an oleander bush, and they want nothing except oleanders. Arrgh! A man isn't a machine!' Perhaps it was not as simple as Secretary of State for Education, Culture and Science Halbe Zijlstra suggested when, outlining the underlying principles of his cultural policy in 2010, he quoted the Frisian artist: 'While I am painting, I am an artist, once the work is finished, I am a businessman'.

Alma-Tadema sold his *Roses of Heliogabalus* to the British parliamentarian John Aird for the sum of £4,000. Today that is the equivalent of at least €100,000. He died in 1912, feted and knighted, and was buried in St Paul's Cathedral. Just in time. With the brutal disillusionment of the First World War his work fell out of fashion, rejected as slick, empty and superficial. In 1934 *The Roses* was sold for £483 and in 1960 the work was worth just £105. Since then the value has risen meteorically again. In 1993 Christie's auctioned it for something over £1.6 million. The tide could change again though. When he was alive Tadema produced art. After his death it appeared to be kitsch. If kitsch is, as Roger Scruton claims, 'fake art, expressing fake emotions, whose purpose is to deceive the consumer into thinking he feels something deep and serious', then Tadema is more than kitsch. Behind the impassivity of some of his paintings, there is something brewing that is difficult to put a finger on.

The Roses will be on display this year in Vienna and London. Go and have a look at them. Tadema has still not given away all his secrets. Perhaps he is what Nietzsche said of the Greeks: superficial. Yes. *Aus Tiefe.* ■

Translated by Lindsay Edwards

A Roman Emperor, 41 AD, 1871,
oil on canvas, 83.8 x 174.2 cm
© Walters Art Gallery, Baltimore

EXHIBITION
Alma-Tadema. Classical Charm

Till 18 June 2017 in
the Belvedere, Vienna.
www.belvedere.at

From 7 July to 29 October 2017 in
Leighton House Museum, London.
www.leightonhouse.co.uk

FURTHER READING

Elizabeth Prettejohn and Edwin Beckers, *Sir Lawrence Alma-Tadema*.
New York: Rizzoli and Van Gogh Museum, 1996
Elizabeth Prettejohn and Peter Trippi (ed.), *Lawrence Alma-Tadema: At Home in Antiquity*. Leeuwarden: Fries Museum, 2016, published in association with Prestel-Verlag, Munich

The Most Industrious of All Centuries

New Perspectives on the Nineteenth Century

[MARITA MATHIJSEN]

Who thinks of the nineteenth century when they strike a match, seal an envelope or open a can of tomato puree? Yet every household is full of objects developed in the course of those one hundred years. It's true that since the introduction of electronic mail and piezo igniters for gas stoves we no longer use matches and envelopes every day, but let's go a step further. Imagine you're booking a trip to Ghana, inspired by the Lonely Planet travel guide, and you need to get vaccinated against yellow fever before you go. Do you realise that the first plane took off in 1890; that the first travel guide multinational, Baedeker, has been publishing its illustrated guide books since 1839; that vaccination against disease only became customary in the nineteenth century (after the smallpox vaccine was developed in the eighteenth century) and that the Dutch Inspection of Public Health, which keeps track of which countries require vaccinations, was set up in 1804? Are you aware, too, that Schiphol Airport is situated partly on a polder that was reclaimed in the nineteenth century; and that the trains that take you there have been running since 1839 in the Netherlands; or that it was impossible to get travel insurance in those days?

In the meantime, it has become common knowledge: the modern world began in the nineteenth century. The fact that time, place and speed have become more or less relative concepts instead of absolutes only became conceivable in the nineteenth century. Till then time was strictly linked to your location and the position of the sun. If it was eleven o'clock in Rotterdam, it was already half past eleven in Hengelo. If you were in one place, you could not be in a different place at the same time, as has happened with the development of the telephone. At the start of the century, the highest speed imaginable was that of a bolting horse.

It is only for the last few decades, however, that this modernity has been generally acknowledged. It took a long time before Dutch historians realised that the Netherlands was no exception in Europe, but was in line with other countries, both big and small. In older studies of the nineteenth century, historians emphasised a relative backwardness and stagnation in the Netherlands. It was thought to be lagging behind other countries economically, entrepreneurially, in its willingness to give up old institutions, and in cultural terms too. Reference was frequently made to an essay written by the leading writer

Everhardus Potgieter in 1842. In it he sketches a Dutch family in which all the sons are called Jan. Some of the Jans are enterprising and behave in an exemplary fashion. Those are the sons who are involved in shipping and trade. The youngest son is called Jan Salie and is a metaphor for the nineteenth century: flabby, indolent, a lie-abed. Potgieter intended his essay as a mirror for the Dutch nation: the country needed more entrepreneurial spirit to get it out of the economic crisis. Subsequently, the 'Jan Salie mindset' became a concept that historians, assuming an economic and cultural impasse, applied to the whole century.

Rijksmuseum, Amsterdam, 1885

Speed, progress and steam power

Over the past few decades historians, including art and literary historians, have been countering this notion. The change coincided with the founding of the journal *De negentiende eeuw*, in 1977, by some young Dutch studies scholars, who were bothered by the contempt for Dutch literature of the period and realised that there was too little research on which to build. There were no surveys of publishers, journals, newspapers, or children's books; there was no knowledge of translation and publication rights, and no survey of contemporary history writers. The journal systematically published research that could be built on. In universities certainly the study of the nineteenth century gained new momentum. Theses appeared thick and fast and certain schools of thought began to form. Professors like Willem van den Berg, Piet Blaas and Niek van Sas supervised young historians and students of Dutch language and

The first train in the Netherlands, 1839

literature, who launched a broadening of the research, with other themes than those that had been customary till then. They were joined by professors with a public profile as well, like Auke van der Woud, Piet de Rooy and myself. This research too brought about a change in the way the nineteenth century was viewed. The sleepy metaphors that had been attributed to those one hundred years changed into metaphors of speed: a century of speed, progress and steam power.

These about-turns in the research are concentrated on a few topics and periods. The history of the early and late nineteenth century had been neglected for years, but now pioneering new research into these periods appeared. The traditional study of literary texts and writers was broadened to include research into reading, publishers, criticism and terminology. The study of nationalism was developing internationally and it was picked up in the Netherlands too. Research into technology, industrialisation and infrastructure was by no means familiar territory for historians, until that too changed both inside and outside the Netherlands. Art history had always been limited purely to art, but broadened its horizons now to take in the art trade, the creation of museums and the collectors. That old favourite, political history had to relinquish its position to social history. The history of poverty, prostitution, migration and education were studied, as was the history of the landscape. The emancipation of Jews, Catholics, workers and women was given a place in history, too, and the internationally developed history of mentality was also practised in the new context. Because so much new research was done in the late 1970s, revised surveys could be published for a wider public in the twenty-first century.

The research into the Batavian Republic (1795-1806) and the periods shortly before and after it can be described, quite simply, as innovative. The Netherlands had wrested itself from Spanish dominance in the sixteenth century and become a republic, under the leadership of a stadholder from the House of Orange. By the eighteenth century, few of those republican principles were still in evidence. The stadholder conducted himself like a monarch and his administrators, who all came from the same ruling families, did his bidding. As of about 1780, there was opposition to this from the so-called patriots. The latter appeared to be gaining ground until the King of Prussia came to the aid of the stadholder, in 1787, causing the patriots to flee in large numbers to France. There they reorganised and, with the help of a French army, invaded the country and drove out the stadholder in early 1795. The Batavian Republic was then

Charles Howard Hodges,
Louis Napoleon Bonaparte,
1809, oil on canvas,
223 x 147 cm,
Rijksmuseum, Amsterdam

established as a vassal state of France, which demanded the maintenance of a French army and a huge sum of money for its help. As of 1800, the most powerful man in France was Napoleon, who regarded the Netherlands as a source of income and a means to increase his influence. In 1806, he appointed his brother, Louis Napoleon, as King of Holland. However, when Louis failed to toe his elder brother's line, he was relieved of his duties and the country was turned into a French province. After the fall of the elder Napoleon in late 1813, the son of the former stadholder returned to the Netherlands and was pro-claimed king. The major powers then decided that it would be clever to amal-gamate Belgium and the Netherlands as a buffer against France, which was still greatly feared, so the so-called United Kingdom of the Netherlands was created. However, in 1830 the Belgians revolted against the politics of William I and declared independence.

This potted history – and particularly the early period of the patriots and the Batavian Republic – had never been recorded and evaluated in all its finer details. Niek van Sas applied the reconciliation thesis to it: both in the early years of the Batavian Republic and after 1814 it was considered necessary for the opposing parties to unite. Patriots and moderate Orangists therefore decided to cooperate in the National Assembly, which had been the most important decision-making body for government affairs since 1796. After 1814, there was tension between the civil servants who had worked in the service of the French and those who had helped drive out the French. The old civil servants were still needed after 1814 to consolidate the by now specialised administration, so it was important not to make too much of a fuss about their misguided past. Thorough theses and studies have been published on the patriot movement, the significance of the exiles in France, the modernity of the first constitution, the opposition press, the civil service and so on, casting a whole new light on this previously neglected period. They show that modernity began in this period, when infrastructure in the Netherlands was tackled on a large scale, primary school education was regulated and the registry of births, marriages and deaths was introduced. In the wake of research into the Batavian Republic came research into the period of the United Kingdom of the Netherlands, another period that had been ignored for a long time before both Belgian and Dutch historians got their teeth into it.

A masked century

This neglect also applies, to a lesser extent, to the late nineteenth century, but research into the period has in any case led to the last decades of it being called a 'second golden age', when new buildings were constructed on a massive scale, huge shopping palaces opened, and enormous projects like the construction of Amsterdam's Central Station were started.

Literary historians extended the boundaries of their research. Readers became the focus. 'Wie las wat in de negentiende eeuw?' (Who Read What in the Nineteenth Century?), an article by Bernt Luger, in 1982, was an eye-opener. Earlier research, full of liberally gratuitous value judgements about literature, was abandoned for research into reading habits, publishers, book distribution, advertising, series, translations and, recently, authors' positioning and the use of literature for political purposes. Joost Kloek and Wijnand Mijnhardt carried out detailed research into the sales of a publisher in Middelburg, to which new conclusions about reading behaviour were linked. The angles taken became more diverse: children's books, censorship, commercial libraries and copyright all became the subject of studies. The precise meaning of various terms was also studied, that of 'realism', for example, 'the true poet' and 'fatherland'. Willem van den Berg was a forerunner in this with his dissertation on the term 'Romanticism', in 1973. I myself linked literature to the history of mentality in my study on the double moral standards of the nineteenth century, which I called *De gemaskerde eeuw* (The Masked Century). The result of the new literary research was that the earlier negative judgements about the quality of Dutch literature no longer mattered. If we look at reading behaviour, we see a growing appetite for reading to which publishers were eager to cater.

The research into nationalism came to some striking conclusions because a comparative approach was used. It became clear that in some respects the Netherlands had an advantage over other countries, which were still struggling for their position as a nation. But during the period of the United Kingdom of the Netherlands it was important to promote the perception of a nation or, better said, to forge one, and that was done by drawing attention to a common past. Joep Leerssen mapped out Dutch nationalism within a broad European context. The extent to which the past was used as if for legitimation has been shown by Leerssen and Mathijsen in various studies. This research had other consequences too. For example, where nationalism used to be interpreted as oppressive and restrictive, it is now clear that no movement is more international.

Art history underwent the same broadening of scope as literary history. The main focus of study was no longer the works and the artist but the art trade, the function of art, the collectors and the museums. The Rijksmuseum, the Van Gogh Museum and the Amsterdam History Museum (now the Amsterdam Museum) widened their horizons and came up with some sensational subjects: 'The ugly period' (*De lelijke tijd*) exhibition of 1995 at the Rijksmuseum, for example, in which neo-historical art forms stood centre stage. The history of the museums themselves also attracted a lot of attention. National museums appear to have been set up all over Europe in the nineteenth century, and that applies to the Netherlands too. Appreciation of nineteenth-century art in the Netherlands, which was previously frequently written off as sham seventeenth century or homely romantic, grew with the organisation of comprehensive exhibitions like the *Meesters van de Romantiek* (Masters of Romanticism) in 2005 in Rotterdam.

National Museum of Antiquities, Leiden, founded in 1818 by King Wilhelm I
© Michiel Hendryckx

Zuid-Willemsvaart, canal connecting Maastricht and 's-Hertogenbosch
© Michiel Hendryckx

We have seen that historians applied themselves to little-known periods in order to shed new light on them, but they also admitted new areas of research to their disciplines. In the 1970s, social history became popular, with the result that studies were published on position and class, poverty and charity. But peripheral areas were researched too, such as prostitution. The emancipatory function that the Society for the Promotion of General Welfare (Maatschappij tot Nut van 't Algemeen) had for education and culture was clear. The Netherlands turned out not to be lagging behind in education, but in terms of literacy rates and regulation, it was actually ahead of other countries. The same applied to infrastructure. The number of paved roads was low, but not proportionally, and thanks to the canal boats public transport was actually highly developed. Though it is true that the existing public transport delayed the construction of railway lines, it was very easy to travel around the Randstad early on. Detailed research into the history of technology was carried out under the supervision of Harry Lintsen, whereby both major and minor changes in everyday life in the nineteenth century could be recorded, from the construction of street lighting to that of sewers, from the arrival of the steam press for newspapers to the founding of large machine industries.

The iron century

All of these studies have contributed to the image of the nineteenth century as a sleepy century being consigned to the past once and for all. The results of the research have been published in books for a wider audience, and some studies have even reached a large public, like Auke van der Woud's, for example.

Of great importance in terms of influencing public opinion about these hundred years are the recent biographies of the three nineteenth-century kings, William I, II and III, written on the occasion of the two hundredth anniversary of the monarchy under the Orange family, and accompanied by exhibitions and TV documentaries. The biographies interweave original and recent research, and because they put the kings in a broad context, a revised image of politics and society has logically emerged. Via King William I, it has become more obvious than ever how completely inappropriate the image of stagnation is, and that there was actually more of a drive for development. He had one canal after the other dug, ordered land reclamation, supported industry with prizes and exhibitions, and promoted the use of steam power everywhere.

The thirteen-part television series *De ijzeren eeuw* (The Iron Century), made in 2015, was also clearly aimed at a large public. In it, the popular presenter Hans Goedkoop presents the developments of the nineteenth century in a very personal way. Here 'iron' is a metaphor for industrialisation, and by extension modernity. There is not a word about stagnation, sleep or decline. The influence of the modernised approach to studying the nineteenth century is clearly visible from the very first episode. In it, the emphasis lies on the infrastructure, modernised according to the Napoleonic model, which was taken over by the kings of Orange. The economic decline is presented as a fact that gave rise to private initiatives and had no influence on idealistic projects, schooling and charity. The fact that patronage was associated with this is something we have seen in many recent studies concerning the patriarchal and sometimes stifling good intentions concerning care for the less fortunate, something which shifted, in the course of the century, to the government. The episodes about manufacturers and businessmen share a great wonder for the energy of those involved and the megalomania of their projects. Every aspect that is covered – feminism, the promotion of hygiene, the emancipation of Catholics, scientific progress, the colonial question – is based on knowledge acquired in recent decades. The series' own merit lies mainly in the beautiful images. And who could ever forget Goedkoop having himself made up as a cholera patient and having leeches applied? The series ends with an image of the flight from modernity, as it was expressed at the end of the century in the various reform movements.

All things considered, the image of the nineteenth century has changed radically in the last forty years. No school textbook today would dare speak of a dull period. The emphasis these days is on the nineteenth century as the cradle of nearly all the developments that continue to evolve now. The famous critic Kees Fens once called the nineteenth century 'the most industrious of all centuries', because of the colossal projects being undertaken in all areas, from dictionaries to museums of antiquity, from the construction of railway lines to water pipes. He might say the same in slightly different words about all the academics who, through their diligence and industry, have made a different nineteenth century common property since 1976. ▪

Translated by Lindsay Edwards

A Wedding of Words

Sylvia Plath and Ted Hughes Revisited

When I heard that *Jij zegt het* (As You Say), the most recent novel by the Dutch writer Connie Palmen (1955), which was awarded the prestigious Libris Literature Prize in 2016, was about the relationship between Ted Hughes (1930-1998) and Sylvia Plath (1932-1963), my first reaction was fairly negative. Hadn't enough been written on the subject? There is the autobiographical work of Plath herself: a sizeable collection of letters, diaries, the roman-à-clef *The Bell Jar* and of course the poems, most of which have a decidedly autobiographical character. In the 1980s one biography after another appeared and in addition an unstoppable flood of memoirs and recollections by friends and acquaintances who had known the American poet in a particular period of her short life.

Moreover ad hoc subgenres emerged around Plath and Hughes: examples include *Her Husband: Hughes and Plath – A Marriage* by Diane Middlebrook, on the two poets' married life (1956-1963), and quite recently – in 2013 – *Mad Girl's Love Song: Sylvia Plath and Life before Ted* by Andrew Wilson, which describes Sylvia's life up to her meeting with Ted on 25 February 1956. In the latter book we find an unbelievably exact record of every boy she ever dated, with whom she corresponded and who were her boyfriends, first in high school and later at Smith College. The most curious book in this category is *The Silent Woman: Sylvia Plath and Ted Hughes* by Janet Malcolm. Malcolm interviewed a series of authors who had written about Plath and Hughes. In order to obtain permission for longer quotations those writers had to submit their manuscripts to the estate of Sylvia Plath, who committed suicide on 11 February 1963. At that point she had been living apart from Hughes for six months. Because they were not yet divorced and no will was found on her death, Hughes became her legal heir. For negotiations on copyright issues relating to her work he appointed his sister Olwyn, two years his senior, as a literary agent. In Malcolm's fascinating book Olwyn Hughes is the central character.

Olwyn Hughes (who died on 3 January 2016) was an unrelenting gatekeeper. After Sylvia Plath's death there was gossip suggesting that Ted Hughes was partly responsible for his wife's suicide. He had supposedly neglected her after leaving her and their two children. Or rather, after he had been thrown out of the house by her because of his adultery. At the time they were living in rural Devon. In the winter of 1962/63 she had moved back to London, where she

Ted Hughes and Sylvia Plath in Yorkshire, 1956

ended her life in dramatic circumstances. She put out milk and sandwiches for the two children, who were sleeping on the top floor, sealed the gaps in the bottom of the door with towels, opened the window and then went into the kitchen, where she put her head in the gas oven. At that time Ted Hughes had published two volumes of poetry, both awarded major literary prizes. Sylvia Plath was the author of the poetry collection *The Colossus* and the autobiographical novel *The*

Ted drawn by Sylvia

Bell Jar, which appeared under a pseudonym. And then came this bombshell: the rumour mill was unstoppable, but Olwyn Hughes had other ideas. Anyone wishing to quote from Plath's work at length had to work via her. And permission depended on the attitude of the author in the Plath-Hughes controversy. Those who did not clearly take Hughes's side had her to deal with. In Janet Malcolm's book you can read the evidence of how she tried to influence authors and pressured them.

Ted Hughes kept in the background as far as possible, especially after 1969, when his then girlfriend Assia Wevill gassed herself together with their young daughter. This could no longer be coincidence. In this the 'libbers' – as Ted and Olwyn Hughes called the feminists – found new ammunition for their attacks on the poet. In the background he may have been, but he was not idle. Little by little the work of Sylvia Plath was published. Hughes edited or collaborated on those posthumous editions – and intervened. He rearranged the poems in her best-known collection *Ariel*, and omitted a few. Passages in the letters and diaries were censored. Moreover, he admitted that he had destroyed the diary of the last few months of her life and that a second diary had vanished without trace.

Janet Malcolm quotes from a letter that Hughes wrote to Plath's biographer Anne Stevenson: 'I have never attempted to give my account of Sylvia, because I saw quite clearly from the first day that I am the only person in this business who cannot be believed by all who need to find me guilty.' That situation changed in 1998 when he published *Birthday Letters*, 88 poems about his relationship with Sylvia Plath. The book appeared in an unusually large edition: it was the fastest-selling collection of poetry in the history of English literature (over 100,000 copies before the end of the year). Ted Hughes was already suffering from cancer when he wrote the majority of the poems. He died on 28 October 1998.

Unconditional love

Such a steep wall of literature is daunting. What can be added to the dossier? No, I wasn't really planning to read Connie Palmen's novel, but on 10 October 2015 I saw on the BBC *Stronger than Death*, a poignant hour-long documentary on Hughes, with testimony from friends and biographers and for the first time a long interview with Frieda, the daughter of Sylvia and Ted, herself a poet and painter, who had designed the dust jacket for *Birthday Letters*. This documentary demolished the wall and my prejudices. The next day I bought *Jij zegt het*.

It is tempting to see everything that has been said and written about the two poets as elements in never-ending legal proceedings: indictment, case for the defence, case for the prosecution, an irrepressible series of witnesses, with echoes and reports in the media. How did Hughes react? In Palmen's novel it recurs like a refrain: 'I kept silent.' 'I said nothing.' 'So I kept silent.' Hughes's silence was not absolute. When in the 1970s a letter to the editor appeared in the *Guardian*, containing the accusation that Sylvia's grave in Heptonstall,

Louis MacNeice,
Ted Hughes, T.S. Eliot,
W.H. Auden and
Stephen Spender at a party
at Faber and Faber,
23 June 1960

Sylvia with Frieda and Nicholas among
the daffodils in Devon, 1962

Her Majesty Queen Elizabeth and
Ted Hughes, poet laureate, at Balmoral
Forest, May 1998

West Yorkshire, the village where Hughes had spent part of his childhood and
where his parents lived, was being neglected and the story was taken up by *The
Independent*, Hughes flew off the handle. The letter had been signed by academics and writers, including Joseph Brodsky. Hughes wrote long indignant
responses to the two papers, explaining that the gravestone had been removed
because 'libbers' (who else?) had scratched out the name Hughes no less than
four times and that the stone was now in the stonemason's yard awaiting his
decision on how to proceed.

Birthday Letters is not so much a speech in self-defence as a public confession, or better still a commentary on a photo album: sometimes business-like,
sometimes in verses where the emotion can be glimpsed. As expressive as all
Hughes's poetry, but for the first time in a relaxed *parlando* style. What is lacking for the reader who is not thoroughly prepared is coherence and clarity. And

that is precisely the aim of Connie Palmen's novel: to bring clarity. As in *Birthday Letters*, Hughes speaks in the first person, but his style is more elaborate and direct, less impressionistic and concealing.

Connie Palmen uses the well-known biographical material available in the many books about Plath; until recently Hughes had to make do with one biography, *The Life of a Poet* (2001) by Elaine Feinstein. *Ted Hughes. The Unauthorised Life* by Jonathan Bate appeared after the publication of *Jij zegt het*. This massive tome, 600 pages long, was rightly criticised because of Bate's predilection for focusing on the poet's extramarital escapades rather than his work. (Hughes married Carol Orchard in 1970.) In *Jij zegt het* the biographical facts are a kind of guideline, the chronological thread around which the novel is woven, but are drowned out by the reflections and comments of the narrator.

The core of Hughes's story is the constant affirmation that his love for Sylvia was unconditional, that he never questioned that love for a moment, and that in the last weeks of her life there were even plans to move back in together. Through the way in which Connie Palmen empathises with Hughes's feelings and has him make, for example, the following confession, we enter the field of the novel (cf. the statement by Bernard Crick, the biographer of George Orwell: 'None of us can enter into another person's mind; to believe so is fiction'):

'Everyone around me thought I was too protective of my bride, thought her too possessive, demanding and jealous, and me an obedient dog, a sleep-walking bridegroom who did not realise he was being manipulated, drilled and trained. They forgot that I experienced everything she saw and felt as if I were seeing and feeling it myself. Her pain was my pain, her fears were my fears; it's just that I reacted differently to them.'

Dominated by literature

Besides the physical attraction – Palmen describes at length their first meeting, when Sylvia kissed Ted on the cheek until he bled and then:

'We didn't embrace, we attacked each other (...) It was cruel, it hurt. It was real. We were each other's prey.'

– there was of course literature. The famous first meeting took place in Cambridge on 25 February 1956. A party was being given for the launch of *Saint Botolph's Review*, a literary magazine that was to cease publication after its first issue. Hughes had published a few poems in it and Sylvia was so impressed that she knew them by heart and recited bits of them as she threw herself at Hughes. They married a few months later on 16 June, Bloomsday, the day on which the action of Joyce's *Ulysses* takes place.

From the outset then their lives were dominated by literature. Sylvia was Ted's muse and Ted was Sylvia's mentor. They read their poems to each other and commented on them. Sylvia typed out Ted's messy manuscripts until she was able to make up a collection and entered it for an important American debut prize. That collection, *The Hawk in the Rain*, won the prize and was published simultaneously in England and America: exceptional for a debut. Hughes had

Ted photographed by his sister Olwyn,
who mirrors herself into the picture

begun on a lightning career. The mentorship of the prize-winning poet consisted in his commissioning poems and also stories from Sylvia, since it was one of
her ambitions to publish in well-known journals like *The New Yorker*. Hughes
felt she wrote too autobiographically and worried so much about the expectations of those magazines that she did not show herself to her best advantage.
He constantly advised her to search deeper in herself for her authentic voice.
Plath found that voice at the end of her life, when in Devon and London in difficult circumstances caused by having to care for two children she was obliged
to steal a few hours in the early morning to write the poems that were to make
her posthumously famous.

Not the last word

In the years when they were still together, their collaboration was so intense
that in the archives of the American universities, where their manuscripts are
preserved, versions of their poems were found on the back of each other's
rough drafts. During the few years that they lived in Devon, they often wrote
about the same subjects. Connie Palmen has Hughes say that at a certain moment the intensity of their collaboration became too stifling and was probably
the deeper reason for their estrangement and split. Ironically, in *Birthday Letters* we find constant echoes of Sylvia Plath's last poems, exactly as if they are
writing on each other's rough drafts again. A special case of intertextuality,
which Connie Palmen expresses brilliantly:

'In the years after her death and now, now I am trying to repair the hole that her suicide blew open in me with poetry, in a posthumous dialogue am having the conversation with her that we can no longer have, am completing the 88 birthday letters to my bride to assert my version of our love, to reclaim my memories as my rightful property, and like an echo let the poetic version of her story be glimpsed in mine, that image often returns to me of the last time we sat together by the fire in the crimson living room and through the glow of the flames could see how our words merged, one body, one mind, a wedding of words.'

Connie Palmen has given a voice to one of the best-known English poets of the last century. She achieves this feat in bravura fashion. The story is believable, incredibly compelling and not at all redundant as I had initially feared. The reader is not given an answer to all the questions. Why, for example, Hughes appointed his sister Olwyn as an intermediary, knowing that the two women were arch enemies and that Olwyn's opinion after Sylvia's death even hardened. I read somewhere that Hughes in that way tried to keep the money from her literary legacy in the family. But enough of that: *Jij zegt het* is a wonderfully structured book, full of passion and empathy, though most probably not the last word. ◾

FURTHER READING

Connie Palmen, *The Laws*, translated from Dutch by Richard Huijing. London: Reed International Books, 1992 [*De wetten*, Prometheus, Amsterdam, 1991]

Connie Palmen, *The Friendship*, translated from Dutch by Ina Rilke. London: Harvill, 2000 [*De vriendschap*, Prometheus, Amsterdam, 1995]

Translated by Paul Vincent

On Duality and on Painting as Sculpture (and Sculpture as Painting)

The Visual Work of Lili Dujourie

In 2015, ten years after the retrospective of the work of artist Lili Dujourie organised by the Centre for Fine Arts in Brussels (BOZAR), her work was again celebrated in Belgium in a new retrospective, *Folds in Time* – a diptych, in fact, held in parallel in Ostend (Mu.ZEE) and Ghent (S.M.A.K.). Together, the exhibitions covered the period from her debut in the 1960s to the present, providing insights into her oeuvre – one that, significantly, is determined as much by its formal character as by the critical development with which Dujourie relates as an artist to the art world around her.

At the end of the 1950s, after attending the *Kunsthumaniora* (School of Art) in Bruges, Lili Dujourie (b. Roeselare, 1941) registered at the Royal Academy of Arts in Brussels. The monumental works of the American abstract expressionists had made a great impression on her during the Expo 58 world exhibition, and she decided to enrol in sculpture as well as painting, finding it impossible to choose between the two. When she began to show her own art several years later, she exhibited a series of works relating to minimal art. Her first exhibition, in 1970 at the X-One Gallery in Antwerp, comprised steel sheets placed on the floor or leaning against a wall, in an exploration of the laws of equilibrium and gravity. The realisations explore the boundaries of sculpture. In these first works, there is already a sense of the problems that she was to explore in her later oeuvre. The steel sheet placed against the wall of the exhibition room had the form of a sculpture but, through the specific way in which it was presented, it simultaneously explored the boundary with painting. Whereas sculpture traditionally occupies space, Dujourie carefully placed this work at the margin, seeking a position between the ground and the wall. It is as if the sheet is a painting waiting to be hung.

Playing with time

Dujourie's art is an unceasing exploration of the artistic medium. In the 1970s, she experimented with slide projections, for example in *Ostend* (1974). In this work, she used slide projectors placed alongside each other to display a series of images of the beach and the sea. Although the projection of the images sug-

gests movement, and thus appears to indicate continuity, the analogy with the principles of photography mainly evokes the past. In this sense, *Ostend* shows how Dujourie plays with the concept of time and how she intensifies it as a series of moments that are by definition transient. From 1972 onwards, she returned to the medium of video, which appealed to her because of the immediacy made possible by instant playback. The work *Effen spiegel van een stille stroom* (Mirror of a Quiet Stream, 1976) depicts Dujourie herself. She wanders in and out of the picture and poses in front of a mirror. In this way, she appears to be interrupting the perception of the viewer who, seeing both artist and mirror image can no longer be sure which of the silhouettes reflects reality – in the knowledge that the image recorded on video is itself already a reproduction, and not reality either. In this work, Dujourie therefore addresses the relationship between 'time and space'. Between 1972 and 1975, she also created the five-part series *Hommage à...*, in which she watches herself while her naked

Lili Dujourie, *Folds in Time*, Exposition, S.M.A.K, Ghent

Lili Dujourie, *Oostende*, 1974

body moves slowly on a bed. Her poses are suggestive as well as intimate, and allude intuitively to images from the history of art. According to critic Wim Van Mulders, it is as if Dujourie's work enables us to 'discover the relative meaning of video as a medium in terms of formulating thoughts.' 'The departure from a linear progression – there is no beginning or end – suggests that time is an elusive, fluid perception.' She frames the work herself through her relationship to the surrounding reality. Because, whereas she 'has always lived in the now', and whereas her work has always been a reaction to the times in which she lives, it was an entirely new medium that enabled her to realise this 'female nude that is both sculpture and painting'. Painting and sculpture brought together by a video recording.

Open meeting and discussions

It is easy to interpret a series such as *Hommage à...* as an exponent of feminism in the art of the twentieth century, a tendency that, in keeping with her video work, is characterised by her use of her own body as a subject. In 2007, for example, her work was included in *WACK! Art and the Feminist Revolution*, the exhibition organised by the Museum of Contemporary Art in Los Angeles to show how the feminist movement 'fundamentally changed' the structures and methods of contemporary art practice in the 1960s and 1970s. The artist herself is well aware of the uniqueness of her position as a woman in the world of art. Several years ago, she observed that at the time of her debut it was 'not usual for women to operate in the art world'. But there is another reason why Dujourie occupies a prominent place in recent art history, namely her critical approach to the way she as an artist relates to the local and international art scene. In 1975, together with Jacques Charlier and Guy Mees, she organised an event in a building in Antwerp's Raapstraat at which Jan Vercruysse – among others – was 'introduced' to the public as an artist – a statement indicating that those involved either wished to define themselves as such or not.

In September 1977, Dujourie held an 'open meeting' – also with Mees and Vercruysse – at Antwerp's Noorderterras to discuss the state of art, an initiative reminiscent of the inauguration of Marcel Broodthaers's *Musée d'Art Moderne* nine years before (Broodthaers opened 'his' museum).

The critical approach that was characteristic of Dujourie during that period was also grounded in her disapproval of the American dominance of the art world. This is the context in which we should place her involvement in actions relating to 'American art in Belgian collections'. Before this exhibition – also held in 1977 – Dujourie, Charlier, Mees, Vercruysse and Panamarenko wrote a letter to a number of Belgian collectors asking them not to loan works to the exhibition. Although she was convinced that there was 'no room' for non-American artists at that time, she acknowledged that her relationship to American art was double-edged. On the one hand, she was involved in writing the letter to the Belgian collectors, but at the same time, through Galerie MTL (established by her husband Fernand Spillemaeckers) she encountered the work of American artists such as Robert Barry, Dan Graham and Sol LeWitt. She nevertheless perceived a lack of poetry in their minimal and concept art, which led in particular to the work *Amerikaans Imperialisme* (American Imperialism), created in 1972 and first exhibited in 1979. A formal reference to contemporary American art, it consists of a sheet of steel leaning against a painted wall. The work also contains an underlying criticism, however, drawing the spectator's attention to what is hidden behind the sheet and thereby attributing a poetic dimension to the work. *Amerikaans Imperialisme* may further allude to Dujourie's decision to study two art disciplines at the Royal Academy since this work, too, explores the equilibrium between sculpture and painting.

Lili Dujourie,
Hommage à ..., 1972

Lili Dujourie,
American Imperialism,
1972

Velvet sculptures

In the 1980s, with works including *Pandora* (1983), *Opus 8* (1984), *In mijn nacht nadert niemand* (In My Night No-One Approaches, 1985) and *Jeu des Dames* (1987), Dujourie realised a series of depictions using velvet, in which her characteristic rendering of painterly folds stands out. Ornament and decoration are accorded a central role in these works, and the artist toys with the sensuality of the velvet material. This is the period in which the influence of the Flemish Primitives became apparent in Dujourie's work, where itis evident not only in the use of drapery as a material. The photograph *Untitled (red nude)* (1980) depicts a nude model posing against a background of carefully draped material. However, it is precisely this background that dominates the image, with an iconographic allusion to the aforementioned tradition. Whereas the velvet sculptures create a tangible imitation of the drapery, the two-dimensionality of the photograph relates to the flat surfaces of the paintings of Primitives such as Jan van Eyck and Rogier van der Weyden. At the same time, Dujourie remained critical in her relationship to her immediate context. In 1986, she took part in *Initiatief 86*, an exhibition at St. Peter's Abbey in Ghent presented by international curators including Kasper König. Ulrich Loock, the then director of the Kunsthalle in Bern remembers the exhibition as 'a smart move' on the part of the Flemish artists who had taken the initiative themselves in order to raise their international profile. That same year, Loock's experience of the exhibition prompted him to invite Dujourie, together with Vercruysse, Guillaume Bijl and

Raoul De Keyser, to stage a joint exhibition in Bern. In the exhibition catalogue, Saskia Bos describes Dujourie's velvet works, again referring to the art-history tradition, as 'Botticelli's Venus without the figures'. They are works that leave the spectator free to experience personal emotions, thereby opening up the path to the 'doors of perception'.

This was followed, several years later, by a solo exhibition at the Bonner Kunstverein in Bonn, Germany. Bart Cassiman, its curator, aimed to take the spectator beyond the cliché of Dujourie as 'the artist who uses velvet and refers to art history' in order to explore the stratification of her practice, primarily by presenting an ensemble of her works that provides a more comprehensive picture, stretched over two decades, of her development as an artist. For Cassiman, this development was largely characterised by a high degree of subtlety, the themes of illusion and 'window-dressing', the opposition of presence and absence, and the idea of duality. The layered nature of Dujourie's work is also reflected in the titles of the video *Sonnet* (1974) and of series such as *Roman* (1979), the collages comprising cuttings from newspapers and advertising material sparsely attached to large sheets of paper. These are titles that give her work a literary dimension and emphasise the importance of the written word in the development of the visual arts. This is also where her work connects with the oeuvre of Broodthaers, who, in the footsteps of René Magritte, embarked on a study of the relationship between word and image.

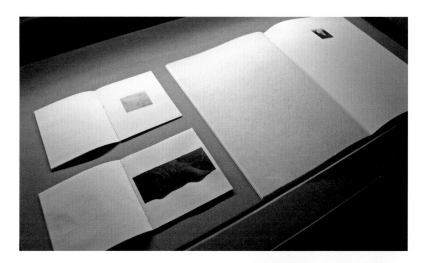

Above
Lili Dujourie,
Novel, 1979

Right
Lili Dujourie,
Red Nude, 1983

Trompe l'oeil

After the period in which she expressed her ideas in velvet, Dujourie explored new techniques using materials such as marble, lead and ceramics. This tendency can be illustrated with, respectively, the modular marble work *Echo* (1989), which is presented on the wall as well as the floor, the lead work *Substantia* (1999) – a subtle allusion to an altar cloth – and the five-piece ceramic work *Sonate* from 2007, the year in which she was the only Belgian artist to take part in the *documenta* in Kassel. In these experiments, too, Dujourie continues to position painting and sculpture in confrontation with each other, for example in the installation *De ochtend die avond zal zijn* (The Morning that Will Be the Evening, 1993) a work that appears to consist of a white cloth spread over two long tables. On closer inspection, however, the cloth and the subtle drapery are merely an imitation of the real thing. At first, the cloth appears to be a soft, classical piece of material, but is in fact hardened plaster. It is as if Dujourie wishes to expose the deception of our visual perception, and she seems to be telling us that nothing is what it seems. She does this by using one of the most traditional artistic strategies: with this work she has created a sculptural *trompe-l'oeil*. But although she borrows references from cultural tradition and art history, she applies these apparently classical forms of expression in a way that is atypical and 'against the rules'. Clay is sculpted not only by hand, but also with a knife. And Dujourie invents techniques that have 'never been used before'. Today she still relates her work to the reality around her. Maelstrom (2009-2010), a series of tactile paper sculptures made – not by coincidence – from pages of the *Financial Times*, expresses her views on the flood of information that is engulfing modern society. She states that this flood is 'so overwhelming,' 'no-one can comprehend it.'

Lili Dujourie, *The Morning that Will Be the Evening*, 1993

Lili Dujourie, *Places Devoted to the Night Remote from Tumults and from Noise*, 1983

Translated by Yvette Mead

In-between space

With *Folds in Time* it became clear that, after fifty years of production, Dujourie has assembled an oeuvre of 'sculptural interventions that fight a battle between painting and sculpture, between balance and gravity', and she has done this in a way that remains entirely consistent with her original artistic principles. It is therefore no surprise that she did not interpret the double overview in Ostend and Ghent in 2015 as a chronological retrospective, but rather as a sample of works from a meaningful whole made up of two different parts, since anyone who wanted to visit *Folds in Time* as an exhibition had to go to both places. This strategy was in line with the duality that is inherent in the exhibited works, which also oscillates between sculpture and painting without choosing one over the other. The title of the exhibition was therefore a reference to folds as the locus of the creative origin, the 'in-between space' from which Dujourie creates her work without making a clear choice in favour of either aspect. Moreover, the works were exhibited in Ostend and Ghent in a carefully considered way in the appropriate rooms, with the artist taking account of the architecture of the museums. The place of Dujourie's oeuvre in recent Flemish and Belgian art history is therefore due to her unique focus on the world and the reality that surrounds her, and on the art world of which she is a part. It is an oeuvre that will certainly not become lost in the folds of time. ∎

The sources for the remarks by Lili Dujourie quoted in this text are:
'A Conversation with Dirk Pültau and Koen Brams', *De Witte Raaf* art newspaper, November/December 2006.
Plooien in de tijd - Folds in time, cobra.be, 7 June 2015.
cobra.canvas.be/cm/cobra/kunst/1.2359861)

The Bluebird of Ghent

One of Europe's Hidden Gems?

'Welcome stranger,' someone shouted to me from on high. It was a mild autumn evening and I was walking back to my room after a book presentation in Ghent, at which I had said a few words. People danced behind lighted windows, a fairy-tale scene that I stopped for a moment to watch. Until someone invited me in and I spent a few pleasant hours at a party in Herberg Macharius, the old gatehouse of a former abattoir, now a neighbourhood community centre.

Two years later I came here to live. There's no connection. The reason for our move from the Netherlands is that my beloved was offered a good job in Jacob van Artevelde's city and it was convenient for me, as Europe correspondent for the Dutch journalism platform De Correspondent, to be domiciled there, not too far from Brussels. Yet it still feels a little as if I accepted that invitation from on high and that destiny chose Ghent for me.

I did get some warnings from people in the Netherlands who thought they knew all about it. Those Flemings, they retorted, they're a friendly lot with a Burgundian streak. If you want a good meal it's the place to be. But as far as they're concerned you'll always be 'the Dutchman', the somewhat churlish, noisy know-it-all with no idea of the charm of the indirect approach, someone who always goes straight for what he wants. You will never break through the shell of the friendly but formal Fleming. They keep their cards close to their chests and only reveal their deepest feelings to a small circle of intimates at the most – and don't think, as a northerner, that you'll be allowed to become one of those.

It'll be fine, I thought. After all, I might have grown up in the Netherlands and have lived there a good forty years, but I first saw the light of day in the hinterland of Ostend and my parents are from West Flanders. I thought I knew the secrets of the culture to some extent; it didn't exactly feel like emigration, more like a return to the land of my roots. What's more, I reasoned, the stereotypes on both sides are gross generalisations. There would be a wide variety of people living in Ghent, who would not allow themselves to be pushed into a box either. And after all, the Low Countries share not only a language but a lot of historical and cultural references as well.

Cultural Centre 'Vooruit',
Sint-Pietersnieuwstraat
© Jonas Lampens

I have lived here in this city in East Flanders for a little under a year now. So were the warnings right, or did my optimism turn out to be well founded? Do I still feel as welcome as on that lovely autumn evening two years ago? And what are my impressions of Ghent now?

Not one of us

One thing is true, it's not that easy to get rid of your Dutch label if you've got a northern accent. The guide at the magnificent eighteenth-century mansion-turned-museum, Hotel d'Hane-Steenhuyse, where Louis XVIII hid from Napoleon, continued to talk about 'your King William II', even when I told her about my West Flemish origins. People in our street talk of 'the Dutch neighbours' too. And although I thought I would never have to explain again that you write my surname the Belgian way, in one word, people still write Van Heste instead of Vanheste based on the idea that I am a Dutchman.

These are the mild irritations of the newcomer who wants to integrate, but feels that others don't see him as 'one of us'. But if that's how it feels for a Dutch-Belgian, I sometimes ask myself, what must it be like for people of a different colour or from more distant parts?

A woman, born and bred in Ghent, who fled the city of her birth, wrote a painful testimony about it in an opinion piece in a national newspaper recently. She is the daughter of a Flemish father and a Rwandan mother who was brought to Belgium during the decolonisation of Rwanda. Thanks to her colour she is asked ad nauseam where she comes from. 'I'm from here, I'm a product of our colonial past,' she used to answer, usually leaving her interlocutor dumbfounded. These days she is mostly indignant that 'my nationality is consistently called into question by the very same nation that severed my link with Rwanda'. She is angry with Ghent, a traditionally socialist city that considers itself to be the Flemish Valhalla of progressiveness and tolerance and thinks that the post-racial society has dawned already.

Peace and quiet

There is no denying it; Ghent does have a rose-tinted image of itself. Many people who ask whether I'm managing to integrate a bit immediately add that they're sure I am, because Ghent is such a friendly and open city. The city profiles itself as a 'city of peace', a place of dialogue and respect, and is organising a 'year of peace' in 2018. The brochure of the Ghent Festival of Flanders 2016 opens with an ode to the city. 'Everyone longs for peace and quiet – whatever his race, beliefs or age may be. In no other city in Flanders, Brabant or Limburg can such overwhelming peace and quiet be found. The reason is the exceptional tolerance of the city authorities and the imagination of the young people who have settled over the years in the provincial capital of East Flanders. Tolerance and imagination have ensured an explosion of festivities.'

The nice thing is that it's true. In the summer, certainly, there is one festivity after the other. The atmosphere here really is kindly and there is a lot to do in the cultural sphere. The 'welcome' that sounded from the Herberg Macharius I heard again in our street, where we were received with open arms and have been invited for drinks at many a neighbour's house. So, very quickly the motley reality turned out to belie the cliché of the friendly but reserved Fleming.

It occurred to me after the attacks on Zaventem airport and Maelbeek metro station, on 22 March 2016, that the desire to be a city of peace is more than just a marketing tool. It is also integral to the city's soul.

As they do every morning, all the children from my daughter's primary school assembled in the hall the next day. The early morning ritual is that the headmistress rings a little bell, after which a sacred silence descends – a rather surprising phenomenon for parents used to the Dutch education system – and the headmistress addresses the children briefly. That day her words

Graslei with Post Plaza Building, Sint-Niklaas Church and Belfry

© Jonas Lampens

were especially charged. She stood there with the flag of 'our Belgium' in her hand. The flag of all of us who live here, regardless of religion, nationality or colour, explained the headmistress. The flag of all the children in this school who come from all over the world and practise all sorts of different religions. She explained that this was a moment when we should all feel like one family, whatever our backgrounds. 'There is only one right word today: love.' She called on the children and those parents present to make a carpet of peace messages in the hall, like the one on the Place de la Bourse in Brussels.

These soothing words were intended mainly for children's ears, of course. But the same message was sounded that afternoon at a wake in the Sint-Niklaas Church in the centre of the city. Representatives of a variety of religious faiths – Christians, Muslims, Sikhs, Buddhists and humanists – joined the Mayor of Ghent in expressing their horror and calling for unity. 'No faith preaches hatred, no faith preaches violence,' said the president of the Association of Ghent Mosques, the VGM. A Zen Buddhist recalled the words of Buddha: 'Hatred is not conquered by hatred, hatred is conquered by love.'

Now those terrible events are behind us, this might all seem rather clichéd or high-flown. But in my view they were exactly the words we needed at the time. They were a sign, amidst all the dismay, of a calm determination not to allow ourselves to be divided, but to defend our open society in solidarity and unity. In those days I almost thought that Ghent was the Valhalla of tolerance that the lady with Rwandan roots, who fled the city, considers a mirage.

Birds of Ghent

The Ghent of our dreams is in my view nicely portrayed by the homegrown band Olla Vogala, which celebrated its twentieth anniversary in the Handelsbeurs, one of the local concert halls, in May 2016. Their respect for tradition is clear from their name. Old Dutch for 'all birds', it is a reference to one of the oldest known sentences in the Dutch language. The group performs enjoyable numbers like 'Met de meeuw' (with the seagull) in their native tongue. But on that lovely May evening there were also performances by musicians from Senegal, Syria and Slovakia. Olla Vogala draws its inspiration from musical traditions from various parts of the world, as well as from different genres and periods. Their music never becomes a mishmash though, in all their eclecticism they succeed in producing a sound that is all their own. Wouter Vandenabeele, the driving force behind the group, presents everything with a pleasant dose of self-mockery and humour.

'Met de meeuw' is inevitably reminiscent of that other Ghent bird 'l'oiseau bleu', or the bluebird, from the 1909 play of the same name by the Nobel Prize winner Maurice Maeterlinck. In the play, which was once madly popular as far afield as Japan, Tyltyl and Mytyl go in search of the bluebird, which symbolises happiness. Although its origins have been forgotten, the symbol is still very much alive in popular culture. The bluebird has been immortalised in many films, including *The Blue Bird* (1976), starring Elizabeth Taylor, Ava Gardner and Jane Fonda, and songs like Paul McCartney's 'Bluebird' (1973).

Maeterlinck was born two hundred metres from the place where I live now. The actual house of his birth is no longer there, but an inconspicuous bronze plaque commemorating the great writer hangs on the front of the present building. The only Belgian Nobel Prize winner for literature is certainly not wholeheartedly feted elsewhere in the city either. There is a Maeterlinck gallery in the Arnold Vander Haegen Museum, which can be visited along with the

Villa L'Oiseau bleu,
Patijntjesstraat
© Jonas Lampens

Herberg Macharius, Coyendanspark, Voorhoutkaai
© Jonas Lampens

Hotel d'Hane-Steenhuyse, but only with a guide and during a limited number of hours. One Saturday in August, which is high season after all, two French tourists, a Belgian and I turned up for the guided tour. At the end of our roam through these two extraordinary mansions there was a quarter of an hour left to look around the Maeterlinck gallery where, besides a nice portrait of the writer by Frans Masereel, you can admire some photos, first prints and newspaper cuttings from the desk and bookshelves brought from his later home in Nice.

It might surprise you that Ghent is so modest in its celebration of one of its greatest sons and that it does so little to exploit him as a tourist attraction. But you might be pleased about it too. In his excellent book *The Other Paris* (2015), Luc Sante, an American journalist of Belgian origin, laments the fact that we have forgotten what a city is. 'The exigencies of money and the proclivities of bureaucrats – as terrified of anomalies as of germs, chaos, dissipation, laughter, unanswerable questions – have conspired to create the conditions for stasis, to sanitize the city to the point where there will be no surprises, no hazards, no spontaneous outbreaks, no weeds.'

Unfortunately he is to a certain extent right. The authorities and big capital do seem to have many cities in an iron grip. They transform them into open-air museums and amusement parks, pushing less wealthy inhabitants out to the fringes. Every neighbourhood and every free space has a director, every asset the city has is used for city marketing. Yet it is the unexpected and unpredictable, the fringes and darker sides that exert such charm.

Ghent has not completely escaped these developments either. In recent years the historic centre has been cleaned up and its old harbour district up-graded with luxury residential and shopping centres, house prices have shot up and cafes for trendies and parents with cargo bikes are mushrooming. There's a risk of a certain museumization and stagnation too. In contrast to a city like Bordeaux, which has a great wealth of contemporary architecture to offer in addition to its UNESCO-listed city centre, Ghent has few exceptional buildings or places dating from more recent years.

But it would be much too pessimistic to decide that Ghent has no surprises anymore or that the city has been sanitised and neutralised. If you stroll around the city you are bound to come unexpectedly upon architectural pearls from the many different layers of time of which the city is built – as Sante says quite rightly, 'the city's principal constituent matter is accrued time' – and places of refuge where people from all layers of the population, with a motley collection of ethnic and religious backgrounds, do their own thing.

On a lovely day recently, I cycled to the house on Sleepstraat where the Flemish poet Karel van de Woestijne used to live. In the busy, messy shopping street, full of Turkish and Bulgarian fabric stores, phone shops and grocers, number 82 caught my eye – a rather dilapidated, but amazingly beautiful Art Deco building that seemed to be classified but not protected. Later I went to the Villa L'Oiseau bleu, a duo of semi-detached middle-class town houses with the names Tyltyl and Mytyl, which were designed by the Ghent architect Geo Hen-derick and built in 1929. On the way, I stumbled across the surprising sign 'Execution site'. It brought me to the 'Execution site for those shot in the head 1914-1918', a rather secluded, hushed, highly impressive monument. Barely recovered from the memory of that abysmal atrocity, the sight of Henderick's houses put me in a heavenly mood. If the bluebird of happiness can be found anywhere, it must be in Ghent. ∎

Translated by Lindsay Edwards

Above left
Execution site 'for those shot in the head 1914-1918',
Offerlaan
© Jonas Lampens

Below left
Art Deco Building, Sleepstraat
© Jonas Lampens

Fiction Is Always Non-Fiction

The Oeuvre of Jan Brokken

I would rather have kept quiet about this, but anyone who makes *entre nous* statements should not be surprised when such secrets emerge. The only uncertainty is *when* that will happen. So, here goes: in the Literary Criticism classes I was invited to teach at universities as a 'guest critic' in recent decades, the writer Jan Brokken (b. 1949) often served as something of a target for me. It's not because I don't like him or because I think he's a terrible writer – on the contrary. I brought him up solely to illustrate the prosaic aspects of literary criticism and the need for an unprejudiced mind.

How does it usually work? A love for literature makes you jump from mountaintop to mountaintop, and in my flat homeland that comes down to: from Louis Couperus to J.J. Slauerhoff, with a long leap aside to S. Vestdijk, and so on, Mulisch-wards. Those who are given nectar to drink long for more of the stuff. But the reality is that every week lesser gods, at worst little scribblers, land on your desk, which is dominated by the latest ephemera. In the Dutch language, a new masterpiece does not come out every seven days, even though those who have faith in hype would have you believe this is the case.

And that's why, in those classes, I would take pot shots at Brokken, in order to temper the flimsy expectations of the aspiring critics. I used to say, 'No one ever wonders: when's the new Jan Brokken coming out?'

Archetypically 'Dutch'

In order to avoid any misunderstandings: I certainly don't consider Brokken to be a scribbler. In fact, whenever I read one of his books, I am generally pleasantly surprised, by the high quality, the subtle pen, the eye for minute detail. To be fair, though, I don't think I would have read a book by him if I hadn't been writing reviews. At most, I would have remembered him as the journalist who conducted such fine interviews with writers in the late 1970s in the now-defunct weekly *Haagse Post*. I owe the *writer* Brokken to the *hic sunt leones* expedition that is literary criticism – a journey into unknown territory.

I'd be perfectly happy to see a new Brokken come out every year. Nevertheless, I cite him in my survey of the latest literary offerings precisely because

Jan Brokken
© Jelmer de Haas

he is not an isolated, stellar talent like Mulisch – which, incidentally, is also true of ninety-five percent of literature written in Dutch. In short, he's lacking in madness. Madness that can result in brilliance – together, the sign of the literary giant. I am sure I am not telling Brokken anything new; I suspect that his role model was first Jean Rhys, then Geert Mak and now Jan Brokken – attainable greats.

Why choose Brokken as an example? Because, to put it euphemistically, he is certainly capable, and yet he seldom features on lists of favourites. Because he has created a respectable oeuvre, but did not make his breakthrough to the general public until his wartime story *De vergelding* (The Reprisal) was published in 2013. Brokken was one of the initiators of the genre of literary non-

fiction in the Netherlands, and can also hold his own in the fields of autobiography and novels. He has twenty-six books to his name and I would recommend six of those to literature lovers who just want to hop from literary mountain to mountain: the novels *De blinde passagiers* (The Stowaways, 1995) and *De Kozakkentuin* (The Cossack Garden, 2015) and the following non-fiction titles: *Jungle Rudy (de Verloren Wereld van Rudy Truffino)* (1999, translated into English by Sam Garrett); *In het huis van de dichter* (In the Poet's House, 2008); *Baltische zielen (lotgevallen in Estland, Letland en Litouwen)* (Baltic Souls, 2010); and *De vergelding (een dorp in tijden van oorlog)* (The Reprisal, 2013).

However, I chose Brokken as an example mainly because it is hard to find Dutcher writers than him. Not the directionless Netherlands of the present day, with its democratized bad taste. But the Netherlands that existed before the era of the overblown ego: respectable, modest, decent to a fault, cursed with a strong work ethic, imbued with the scent of a Calvinist past, and the active awareness of an educational ideal. The Dutch identity exists, as a residue of shared history and collective qualities. As evidence, I point my finger at the prose of Jan Brokken.

He will presumably go down in Dutch literary history as a writer of literary non-fiction, mentioned in the same breath as Geert Mak, Frank Westerman and Annejet van der Zijl. Within that genre, he has written travel books, interviews, articles, portraits, essays, autobiographical prose, and works of popular history. That sounds clear enough, but such genre divisions are imprecise and therefore arbitrary: his autobiographical 'novel of a friendship', *In het huis van de dichter* (In the Poet's House, about Youri Egorov), forms a diptych with the non-fictional portrait gallery *Baltische zielen* (Baltic Souls) – a superb standard work of cultural history. His recent title *De vergelding* (The Reprisal) is a novel-like reconstruction of the hidden history of the village of Rhoon, involving the murder of a German soldier during the Occupation. Brokken, born in Leiden, grew up as the son of a minister in Rhoon; the village is a setting that his readers already knew well, with a certain amount of duplication, from his debut novel *De provincie* (The Province, 1984) and his autobiography *Mijn kleine waanzin* (My Little Madness, 2004).

No one escapes their origins

Fiction is always non-fiction in Brokken; reality cannot be denied. Take his novel *De droevige kampioen* (The Sad Champion, 1997). The two quotes at the beginning of the book relate to the place where the story is set: the island of Curaçao. Brokken quotes Cola Debrot, who, after the violent riots in 1969, wrote 'Droevig eiland droevig volk / droevig eiland in de kolk / van de maalstroom van de maalstroom / droevig eiland zonder tolk' (literally: Sad island sad people / sad island in the vortex / of the maelstrom of the maelstrom / sad island with no interpreter). The first two of the seventy-five chapters show us Riki Marchena at the height of his fame, acclaimed by the entire population of Curaçao as a table-tennis champion, and then later becoming a ragged and dirty 'choller' (junkie), washing cars to fund his crack addiction. So both Marchena and his island are sad champions.

There is a warning at the beginning of *De droevige kampioen*: 'Most of the facts in this book are based on reality, but *De droevige kampioen* is a novel, and all the characters are depicted so as to have no similarity to existing people, with the exception of the politicians Papa Godett and Miguel Pourier, who appear under their own names.' Presumably Brokken intends that the backdrop against which the story takes place – the Antilles of the past forty years – should not be dismissed as fictional. Not because that would be a waste of his thorough documentation, but because harsh words of social criticism are spoken about the island. Words that, in his opinion, need to be heard.

The idea, accepted and lauded in progressive circles, of the island's demographic composition as a friendly racial melting pot is shown to be an illusion. Within all strata of society, it matters whether someone is a shade lighter or darker; great importance is also attached to people's ancestry: 'On Curaçao, no one escapes their origins.' The postcolonial joy at independence is in retrospect tempered by the facts: 'We believed everything would be better and we set our own city on fire. We turned our backs on the colonial past and created such a favourable fiscal climate that the whites came in droves. We said we should finally become independent and yet held out our hands wherever we could.' The mentality in particular is no good in this Antillean society, where corruption is part of the amoral order of the day. The writer, speaking through his mouthpiece, Riki: 'Everything was permitted here, as long as it paid; the centuries of piracy, robbery and plundering had corrupted the mentality to such an extent that everyone was merely out for a quick profit.'

Brokken also makes use of informative footnotes, which serve to reinforce the suggestion of truth. A note referring to one character, for instance, informs us that 'Grandfather: Doctor Capriles, Diane d'Oliveira's grandfather, was the first doctor in the West Indies to treat the mentally ill.' So it seems Brokken's story is less fictional than he indicated. His own protagonist also gets it in the neck: 'Riki Marchena is confusing two events here.' The historic accuracy of the facts – about his actual protagonist: Curaçao – clearly takes precedence over the imagination for Brokken. After finishing the book, then, it is not so much Riki's parable-like experiences that linger with the reader. Rather, *De droevige kampioen* – like a report delivered from the inside – draws attention to the tragic situation in a society in which everyone since time immemorial has just tried to get whatever they can for themselves and 'dirty hands don't matter'. So this is a novel à la Jan Brokken.

An old-fashioned storyteller

I will now search his oeuvre for variation, for cracks, because such dissection offers ways in. But, in his case, this seems rather unnatural. Because what actually lends his work its unforced unity is its unobtrusive personal tone. Whatever he writes, whether it is his inimitable portraits of writers and artists, an indictment in the form of a novel, such as *De droevige kampioen*, or a neo-romantic novel like *De blinde passagiers*, it stems from his own concerns. He clearly does what he wants to do, goes where his wide-ranging interests take him, and that is evident in his unfashionable oeuvre.

Unfashionable, yes. As a novelist, he is an old-fashioned, realistic storyteller. In the Netherlands, this description is often wrongly perceived as an insult; obviously, people have forgotten that Guy de Maupassant was also a storyteller and that three-quarters of British literature is 'litertainment'. The maritime novel *De blinde passagiers* could not have been written without great admiration for storytellers such as Johan Fabricius and Jan de Hartog. Yet, in that novel, I also hear the breath of F.C. Terborgh, that slow Slauerhoff. The novel as homage, then. And that makes it closely related to his travel story *Goedenavond, mrs. Rhys* (Good Evening, Mrs. Rhys, 1992) and the empathetic and admiring portraits of artists and writers in his collection *Spiegels* (Mirrors, 1993).

The hermit of his own dreams

In the space allocated to me here, I would like to speak up for a Brokken title that I am fond of, but which is largely unknown to the wider public: the biographical sketch *Jungle Rudy*. It is 1975 and the prince consort Bernhard is at the controls of a plane. His destination – and that of his extensive retinue – is the Venezuelan jungle encampment built by expatriate Dutchman Rudy Truf-

fino, the director of an enormous nature reserve. It's a legendary encounter. Bernhard was immediately impressed by Truffino. 'What that man has achieved in the jungle,' he declared two days later to *Telegraaf* journalist Stan Huygens, 'verges on the implausible.' Truffino, however, had soon had enough of His Royal Highness. 'He kept going on about how he looked so young for his age and I looked so old. Eventually I got fed up with it. So I said to him, "Hey, hang on a moment, man, that Holland of yours is a shitty little country and how many people have you got to manage it? And this park here is thirty thousand square kilometres and I run it on my own." Bernhard looked a bit taken aback for a moment, then he took his pipe out of his mouth and, with a hiccupping laugh, admitted defeat.'

It's a typical anecdote, dished up by Brokken with gusto. Not only does it say something about Bernhard's machismo and the adventurer 'Jungle Rudy'. It also reveals Truffino's feudal attitude to the world and shows how that inspired respect in Bernhard – two aristocrats, above the law and man to man. It should be noted that Truffino could boast of some illegitimate royal Oranje blood in his ancestry.

And yet Truffino had to travel to the other side of the world and detach himself from everything that bound him to his fatherland, the education he had enjoyed and his family background before he was able to become 'Jungle Rudy'. 'He was uncompromising, in many respects extreme, and could only get along with unconventional types,' writes the romantic realist Brokken in his account of his search for Truffino. But Jungle Rudy was also an expert on the local fauna and flora, and an explorer in territory that was previously unknown to Westerners – in these areas he was an undisputed authority.

He was an authority, for he is no more. His fate was tragic. He died of a tumour, in complete isolation in his beloved jungle. He had become 'the hermit of his own dreams', alienating almost everyone. His Dutch family lived too far away to support him and, Brokken reports soberly, his three daughters from his marriage to the Austrian Gerti, who were brought up in the jungle among the local tribespeople, lacked a certain trait: tenderness. Truffino's life and particularly its end would not have been out of place in a novel – King Lear in the jungle.

Brokken saw good material in Truffino's life – his keen nose for subject matter is also a talent. It is naturally all too good to be true: Truffino emerged from the pre-war upper class of the Netherlands and was ejected from this milieu as a result of his father's profligacy and financial failings. Thrown out of schools, unwilling to learn, after the war he left for Tunisia, where he almost died. Then he started work as a zookeeper for the dictator of the Dominican Republic, subsequently being arrested during a coup and coming close to execution by firing squad. Venezuela followed next, where he was first a homeless street vendor and later the manager of a successful business. Crashed in the jungle, bitten by a venomous snake, saved just in time by members of the Pemón tribe... The rest of his life story is jungle: 'For Truffino, the real jungle was far from the tropical forest and, as night fell, he would read about Nostradamus or nightmarish murders in San Francisco and Los Angeles.' Safe in the jungle, classical music and books within reach, as far as possible from the masses.

But Brokken was also fascinated by him because Truffino dared to venture where he feared to go. He did not belong anywhere – not in any country, not in any time. *Jungle Rudy* is both an adventurous travel story and a psychological portrait. But the true protagonist is the jungle itself, a place where nature is stronger than man. Where snakes have their eyes on you, an ant bite can prove fatal, 'vampires' are out for your blood, dinosaur-like creatures hop around, former members of the SS make their home, and the locals enjoy being drunk. Photographs corroborate the facts in Brokken's masterful report: Truffino degenerated from an attractive man into an emaciated corpse. The jungle won.

In terms of genre, *Jungle Rudy* is indisputably non-fiction – the arch-Calvinist Brokken's preferred path. And behold, now that he no longer has to battle against the frivolous fortitude of the novel overwhelming his beloved facts, he loosens up and paradoxically writes with the panache of a gifted novelist – which, having taken this route, he is. In this case, the truth is strange enough for this champion of literary non-fiction.

Away from the fanfare

His most recent novel, *De Kozakkentuin* (The Cossack Garden) is a perfect testament to this. Brokken climbs inside the head of the nineteenth-century German-Baltic baron Alexander von Wrangel, equipped with his unpublished memoirs. Through Fyodor Dostoyevsky's friendship with this young public prosecutor, whom he met during his exile in Siberia, Brokken succeeds not only in casting light on the fascinating subject of gender roles in Russia, but also on Dostoyevsky's literary development. It was Von Wrangel who urged this genius to write his most important books: *Crime and Punishment*, *The Idiot* and *The House of the Dead*. Another homage then, this time to a man who, away from the fanfare of great fiction, modestly performed his own essential part. Like Jan Brokken himself. ■

www.janbrokken.nl

Jan Brokken, *Jungle Rudy*, translated by Sam Garrett. London – New York: Marion Boyars Publishers, 2004 [*Jungle Rudy*. Amsterdam: Atlas, 1999]

Jan Brokken, *The Rainbird: A Central African Journey*, translated by Sam Garrett. Melbourne; Oakland; London; Paris: Lonely Planet, 1997 (Lonely Planet Journeys) [*De regenvogel*. Amsterdam: De Arbeiderspers, 1991]

Jan Brokken, *The Music of the Netherlands Antilles: Why Eleven Antilleans Knelt before Chopin's Heart*, translated by Scott Rollins. Jackson: University Press of Mississippi, 2015 (Caribbean Studies/World Music) [*Waarom elf Antillianen knielden voor het hart van Chopin*. Amsterdam: Atlas, 2005]

Translated by Laura Watkinson

An Extract from *De Kozakkentuin* (The Cossack Garden)

by Jan Brokken

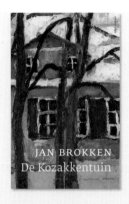

The conspiracy

The first time I saw him he was standing in front of the firing squad, wearing a white shroud. He: a man approaching thirty preparing himself for death and kissing a silver cross that the priest held out before him. I: an inquisitive youth looking from a safe distance at what injustice was.

There was no school that day. 1849 was the year of the cholera; masses of people died in Saint Petersburg. Because of the danger of infection, our grammar school had closed before the start of September. I was living in the house of an uncle and for months I'd been simply mooching about.

In December the school advised us to go back to our families for the holiday season. Outside the city fewer people were falling victim to the disease and I contemplated travelling to Terpilitsy. The estate was only seventy versts from Petersburg and could be reached within a day. We hadn't yet had any heavy falls of snow, so the roads would be passable, it could be done, but instead I stuck around with my uncle, Baron Nicolai Korf,[1] who lived in a small wooden house on the corner of the Liteyny Prospekt and Kirochnaya Street. At seventeen you're not interested in your family and the city is many times more exciting than the countryside, especially in winter. In actual fact there were three months to go before my seventeenth birthday,[2] but I felt a real young man already and I was remarkably tall for my age. Still, I would have wanted to be home for Christmas alright, had I not known for certain that my father would hurl an endless series of reproaches at me. He felt very strongly about order and discipline and believed 'people like us' needed to set an example to others in all things.

The execution

Uncle Vladimir asked me to go with him to the exercise yard. I initially put on my unlined summer coat, then realized it was cold and exchanged it for my uniform jacket[3] and donned a cocked hat. I didn't have a winter overcoat because my father thought it was a luxury and a lad shouldn't be spoilt but instead toughened up.

We took a hired coach, a 'crock'. It was an overcast day, a real grey Petersburg morning, around four or six degrees, damp cold. From time to time a little snow fell. Dostoevsky would remember that it was 'icy cold', especially at the moment when they made him put on the shroud.

The exercise yard was a huge field where the snow had mixed with slush. When we got out of the coach we saw a group of people in the distance, soldiers in square formation, and what at first sight looked like a rather rickety structure, a platform of planks on long wooden poles with steps at the front. Was that a scaffold? We thought the men were to die facing the firing squad, yet it did indeed look like a scaffold. We tried to get closer but police and gendarmes held us back.

Another uncle came over to us, Uncle Alexander Mandershern. He bragged with a barely concealed appetite for sensation that he had wanted to be present at the execution along with his Chasseur Company. When he caught sight of me he was astonished.

'For God's sake boy, get away from here. God forbid your headmaster finds out you've been to the execution. Soon they'll suspect you of being a political and expel you from the grammar school.'

When he'd finished scolding, Uncle Alexander leaned over towards us, as he had major news he couldn't keep to himself.

'In the strictest confidence,' he whispered, 'I can tell you that there's not going to be an execution.'

'Not?' asked Uncle Vladimir, who suspected he had misunderstood.

Uncle Alexander shook his head categorically. All lives would be spared, but the condemned men did not know that. The tsar wanted the firing squad procedure to be carried out in its entirety and then, at the last moment, when it was time to give the command 'Fire!' the adjutant would come galloping up with orders from the most high: execution to be halted.

I didn't believe him, and neither did Uncle Vladimir. At least, so I deduced from the dazed look in his eyes; he didn't think the tsar was capable of such a cruel charade.

'Come on, we're going,' he said to Mandershern, almost angrily.

My uncles went to their units. I mingled with the grey masses. The distance between me and the men in square formation was hard to estimate, but at any rate I was a fairly long way from them. The exercise yard had by now filled with inquisitive people who happened to be passing by. The date and time of executions was kept secret; the bloodthirsty crowd, which attends such performances as if they're a fairground attraction, could not possibly have been informed in advance. The mood among them was serious. Everyone felt sympathy for the 'unfortunates', although hardly anyone knew of what crimes they had been convicted.

It seemed as if the condemned men felt freedom for a brief moment when they stepped out of the coaches. They looked at the early light above the city – the sun had just risen – and then at each other. During their imprisonment they had been kept separate and for eight months they had heard nothing about the other members of the group. It had something of the reunion about it: they walked up to each other, greeted and embraced, until a general called them to order in a thundering voice and demanded silence. I heard that voice, but because of the distance the prisoners remained indistinct.

Another voice called out the names of the condemned men and asked them to take their places in line promptly, one by one. It didn't surprise me that Petrashevsky and Speshnev were at the top of the list; the other names were lost on the wind.

Several figures climbed the scaffold, following a priest with a cross. A little while later they came down the wooden steps again and walked slowly past the formations of soldiers and my uncles' units. The officers among the condemned had to demonstrate to their garrisons that they had been reduced to the ranks. Everything was aimed at humiliation and at inspiring mortal fear.

Close to the scaffold the prisoners were split into two groups. Again a voice rang out. It seemed a functionary was reciting a specific verdict to each condemned man, but he spoke quickly and stumbled over his words. Nevertheless, the reading of verdicts took up a good deal of time. The final sentence alone came out clearly: 'The court martial has condemned you all to death by firing squad and on 19 December His Imperial Majesty personally wrote below that verdict: "Upheld".'

Dostoevsky told me later that, dumbfounded, he turned to Sergey Durov (who was closest to him) and cried out indignantly 'It's not possible that we'll be executed.' To himself he murmured, 'It can't be true. It can't possibly be. It's impossible that I, in the midst of all these thousands who are alive, will no longer exist in five or six minutes from now.'

He believed it only when all the condemned men were ordered to put on long white shrouds.

From *De Kozakkentuin* (The Cossack Garden), Uitgeverij Atlas/Contact, Amsterdam, 2015

Translated by Liz Waters

NOTES

1   The uncle was actually called Baron Nicolai von Korff. German Baltic barons who held public office in Russia often adopted more Russian-looking names. The Von Wrangels dropped the 'von' and sometimes spelt their name 'Vrangel'. Baron von Korff likewise abandoned the 'von'. Baron Nicolai von Korff was married to a sister of Alexander's father. The Von Korffs owned the Raskulitsy estate, close to the Terpilitsy estate owned by the Von Wrangels.

2   Alexander Egorovich was born on 23 March 1833 according to the Julian calendar and on 4 April 1833 according to the Gregorian calendar.

3   Pupils of the Imperial Alexander Lyceum wore a school uniform that had a military look.

What You See Is not What You Get

The Architectural Fiction of Filip Dujardin

[DIRK LEYMAN]

Messing around with buildings, until a completely new architectural reality emerges. The photographs of Filip Dujardin explore the twilight zone between reality and fiction, often with consequences that are both mildly comical and slightly discomfiting.

Where might they be found, these remarkable structures portrayed by Filip Dujardin? Who dreamt them up and designed them? And what is their precise function? These are questions that automatically arise on first seeing his photos of strange-looking apartment blocks, desolate villas in the middle of nowhere, exorbitant but pointless bridge constructions or apartment blocks with a corner missing. Google Earth will not help you here, and an architectural catalogue will be no use either. Dujardin creates confusion in the brain with his ingenious photographic and architectural portrayals. But hang on... Do these images not challenge gravity in a rather subtle way? Are we trapped in a progressive illusion à la M.C. Escher? Or is this locational art?

It soon dawns on the viewer that Dujardin is playing tricks and has been showing off what Photoshop and other image processors can do. This does not make his images any less intriguing, however. There is something both uncomfortable and dryly comic about them. They represent the art of the impossible. At other times they look surprisingly real, as if the building style of the former Eastern Bloc has come back to life, with those grey, desolate colossuses, apparently unceremoniously dumped where they stand, without the merest scrap of town planning. And what about that mysterious villa with its closed shutters that has suddenly appeared in the landscape? Dujardin creates castles in the air which stimulate the imagination, though only rarely is there a living being to be seen. Things become even more intriguing when we learn that the photographer began by simply photographing everyday buildings in and around Ghent. Dujardin uses them to piece together a new world, not so far removed from ours, it seems. He creates 'an ironic pleasure with his surrealist juxtaposition', writes Pedro Gadanho from the MoMa in New York in the compilation *Fictions* (Hannibal, 2014), in which Dujardin's imaginary structures and hybrid creations are brought together, supplemented with more recent work. 'His "tinkerings" open up unexpected insights into the contemporary building culture and its contexts.' In creating these images, Dujardin

is surfing on the crest of a wave of architectural photography which is also a great source of inspiration for photographers such as Jan Kempenaers and Bert Danckaert.

Virtual dabbler

The art historian, architect and photographer Filip Dujardin (b. Ghent, 1971) acquired international renown with the series *Fictions*. The work even led to him being dubbed the 'Le Corbusier of contemporary photography', primarily because the series is chock-full of nods to architectural and art history.

Dujardin certainly did not develop his projects overnight, but took plenty of time to unfold his talents. He studied art history at Ghent University, specialising in architecture, and later went on to study photography at the Royal Academy of Fine Arts (KASK) in Ghent. He initially earned his spurs as a technical assistant to Magnum photographer Carl De Keyzer. From 2000 to 2006 he worked as an architectural photographer, mostly in partnership with Frederik Vercruysse, building up a more than solid reputation. In 2007 Dujardin decided to follow his own path, taking on work for a variety of private and public sector publishers. This was precisely the moment that his *Fictions* project really began to spread its wings. Or, as Gadanho puts it dryly: 'He developed an interest in architectural structures that may have conflicted with the architectural photoreportages he was creating at the time.' The photo montage would become 'the expressive vehicle of choice for the virtual dabbler'. Dujardin's background in art history would prove extremely useful to him in this endeavour.

Remote sculptures

But first there was the series *Sheds*, which harbours the embryo of the *Fictions* series. Dujardin himself gave the following account in an interview on the *De favoriet* website, where photographers talk about their favourite photograph: 'The idea for *Fictions* really started with the *Sheds* series, which I photographed several years ago. Typical Flemish sheds standing in fields, which have never seen an architect. With these "sheds", it's the farmer who builds structures in his fields; in the "fictions", it's me sitting at my computer screen building fictitious structures.' Wandering through the Flemish countryside, Dujardin's eye was caught by ramshackle farm buildings or sheds, improvised and knocked together haphazardly, simply planted there, with no aesthetic or decorative intent. They were merely a means of providing shelter for cows, hay or animal feed. *Sheds* was a testament to Dujardin's budding fascination with the absurdities and contradictions in the landscape.

In the *Fictions* series, Dujardin bends architectural reality to his own will. Art assumes the upper hand. The urban landscape is turned on its head and a diversity of architectural atmospheres are juxtaposed in an unfathomable interplay. Starting from photographs of existing buildings, Dujardin creates highly innovative new structures. A slab of shabby Belgian dwellings or soulless flats is transformed into a striking example of modernist architecture. Very ordinary buildings – usually depicted against a filtered, grey sky – are transformed into remote sculptures. But older buildings too are stripped bare and relocated, completely rebuilt, as it were. All done with Photoshop. The absence of win-

dows also often creates a sense of alienation. 'The typical disarray of a city backstreet is reproduced with a disconcerting realism, in which only the absence of windows betrays a fictitious element', records Gadanho. On another occasion, Dujardin appears to create a building which, by contrast, contains a full complement of every possible window imaginable. An image in which everyone breaks away from the shackles of the collective residential block with its strictly defined ideology, and follows what their heart dictates. All mixed with tightly configured Mondrian-like motifs which add a touch of colour. Now and then, the images stop you in your tracks. Gentle humour remains one of the trademarks of Dujardin's photographs.

Boundary between reality and fiction

Dujardin is mad about collage and composition, and he has undoubtedly drawn on the architectural visions of the Russian constructivists or Mies van der Rohe, as Gadanho makes explicit. 'Fiction becomes a critical tool for examining architecture.' And of course there are the very obvious references to Le Corbusier's *unités d'habitation*, giving rise to a sort of 'mathematical lyricism'. Dujardin gives his fictitious buildings extensions, balconies and extra storeys. They are not so very far removed from real, existing buildings. One only has to look out of the window of a train riding through the Flemish – and, by extension, European – landscape to see residues or derivatives of Dujardin's photos.

The fact that the photos are untitled is also interesting. Dujardin leaves us to guess and puzzle for ourselves. No neat keys are provided to explain his images, though in an interview with Stefan Devoldere he does lift the veil a little: 'I focus on the intrinsic quality of the urban landscape. What is a city, and how does one city define itself compared to another? What is left if you take away everything that is typical? I create a more universal image of the city.' And, he contends: 'I play on the boundary between reality and fiction: is what you are seeing real?' Dujardin deliberately throws the viewer off balance and refines

our gaze. He himself says that he is continually reacting to the Belgian context: 'I see examples every day of that "knocked-together" residential fabric. The backs of the buildings are interesting from a formalistic point of view because there's a sort of untamed architecture going on which eschews any planning rules.' He also sheds light on his working method. Starting from actual buildings, he begins by making models using Lego blocks, before later switching to computer models. He adheres to a set format and ensures that the perspective is accurate, so as to retain the 'realistic' element. First comes the design, and only then the photos and the processing. One might suspect otherwise. 'My images sometimes have a very "high-tech" starting point but a "low-tech" outcome. I find that tension interesting.'

Universal resonance

Yet the question that keeps on popping up is whether Dujardin's buildings really are entirely imaginary and technically impossible constructions. It is a question which also intrigued Nynke Vissia. On the website *De Optimist* she presented the photos to the architect and architectural historian Cornelis van Wieren. 'I have looked at almost all the buildings, and I see little that would be impossible to build', was his response. 'Sometimes illogical, but not impossible. Just because something appears to be made from concrete, doesn't mean that it actually is. There might be a steel structure hidden beneath a (thin) concrete cladding, for example. That makes large spans possible. And as long as the facade with its differently dimensioned and distributed door and window frames is not load-bearing, that too is something that could be built in reality.' While it may not be Dujardin's ambition, it is a fascinating idea that fiction drawn from a photographic reality could perhaps actually be implemented in practice. Dujardin balances on the cusp of possibility and impossibility. And the purified simplicity of the visual narrative finds a universal resonance. That is also evident from the number of places where his work is shown. A selection from *Fictions* was displayed for the first time in 2008 in the BOZAR Centre for Fine Arts in Brussels, during the *IMAGE/CONSTRUCTION* exhibition. He quickly found an international response, with exhibitions in South Korea and San Francisco. Recently his work was also purchased for the Metropolitan Museum of Art in NYC and the MoMA in NYC and in San Francisco. His photographs can now even be found on postcards, in any number of magazines and publications and of course all over the web.

In the compilation published by the Flemish publishing house Hannibal and the Flanders Architecture Institute in Antwerp, we also discover the new horizons that Dujardin has been exploring in the recent period, with photographs commissioned by cities such as Guimaraes, Deauville and Middelburg. In the Portuguese city Guimaraes in 2011-2012, he approached the historical context and the castle that symbolises the birth of the nation with great irreverence: 'I created a bad restoration of the picture postcard that is Guimaraes. The message was: what you see isn't real, but a political, romantic reconstruction.' Dujardin intervenes and falsifies with secret pleasure. But he also quietly sets

about building himself, as in the Z33 House for contemporary art in the Belgian town of Hasselt, for the group exhibition *Atelier à Habiter*. And he has also turned architect again: between December 2013 and March 2014 he erected a plinth, a screen and a prefabricated wall, using 3-D installations and photomontages. Cool brick interventions in bare, empty spaces. But they heighten the emphasis, 'introduce corrections to the architecture of the building', as the accompanying text puts it. 'They sharpen the awareness of the visitor of its existing condition and make an alternative visible, whether sensible or senseless. The sections of brick wall nestle and sprawl like parasites in, on and over the folds of the building and insinuate what could be, what could come ...' Dujardin derives a devilish pleasure from this: 'Pimping or upgrading wholly banal things is something I really enjoy. Put a column somewhere else, or put it next to another column, and it loses its power.' Or, as Jan De Vylder from the architects' firm architecten de vylder vinck tallieu comments in the book: 'A small definition for architecture. Perhaps that is what architecture should be seeking out; the same thing that Dujardin is seeking. Lessons in differences.'

In any event, Dujardin is now a much-in-demand photographer and imaginary builder. He was also asked to develop a new vision for the upgrading of the open-air heritage museum and Flemish tourist hotspot Bokrijk, and to capture the results in a photograph, which is even available as a poster. He opted for a typical 'Dujardin structure': 'I used the wooden skeleton technique to build a tower', he says at the museum site. 'What's interesting about the tower is that the lines of the timber skeleton define both the graphic elements and the relief of the structure. Within this tower structure you can observe an evolution in abstraction, from the bottom to the top. At the bottom, the authentic Bokrijk

buildings can be clearly seen, gradually transitioning into purified volumes and ending in an open structure, as if the tower is awaiting completion.' And he talks of the 'openness that refers to the transition that Bokrijk is currently undergoing', seamlessly binding together past and present.

Photographer? Architect? Theoretician? Art critic with images? In reality, the epithet doesn't matter much. This is in any event clever photography and installation art that you can continue looking at attentively for a long time. It is an oeuvre which subtly removes architecture from its pedestal and at the same time brings it into sharp focus. The fact that Dujardin aligns *en passant* with the Belgian surrealist tradition whilst subtly commenting on it is an added bonus. What's the betting that, after looking at the *Fictions* images, on your next road trip through Belgium you will also find yourself looking out for potential subjects in the buildings you pass? ∎

www.filipdujardin.be

FURTHER READING

Filip Dujardin, *Fictions* 2007-2014 (Hannibal, Veurne, Architecture in Belgium A +, 2014), texts by Jan De Vylder, Stefan Devoldere, Pedro Gadanho.

Translated by Julian Ross

Managing Climate Change

Adopting a Macho or a Modest Approach?

[PIETER LEROY]

Under the headline 'Macho Plants', a Dutch-Flemish gardening magazine recently published an eye-catching article describing ten garden plants which are not only resistant to exceptionally heavy rainfall but also to long periods of drought. 'Macho' because they can apparently survive the anticipated effects of climate change on our part of the world. As an amateur gardener I have always tried to make sure that our garden plants are well adapted to the soil, humidity and climate of our garden; hence my interest in these climate-proof plants. Yet climate change will create more urgent and pressing problems than those which can be solved by a handful of 'macho' plants. This article will explore the extent to which the idea of adaptation to climate change has penetrated society: might it also reflect the lengths to which we will go to accommodate this self-created problem?

Climate change, mitigation and adaption

The story of climate change is a familiar one. Since the industrial revolution, we have been pumping out ever-increasing quantities of so-called greenhouse gases, of which CO_2 is the best known. They create a kind of blanket around the earth preventing it from losing heat, which leads to global warming: i.e. a gradual rise in the average temperature on Earth. In recent years, record after record has been broken and average temperatures have risen faster than the most probable scenarios had predicted. Global warming leads in turn to a range of regionally specific climate changes: more, as well as less, rainfall, warmer winters, disrupted rainy seasons etc. Furthermore, global warming is causing the ice caps to melt and the seas to become warmer, all of which leads in turn to rising sea levels and changes in the ocean currents.

As an optimist or pessimist, the world seemed to react either quickly or slowly to the effects of climate change. It was the scientists, especially meteorologists, who first fired off early warnings about these changes, and climatology rapidly grew into a large, multi-disciplinary and influential discipline. But it took some time for politicians to heed their warnings and take any action. The setting up of the intergovernmental panel on climate change, IPCC (1988), and

The Blue Marble,
Earth as seen by Apollo 17
in 1972

the signing of the United Nations Framework Convention on Climate Change, UNFCCC, in 1992 marked the start. Since then, more than twenty Conference of the Parties (COPs) sessions have been held, most recently in Paris in December 2015. The frustrations created by the Copenhagen meeting in 2009 gave way to a sense of euphoria in Paris when it was agreed to limit the rise in the average temperature to 2° Celsius and even to aim at 1.5°. However, it is clear from the figures that even if all the promises made in Paris are fulfilled, we shall still see an average temperature rise of 3°C. The scepticism surrounding those promises was well expressed in a cartoon showing a world under water and the caption: 'First there was the Paris agreement, then Trump became president of the United States'.

Sceptical or not, climate change requires a two-fold response: mitigation and adaptation. Mitigation means tackling the root cause: the emission of greenhouse gases. That involves a tiresome process of change in energy production, in agriculture and industry, in our transport systems and so on. Our whole economy will have to be weaned off its addiction to fossil-based energy and switch to low carbon, in a sustained effort over several decades. How difficult this will be can be seen in the Low Countries and elsewhere in Europe. Coal-fired power stations will have to be decommissioned; those burning lignite ought to close immediately; atomic energy is no longer an acceptable alternative; and to introduce wind, sun and other renewable sources will demand a huge effort. The German and Danish transitions in energy production are exemplary, but they are neither straightforward nor easy to copy. In Belgium, the

'In 2015 all countries agreed to fight global warming.
And then President Trump came.'
© Steven Degryse

nuclear option is digging in its heels while the Netherlands is finding it difficult to close down even recently built coal-fired power stations. In both countries, the transition to renewable energy is being frustrated. But in this respect, the Low Countries are little different from many other countries. Traditional technologies and economic practices are backed by powerful lobbies, while energy prices are far too low to encourage restraint and innovation.

Adaptation appeared somewhat later on the international agenda. Initially, the call for action came from the poorer countries, since they suffer the consequences of climate change without having the means to combat them. The hurricane that swept over the low-lying island of Vanuatu in March 2015 revealed the extreme vulnerability of some regions. The progressive desertification of Africa and the more frequent periods of drought in Southern Europe have also highlighted the need for adaptation. Vulnerable countries and regions want financial and technological assistance from richer countries to adapt their water resources, agriculture, and economic development to the rapidly changing circumstances. Meanwhile, even the wealthier countries have seen the need to adapt. After all, climate change is here to stay and adapting to it is essential.

Whereas mitigation imposes similar requirements everywhere, namely the reduction of greenhouse emissions through wide-ranging and difficult changes, adaptation necessarily involves regional variation. There are three reasons for this. In the first place, climate change has widely differing effects on different regions: drier here, warmer there; more rainfall here, earlier monsoons there. In Europe the scenario for climate change in Portugal, for instance, is entirely different from the situation in Finland. In Asia, Africa, America and elsewhere regional differences will be even more obvious. Secondly, not only do the effects of climate change wildly vary, but regions, cities and rural areas also differ in their vulnerability. Some regions in Northern Europe can expect an increase in agricultural land while Spain and Portugal are facing more periods of drought. Coastal towns and coastal regions in general, such as the Low Countries, are vulnerable in the short term, less because of rising sea levels than because the silting up of ground and surface water will make agriculture more difficult. Drought and rising temperatures will increase the danger of forest fires. In mountainous areas, greater precipitation and more rapidly melting snow will require impossibly expensive measures for managing peak flow. The mention of expense links up with the third reason for regional differences in adaptation. Countries and cities differ widely in their resilience and their capacity to respond or adapt to climate change. Classic examples of this are river deltas such as the Scheldt and Rhine, Danube, Mississippi, Niger, Mekong, Ganges and Brahmaputra, to mention but a few. Although they are all physically and geographically very different, climate change affects each one of them through mechanisms and processes that are broadly comparable. However, it is hardly necessary to point out that some of these regions are far better equipped, financially, technologically and politically, to face the challenge of climate change.

Adaptation: nothing new under the sun?

The concept of adaptation, like climate change itself, has become extremely popular: one now has adaptation research, adaptation strategies, adaptation opportunities, adaptation platforms and so on. We shall return to them shortly. The concept has thereby acquired rather too narrow a meaning, typically associated with climate change, which needs correction from the standpoint of both evolution and history. With regard to the first, Darwin showed convincingly that the whole of biological evolution was the result of continual adaptation by species to their changing environment. Species which failed to adapt sufficiently died out. Human beings themselves are the product of that mechanism of adaptation and selection.

As for history, human beings have through the centuries proved astonishingly good at adapting. Much more than an evolutionary or biological development, this has been primarily a cultural and political process, which similarly produces winners and losers. For example, I have long been an admirer of Cistercian abbeys. Certainly because their simple architecture and their spirituality speak of such moderation and humility. But equally because their location, structure and organisation reveal the ingenuity with which eleventh-century

Philadelphia, USA
© Fabien Dupoux

monks were able to adapt to the irregularities of relief, landscape, soil, precipitation and so on in order to make full use of available resources such as water, wood and agricultural land. All in harmony, and in consequence with little disruption. Was that dictated by morality? Undoubtedly, but the technology of the time did not allow them to do much more.

Since then, people have become much less modest and less restrained. Adaptation to nature has increasingly turned into the adaptation *of* nature. The combination of science and technology has produced an ever-improving control over natural circumstances: floods and drought, sterile land, lightning damage, diseases affecting plants, animals and humans, all these natural dangers have steadily become easier to manage. Or, as Peter Sloterdijk put it: humanity has exceedingly learned to immunise itself against the vagaries of nature. Think irrigation systems and manure, lightning conductors and vaccinations, and other comparable 'modern' technologies. Modernisation is virtually synonymous with the degree to which we are able to free ourselves, defend ourselves and immunise ourselves from the unpredictability of nature. Historically it is clear that replacing unpredictability by stability has been a precondition for investment, innovation, capitalism and prosperity. Likewise, there has been a progressive shift from adaptation to nature to the adaptation *of* nature. And the power to adapt has been and still is unequally distributed, with winners and losers.

Among the losers, we find not only a large proportion of humanity but also those parts of nature which have been adapted to our wishes: forty percent of the world's surface has been turned into agricultural land at the cost of ruthless deforestation and enormous interference in the natural cycle of phosphates and nitrates. Although water management has admittedly enabled countries such as the Netherlands to exist at all, it has also brought about the destruction of enormous wetland areas and has affected the water cycle to such a degree that we cannot yet foresee its consequences. And our capacity to produce so much extra energy from coal and oil that we no longer have to be either frugal or careful, has brought about climate change.

For stubborn modernisers, climate change primarily represents a challenge by which human adaptability can be developed further. These strange creatures who still doubt that climate change is brought about by human beings, believe that the answer lies in geo-engineering. Geo-engineering embraces a number of technologies, and ranges from creating artificial clouds, lowering the planet's temperature by injecting sulphur into the atmosphere, to placing gigantic mirrors around the earth in order to reflect sunlight back into space. Such technologies hardly suggest modesty or restraint, rather brazen macho-adaptation of nature – though unfortunately lacking the irony of 'macho plants'.

Adaptation to climate change: the Low Countries' strategies in a European perspective

Fortunately, most discussions on climate adaptation steer clear of such schemes. The European Union has asked its member states to prepare national adaptation plans by 2017. So far, all that is known of them is that they differ widely in procedures and content. Some countries see the plans primarily as an exercise by and for governments and experts, while other countries are involving their populations in order to spread awareness of climate issues. The proposed measures also differ since they naturally reflect the climate scenarios and risks specific to each country. Adaptation around the Mediterranean is not the same as in Scandinavia, or Northwest or Central Europe. Incidentally, it is striking how the emphasis of each country is dictated less by climate as by dramatic experiences from their recent past. Portugal and France, for instance, focus on forest fires; Poland and Germany are concerned about floods; Spain expects to face problems of drought. After the heatwave of 2003 which led to more than 10,000 deaths in France, many measures have been introduced to protect children and the elderly during hot summers and in so-called urban heat islands from the effects of dehydration.

Dacca, Bangladesh © Yusuf Ahmed

Above
Calcutta, India. Young boy studying with the aid of a potato-powered oil lamp

Right
Garden of the disappeared plants, designed by Denis Valette and Olivier Barthélémy, Chaumont, France, 2011

Furthermore, there are wide differences in how various measures of adaptation are perceived as a whole. For example, a long hot summer can lead to a reduced harvest and to reduced electricity production through a shortage of cooling water; it can make canal navigation impossible; it can bring down ICT systems, cause forest fires and so on. To protect society against such wide-ranging disruption requires the coordination of different sectors and fields and different levels of government. Although politicians tell us that climate change will force us to introduce institutional change, there are as yet few signs of this kind of all-embracing intervention.

In the Netherlands and Belgium, adaptation plans are also being developed though not with any great enthusiasm. In The Hague, the idea prevails that the Delta programme already constitutes an adaptation plan. The Delta Act was put into effect in 2012 and the Delta programme which is updated annually constitutes five packets of 'Delta Decisions' currently relating to flood risk management, fresh water, the river deltas (Rhine and Maas), the IJsselmeer region and spatial adaptation relating to water. Such concern with water is understandable in the Netherlands but can hardly be said to address all the effects of climate change. Even the Dutch Court of Audit considered the exclusive emphasis on water to be too one-sided. So they are now working on an adaptation plan to be presented in 2017 that also includes agriculture, energy supply, the ICT infrastructure, transport, public health and so on. Most likely, this will consist of little more than a risk-assessment and a preliminary summary of the measures to be adopted. After all, 2017 is also election year in the Netherlands. Furthermore, and this applies to both the Netherlands and Belgium, the Paris Agreement mitigation will need full attention, at least in the short term. The Netherlands will certainly have to revise the weak Agreement on Energy of 2013 to meet the Paris conditions. A range of fossil fuel energy sources, in particular its coal-fired power stations, will have to be decommissioned and the contribution of renewable energy, which is currently extremely low, will have to be ramped up rapidly.

In Belgium too, as we have already indicated, there is an urgent need to begin the transition to a low carbon economy in energy, industry, transport, agriculture and households. The division of authority between the regions is an obstacle to both mitigation and adaptation since both will need comprehensive inter-regional agreement. In light of the present over-burdened political agenda, this is unlikely to come about. The most that will happen in 2017 is that Belgium will present three regional adaptation plans to the EU which we can safely predict will be unexceptional in content and not politically binding.

That does not sound optimistic and it is not very positive. But fortunately, more convincing schemes are being planned and carried out elsewhere. Cities in particular, not only in the Netherlands and Belgium but throughout Europe, are very active on the climate front. Many have opted to apply a thematic approach to both mitigation and adaptation: energy, construction, mobility, environmental planning, urban development, urban green and water management, all have led in various imaginative combinations to some attractive projects. In addition, care is taken not to present climate change as negative or threatening but as an opportunity for innovation. Cities like Rotterdam and Ghent, for example, use their climate policies to promote the city itself: city marketing through climate change. In doing so, they have involved not only the general public but also businesses, such as companies involved in construction, tourism, public transport, energy, food and other related industries.

The net effect of all these projects on mitigation of and adaptation to climate change is undoubtedly more limited than one would want. What is needed is support from the top but so far there is little sign of that happening. However, their long-term importance lies elsewhere: in the first place in creating opportunities for innovation, in experimentation, and the exchange of different adaptation strategies. The effect will be that cities and countries alike can expect a diversity of adaptation platforms and the sharing of experience, from which, in the long run and true to Darwin, the most effective projects and strategies will emerge as winners – hopefully without too many losers. Secondly, while undoubtedly certain burgomasters indulge in vanity, are even flashy to the point of megalomania, when it comes to urban planning, there are also many who are deeply conscious that we as human beings must learn to adapt; that we have brought this unpredictability in weather patterns upon ourselves; and that a sober and modest approach to our energy needs, to our housing and to our mobility is the best way forward. Who knows, perhaps adaptation to climate change will lead to a new and improved form of modernisation: a style of management which is modest and restrained. ∎

Translated by Chris Emery

The Oldest Museum in the Netherlands

Arts and Sciences at Teylers in Haarlem

[ILJA VELDMAN]

Teylers Museum is the oldest museum in the Netherlands. No other museum from the same period has been as beautifully preserved. When a museum is named after someone it is often because it was commissioned to display an individual's large collection of artwork, but the history of Teylers Museum is more unusual in this respect and more interesting for it.

Pieter Teyler van der Hulst (1702-1778) of Haarlem was a prosperous Mennonite cloth and silk merchant whose forebears emigrated from Scotland to the Netherlands in the sixteenth century for religious reasons. Teyler and his wife, Helena Wijnands Verschaaven, initially lived in the house called *De Hulst* in Damstraat, but moved into the grand property at no. 21 in 1640. After Teyler's death, this became the seat of the foundation and societies he established. Mennonites are known for their belief in charitable work. In 1752, Pieter Teyler bought a *hofje* (almshouses built around a courtyard) at Klein Heiligland. After his death this was replaced with a new, larger *hofje* at Koudenhorn, which was managed by the Teylers Foundation until recently. As a follower of Enlightenment ideas, Teyler was convinced that the arts and sciences help to enrich people's lives and would help the advancement of society. In 1732 he developed plans for a society designed to promote the study of theology and natural history – liberal believers regarded the study of nature as a means of studying God's wondrous creations. Teyler was also a co-founder of the Haarlem Drawing Academy (*Haarlemse Tekenacademie*), for artists and craftsmen, and he placed *De Hulst* at its disposal. At his home at no. 21 he began to build a library and a modest collection of coins and medals, prints, drawings, paper cut-outs, stuffed birds and preserved animal specimens.

In 1756, childless and now widowed, Teyler drew up a will in which he stipulated that his fortune should be used to promote the arts and sciences. For this purpose he created the Teylers Foundation (*Teylers Stichting*), governed by five directors, and two societies: the Theological Society (*Godgeleerd Genootschap*) and Teyler's Second Society (*Teylers Tweede Genootschap*), which was intended to promote the arts and sciences. His home, since known as Foundation House (*Fundatiehuis*), was never to be sold and should instead become the meeting place for the foundation and societies. It was also to be a residence for a 'painter or other lover of the arts and sciences', who would be the keeper of the Cabi-

© Teylers Museum, Haarlem   Entrance hall © Teylers Museum, Haarlem

net of Prints and Drawings. The person Teyler had in mind for this position was the portrait painter Taco Jelgersma who was commissioned to make a pastel portrait of Teyler, showing him with his books and items from his collection of coins and medals. When the will was executed, however, Jelgersma felt that he was too old to take up the position, and the painter Vincent Jansz van der Vinne was appointed keeper instead. Notably, in drawing up his detailed plans, Teyler did not envisage a museum in the modern sense of the word, but a scientific institute supported with study collections.

Testament to the Enlightenment

Pieter Teyler died in 1778. Because he had left the textile industry and become a successful banker, Teyler bequeathed not only his home, library and a modest collection, but also a fortune of some two million guilders (roughly 80 million euros), at that time an unprecedented sum that brought unparalleled opportunities. The directors he appointed were all members of Haarlem's Mennonite community and 'regent' class, and took up their task with great enthusiasm. Already the following year, they decided to build a public room behind the Teyler residence in Damstraat. The young Leendert Viervant was commissioned, and he produced a striking neo-classical design. The Oval Room could be used by members of the societies to give demonstrations and lectures in which they could refer to the art and science objects displayed in the tall wall cabinets with glass doors and in various glass cases. The natural history library was housed on the gallery, and an astronomical observatory was built on the roof.

The creation of an encyclopaedic museum was entirely in keeping with the ideals of the Enlightenment. There were five main collecting themes: scientific instruments, fossils and minerals, prints and drawings, coins and medals and the library. The collections were not only open to society members, but were also intended 'for the benefit of the common good'. Haarlem residents could visit the collections on Tuesday mornings, and those from outside the city could visit on weekdays between 12 noon and 1.00 p.m. Visitors' books from as early as 1789 still survive in the foundation's archives. Even when the museum first opened, visitor numbers were relatively high: 200 to 300 per year.

There were ample funds for acquisitions. In 1780 the library was enhanced with Diderot and d'Alembert's 35-volume *Encyclopédie*, the standard work of the French Enlightenment. Various illustrated botanical reference works were subsequently purchased, including the well-known five-volume *The Birds of*

Taco Hajo Jelgersma, *Portrait of Pieter Teyler van der Hulst as a Collector* (ca. 1760-1778) © Collection Teylers Museum, Haarlem

America by John James Audubon. From 1780 onwards, drawings by sixteenth- and seventeenth-century Dutch masters were purchased. The most important acquisition, however, was made by Willem Anne Lestevenon of Teyler's Second Society. In 1790, while travelling in Italy, he managed to acquire some 1,700 drawings from the heirs of Duke Livio Odeschalchi. Most of the drawings had previously belonged to the collection in Rome of Christina, former queen of Sweden, and included many works by Raphael, Michelangelo, Guercino, Claude Lorrain and Hendrick Goltzius.

Admired by Napoleon and Einstein

Two figures were influential in the early days of the museum: Martinus van Marum (1750-1837), the museum's first director, and the painter Wybrand Hendriks (1744-1831), who succeeded Van der Vinne as keeper of the art collections. Van Marum was a renowned and versatile scholar who had great ambitions with respect to the natural sciences. He acquired an important fossil collection, which was the foundation of the Palaeontological and Mineralogical Cabinet. On a journey through Switzerland he also acquired the skull of *Homo diluvii testis* (Man, a witness of the Deluge), one of the world's most coveted fossils. The Physics Cabinet comprised his most important acquisitions. He had managed, with some difficulty, to convince the directors that it was necessary to commission the building of the world's largest electrostatic generator. The gigantic machine was installed in the Oval Room on Boxing Day in 1784, and Van Marum used it for various experiments, some of which involved a battery of Leyden jars. Later, his interest shifted to combustion apparatus, which he built himself. By 1812, according to a catalogue compiled by Van Marum himself, the Physics Cabinet already comprised 435 objects, thanks to numerous acquisitions from all over Europe that included Volta's voltaic pile. He used some of these objects in his public teaching and experiments. Because he had good contacts in France, the collections were not confiscated during the 'French period' in the Netherlands. In 1811, Napoleon visited Teylers Museum. According to Van Marum, the emperor had personally urged him to continue with his educational activities.

The directors of the Teylers Foundation not only managed its finances but also faithfully carried out Teyler's wishes with regard to supporting the visual arts. Wybrand Hendriks purchased important drawings and also laid the foundation for the collection of graphic art, including almost the complete graphic work of Rembrandt and Adriaen van Ostade. Drawings by living artists were also purchased. When Hendriks was succeeded in 1820 by the landscape painter Gerrit Jan Michaëlis, the directors further decided to establish a collection of contemporary painting – a 'first' in the Netherlands.

The collection grew rapidly and the museum soon ran out of space. Between 1824 and 1826, on the east side of the Oval Room, the Fossil Room was built, along with the *Eerste Schilderijenzaal* (first art gallery), a larger room with cabinets for drawings and prints that was designed for exhibiting works by living masters. A library and reading room were built above the gallery. A second art gallery, also designed to house large works, was built in 1893. In the centre of the room, in accordance with the fashion of the time, there was an oval seat

Oval Room
© Teylers Museum,
Haarlem

surrounding a radiator, on top of which stood potted palms. The keeper of the art collections, J.H. Scholte, published a catalogue of the paintings in 1894. A catalogue of the Dutch, French and German drawings was published in 1904.

The museum also kept pace with developments in the exact sciences. Acquisitions made under Van Marum's successors included a daguerreotype camera, a spectacular Powell & Lealand microscope and a model of Foucault's pendulum. The increasing lack of space was an incentive to mark the museum's first centenary with a major expansion in the form of three exhibition rooms for fossils and instruments built onto the Oval Room, with a completely new entrance on the Spaarne. An international design competition was held in 1877 for this purpose. The imposing façade, in the Viennese Classicist style, was designed by Christian Ulrich. A staircase leads from the lobby, with its glass cupola, to a gallery which gives access to two auditoriums and the library extension. Along the ceilings of the upper floor there are cartouches bearing the names of famous Dutch natural scientists. Over the years, some of the names have been overpainted with those of scientists who have made greater discoveries, most recently in 1971.

The catalogue of instruments in the Physics Cabinet, published in 1882, was intended for specialists. The guide published in 1898 was for the lay public. This illustrates the double function envisaged for the museum. The sciences were given a major stimulus in 1909, when the internationally renowned Nobel Prize winner H.A. Lorenz was appointed keeper of the Physics Cabinet. He had the use of a brand-new well-equipped laboratory, where he was visited by Albert Einstein, among others. Teylers Museum was a centre of physics research for many years until the laboratory was closed in 1955 due to funding problems. Another renowned scholar who was affiliated to the museum in the first half of the twentieth century was Eugène Dubois, who discovered Java Man (*Pithecanthropus erectus*). The museum has him to thank for its collection of fossils and casts of skulls. The Numismatic Cabinet was established at the end of the nineteenth century, thanks to donations from the collector and archivist Adriaan Justus Enschedé.

Steamed fish with carrots and mashed potato

For Pieter Teyler, the founding of the two societies, each with six members, was an essential part of his will. The task of the Theology Society was to consider all subjects relating to religion, particularly subjects relating to the freedom of religion. The society's members are scholars of the philosophy of religion, religious studies, the exegesis of the Old and New Testaments, the history of Christianity, and practical theology. The society was recently expanded following the endowment by the Teyler Foundation of the chair of 'Enlightenment and religion in historical perspective' (Leiden University).

The areas of expertise of the six members of Teyler's Second Society encompass physics, biology, literature, history, art history and numismatics. Within this select company, the exact sciences and the humanities still co-exist in harmony. Since 1928, the chair of the history of science, also endowed by the Teyler Foundation, has traditionally been a member of the Second Society. Various scholars played an important role not only as members, but also as keepers of the various cabinets: the aforementioned Van Marum, Enschedé, Lorentz and Scholten, as well as Jacob Kistemaker, the pioneer in uranium enrichment, and the art historian Johan Quirijn van Regteren Altena. Members of the Second Society have also included renowned historians such as Robert Fruin and Johan Huizinga.

Raphaël, *Study for Two Angels* (1517-1518)
© Collection Teylers Museum, Haarlem

Library © Teylers Museum, Haarlem

In his will, Teyler stipulated that members had to give regular lectures at the museum, and that each society should hold an annual essay competition. The writer of the best essay was to be awarded a gold medal, depicting personifications of Freedom, Religion and Truth. Since 1778, a precise record has been kept of the essay subjects and the entries deemed worthy of an award. Many of the essays submitted are now standard works in the relevant field of science. Only occasionally have the essay subjects strayed into the realm of inanity. One example was the 1834 competition: 'The causes of the increased lack of taste displayed in Dutch theatre', for which, incidentally – as was often the case – no prize was awarded. Both a gold and a silver medal were awarded for entries on the subject 'How has poetry, particularly that of previous centuries, influenced the civilising of the human mind?' (the essay competition of 1799). Entries are still submitted to the directors anonymously, under a motto or aphorism, as Teyler originally stipulated in his will. The envelope containing the entrant's real name is not opened until the decision has been made.

Until recently, the directors' meetings were held in the *Grote Herenkamer* (Large Boardroom) and society meetings in the *Kleine Herenkamer* (Small Boardroom) of Foundation House, observed by Pieter Teyler looking down from the posthumous portrait by Wybrand Hendriks (1787). The pewter inkstand in the painting is still in the possession of the foundation. The interiors of the rooms in Foundation House have remained virtually unchanged since the end of the eighteenth century, and on the first Friday of November, the society members have lunch there. The dinner service was originally owned by Pieter Teyler, and the menu consists of steamed fish with carrots and mashed potato, a dish that, as tradition has it, was enjoyed by the legator. After lunch, the annual meeting of the directors and society members is held. As Foundation House is currently undergoing extensive restoration, the meetings are held in the museum.

Creaking chairs

It has always been the museum's policy to preserve the authentic character of the building and the way in which the collections are presented – the building was lit by gas lamps until 1970. Clearly, however, modifications had become necessary by the twentieth century. However, in a country where the urge to modernise is widespread, Teylers Museum has fortunately escaped disastrous modernisations. Entering the monumental entrance hall, visitors still feel transported back to the nineteenth century. The lobby, decorated with stucco reliefs depicting personifications of the various scholarly disciplines, leads to three dimly lit rooms where the collections of fossils, minerals and physics instruments are displayed in large glass-fronted cabinets. The pattern on the marble floors of the 'new museum' is the same as that in London's Natural History Museum. The cast-iron gratings were installed for central heating. The various rooms lead into the Oval Room, which greets visitors in its restored glory. The art galleries have been embellished with new acquisitions. A high-light of the collection is the large painting *De Tuin* (The Garden, 1893) by the Haarlem painter Jacobus van Looy, which the museum was able to acquire in 2013 thanks to contributions from various funds. The museum now also has a modern café and a large space for temporary exhibitions, which has hosted various popular international exhibitions in recent decades, such as drawings by Michelangelo and Raphael.

Work on the academic appraisal of the permanent collection continues; the series of catalogues of the drawings collection is almost complete. Art books and catalogues can be purchased from a modern, spacious museum shop that has been built to the left of the entrance. The museum publishes a periodical, *Teylers Magazijn*, and has a very informative website. Today, the essay competi-tions are announced online. However, lectures and presentation ceremonies still take place in the nineteenth-century auditorium – using PowerPoint rather than a slide projector – and audiences are happy to take a seat on the creaking, slightly uncomfortable chairs. ■

www.teylersmuseum.nl

John Cuthbertson (1743-1821) after a design
by Martinus van Marum (1750-1837),
The Great Electrostatic Generator, 1784
© Collection Teylers Museum, Haarlem

Translated by Yvette Mead

The Fierce Talent of an Unpolished Chronicler

Dimitri Verhulst's Prose

[ELSBETH ETTY]

When Flemish author Dimitri Verhulst (b. Aalst, 1972) took the literary world by surprise with his tragicomic autobiographical novel *The Misfortunates* (*De helaasheid der dingen*) in 2006 he was still a complete unknown. Of the nine books he had published since 1992, the only one that had received any attention was *Problemski Hotel* (2003), a fictionalized reportage from a centre for asylum seekers, where he stayed for a while disguised as a refugee. The book made an impact because of Verhulst's merciless portrayal not only of the asylum policy but also of the asylum seekers themselves. Fourteen years ago that sort of thing was just not done. Asylum seekers were by definition victims and therefore beyond criticism. But because Verhulst had himself experienced homes, institutions and clinics he could see through all the facades. He revealed how the asylum seekers in the centre accused each other of racism and came to the conclusion that there are creeps everywhere, refugee centres included. Meanwhile the issues depicted with biting humour in *Problemski Hotel* have only become more topical, as evidenced too by the successful film adaptation in 2016 by the acclaimed documentary maker Manu Riche.

It was the jury of the AKO literature prize that gave the starting shot for Verhulst's triumphal procession, when it put *The Misfortunates* on its shortlist in 2006. The highpoint of this novel about the dissolute lives of aimless losers and antisocial semi-criminals in filthy Flemish backstreets is the chapter titled 'The Tour de France'. In it, an uncle of the youthful main character Dimitri organises a drinking contest in the form of an alcoholic Tour de France. This Pub Crawl was the best scene in Felix van Groeningen's 2008 film of the book. But however amusing it may be the film is not a patch on the book, because what Verhulst writes is pure literature. It's all about eruptions of language and word explosions, which just can't be filmed. In the meantime, a good hundred thousand copies of the novel have been sold. Its strength lies in its use of contrast, as it exposes not only the underbelly of society but the 'upper crust' too, and the hurtful smugness of so-called decent people in their model families.

Dimitri Verhulst

De helaasheid der dingen (The Misfortunates, 2009).
A film by Felix Van Groeningen

'Family polka'

For those inspired by *The Misfortunates* to pick up Verhulst's other work a new linguistic universe and a skilfully fictionalised autobiography opens up, providing insight into the ills of Western society. All his books deal with topical social problems. That was already clear in *De verveling van de keeper* (The Boredom of the Goalkeeper, 2002) a novel in which he pokes fun at Flemish nationalism by having a Flemish national football team become world champion. He himself called the book an attack on Vlaams Blok, the xenophobic party that later changed its name to Vlaams Belang. His self-declared commitment puts Verhulst in the tradition of great Flemish writers like Louis Paul Boon, Hugo Claus and, more recently, Tom Lanoye.

Verhulst's stories are almost always set in institutions where people go to deal with their misfortunes, but often his characters, frenetically trying to adapt to what is considered to be normal, end up worse off. In *The Misfortunates*, Dimitri is himself removed from his home by child welfare, an autobiographical detail with which nearly all his books deal. His themes are parents who fail and the children they neglect, who are dumped in children's homes or with foster families.

This is also the subject of Verhulst's 2015 Book Week Gift (a free novella, subsidised and distributed by the Dutch government, for which a prominent author is honoured with the commission each year). *De zomer hou je ook niet tegen* (You Can't Stop Summer Either), printed in an edition of 723,000 copies is not Verhulst's best work, but it is an interesting introduction to the rest of his oeuvre. The story features the multiply disabled Sonny, whose deceased mother once had a love affair with Pierre, a man in his sixties. Pierre abducts the dribbling, incontinent youth and takes him to the top of a mountain in the French Provence to tell him, as a gift for his sixteenth birthday, the story of the love between Sonny's mother and himself. Their relationship ended because Pierre did not want a child with her, but neither did he want to hinder her in her desire for a baby. So she became pregnant by an anonymous other man and gave birth, in the words of Pierre, to 'a pot plant'. Pierre did not want a child with his great love because he didn't fancy what he called the 'family polka'.

Family values

We can gather from all his books why Verhulst's characters are so averse to family life, beginning with his collection of autobiographical stories *De kamer hiernaast* (The Room Next Door, 1999). In it, the writer portrays his biological mother with her own name as a revoltingly fat, stupid and monstrous person. It is a brutal settlement of accounts, which led Verhulst's mother to sue her own son for defamation. She lost, by the way.

What he hates most about his mother are her attempts to lead a nice bourgeois existence, as he described again grotesquely in the novel *De laatste liefde van mijn moeder* (My Mother's Last Love, 2010). Chronologically this part of Verhulst's autobiography precedes *The Misfortunates*. *De laatste liefde van mijn moeder* (My Mother's Last Love) is about the episode that ends with the child, called Jimmy in this case, being thrown out onto the street by his mother Martine. The mother, an uneducated thirty-year-old fatso, works in a factory where she assembles bicycle saddles and spends the rest of her time stuffing herself with food and watching soaps on TV. After her divorce from Jimmy's father, she wants to establish a model family with her new lover Wannes. She herself and the eleven-year-old Jimmy must therefore be provided with fictionalised identities. Verhulst offers a merciless exposé of his deep aversion to Wannes and Martine's petty-minded bourgeois ideal in this book.

The two of them personify the kind of people portrayed in *Godverdomse dagen op een godverdomse bol* (Godforsaken Days on a Godforsaken Planet): unscrupulous, aggrieved, thoroughly stupid creatures, who live only for themselves, without love or real ideals. *Godverdomse dagen* was offered free as a supplement to the Flemish weekly *Humo*, in 2008, and was awarded the Libris Literature Prize in 2009. The jury praised it as a sardonic comedy, a firework display of language and a literary performance worthy of someone who had mastered the art down to the finest details. 'It is a book that corners the reader and forces him to make a choice.'

Kaddisj voor een kut (Kaddish for a Cunt, 2014) is another novel that forces the reader to think about choices, namely about bringing children into the world. Conditions in the children's home where Verhulst sets the novel are as

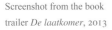

Screenshot from the book trailer *De laatkomer*, 2013

heartrending as they are realistic. The main character describes how two of his former housemates from the 'Sunchild Home' (Home Zonnekind) get into the newspapers after murdering their own children. According to the narrator, that is a logical consequence of their youth in a children's home, because such children have never learned about family life and have no idea how to cope with it. As so often when he refers to his own experiences in children's homes, Verhulst comes over as a bit of a preacher here, extolling family values. But in his stronger moments he uses great humour and stylistic brilliance to show his loathing for both family life and the abhorrent way in which children, the elderly, the disabled, the demented and all the other people for whom family life is not an option (any more) are treated in many institutions.

Dadaistic praise of folly

The novel in which Verhulst brings all these themes together in sublime fashion is *The Latecomer* (*De laatkomer*, 2013). Once again, it is about his aversion to marriage and family and an institution in which the main character, seventy-four-year-old Désiré Cordier, has himself detained voluntarily. He pretends to be demented, because that is the only way he can be rid of his ghastly wife Moniek. After serious medical tests, he ends up in the closed geriatric centre Winterlight. The descriptions of Désiré's horrendous marriage and his increasingly crazy efforts to escape it are bitingly funny. To be officially declared demented, he must consistently behave like a completely brainless idiot with no memory. That is by no means easy, but then life isn't easy for anyone.

Little by little the realisation dawns that Désiré's marriage and the whole passionless bourgeois existence, in which he vegetates both physically and mentally, is a metaphor for life. Désiré seems to find his escapist endeavours 'delightful' and is consumed with regret that it had not occurred to him sooner to live life as if he were playing a role in a Dadaistic play instead of taking it completely seriously. He considers the bizarre antics he gets up to, in his efforts to convince his wife, children and the neighbours in his oh-so-respectable street that he is demented, as the prelude to his absurdist performance. The main action is set in 'Winterlight Geriatric', a centre where the demented can pretend to be 'normal' in a Dadaistic decor specially designed for them. There is a fake bus stop, for example, complete with a signpost to a non-existent town, to give the demented inmates the impression that they can escape at any moment. Désiré would much rather hang around at the stop on this 'phantom route to somewhere else', waiting for a bus that never comes, than in the blind alley of 'real' life. As a budding librarian, he had once written a theoretical essay on Erasmus. Once he has passed the entrance exam for the psychiatric home he can finally sing the latter's *Praise of Folly* at the top of his voice.

A bag of cocaine or a box of explosives

Dimitri Verhulst is by definition a humanist writer, with a deep-rooted aversion to institutionalised religion and the associated commandments and prohibitions, without falling into banal nihilism. In what he himself considers to be his best novel, the slightly absurdist winter tale *Madame Verona Comes Down the Hill* (*Mevrouw Verona daalt de heuvel af*, 2006), which is set in Wallonia, he sings the praises of a (life) artist's love for her deceased husband. Her capacity for love, even beyond the grave, sets this character apart from the local villagers, who know neither love nor beauty and live like animals. They elect a cow as mayor, and the female vet to whom they turn in the absence of a doctor treats them like ageing cattle on their way to the slaughterhouse. Love takes the place of God. Madame Verona has organised her life like a religious service for her deceased husband. How pathetic then are the lives of her fellow villagers, who must do without God or love.

Almost all Verhulst's books are allusions to classics from world literature and art. The essayistic prose poem *Christ's Entry into Brussels* (*De intrede van Christus in Brussel*) refers expressly to James Ensor's eponymous impressionist painting from 1888, and in a somewhat more veiled fashion to Dostoyevsky's

de intrede van Christus in Brussel

DIMITRI VERHULST

PROBLEMSKI HOTEL

Letters from the Underworld. In fluent effing and blinding vernacular and with a large dose of humour, Verhulst once again delivers razor-sharp social criticism of everyone and everything, from the Catholic Church to the monarchy, from baby boomers to the youth of today and from established politicians to shrill populists on the internet. In retrospect, Verhulst himself was not pleased with his 'little chronicle'. In an interview in the *NRC Handelsblad* newspaper dated 18 May 2013, he referred to *Christ's Entry* as a complete failure.

'It is not sufficiently developed, I was too lazy and not courageous enough. I realised that about six months ago. Unfortunately the rights had already been sold and it will be published in England next week. I'm dead embarrassed. I advise any readers who haven't bought it yet not to.'

Verhulst is mistaken. Since the terrorist attacks in Brussels on 22 March 2016, we know how prophetic his analysis of hypocritical Western society was. Like *Problemski Hotel*, *Christ's Entry into Brussels* has only become more topical as the years pass. Take the passage about Ohanna, an illegal immigrant living in Brussels, stigmatised by most Belgians as 'the personification of a bag of cocaine or a box of explosives'. 'Illegal: imagine hearing it about yourself! That your existence is unauthorised! That your birth was non-statutory! That you weren't actually allowed to exist!' writes the nameless first person narrator. The illegal girl may stay in Belgium if she is prepared to act as an interpreter for Christ, who is expected to speak only Aramaic. But if Jesus calls off and doesn't turn up in Brussels, she and her family will be deported without mercy.

A modern evangelist

Christ's Entry reads like a pastiche of the New Testament. It was followed in 2015 by *Bloedboek* (Blood Book), Verhulst's rewriting of the Pentateuch, or the first five books of the Old Testament. Although the creation myth and the stories of Noah, Abraham, Joseph and Moses remain basically the same, Verhulst's raucous narrative style and brutish choice of words put them in an even starker light than was already the case. And even though the original is better, in *Bloodboek* this modern evangelist once again succeeds in both amusing his readers and confronting them with a terrifying analysis of the human condition.

Dimitri Verhulst has already been referred to as a Flemish Jacques Brel. A fierce talent and an unpolished chronicler of a lot of what is squalid in the world and especially in Belgium. ∎

Translated by Lindsay Edwards

FURTHER READING

Problemski Hotel, translated by David Colmer. London/New York: Marion Boyars Publishers, 2005

Madame Verona Comes Down the Hill, translated by David Colmer. London: Portobello Books, 2009

The Misfortunates, translated by David Colmer. London: Portobello Books, 2012

Christ's Entry into Brussels, translated by David Colmer. London: Portobello Books, 2014

The Latecomer, translated by David Colmer. London: Portobello Books, March 2016

The National DNA

Boardroom Portraits by Taco Anema

Sitting on an administrative board means coming to the table, taking seats face to face. Furniture features prominently in Taco Anema's boardroom portraits. In some cases seats contribute to the aesthetics of the composition, a pair of red armchairs providing a pleasant balance, but often they make it messier. That tells us that Anema is an honest photographer. He does not make things prettier than they are; he composes a document. The empty chairs in the foreground are the consequence of a decision to photograph all members of the board head on. At the photographer's request those in the foreground, whom viewers would see from behind on entering, have moved to stand behind those they normally face. All members gaze with deadly seriousness into the lens. The photo moment confirms their communal task.

Everything must be equal

The Netherlands seems to have more administrative boards than any other country. An urgent decision, a course of action to be mapped out, the survival of a charity: it is always the board which gets stuck into the task. The board talks, each member takes a turn, until a decision is reached. For a country largely under sea level, agreement on keeping polders dry and maintaining dykes has been a matter of survival for centuries. The Netherlands was already strewn with dyke boards in the Middle Ages. Even after recent mergers there remain twice as many district water control boards as provinces. Like the nobility, the water control boards possess a distinguished coat of arms and tend to meet in old buildings with antique furniture. Of course, the members originally hailed from the better circles, where it was customary to underline one's status with a portrait. The gentlemen therefore had the high-ranking company depicted by a good painter. It became all the rage in the seventeenth century. All kinds of professional groups and associations posed before the easel. Frans Hals painted various militia group portraits full of cheerful shows of testosterone, and Rembrandt's *The Night Watch* is the major attraction of the Rijksmuseum in Amsterdam nowadays. Female board members, generally responsible for managing orphanages and caring for the poor, also had themselves immor-

talised in times gone by. Their expressions exhibit style and discipline. The subtle *Regentesses of St Elisabeth's Hospital* with its beautiful lighting, painted by Johannes Verspronck in 1641, was recently donated by the current members of the same board (no doubt after earnest deliberation) to the Frans Hals Museum in Haarlem, where it had already long been displayed.

The custom among Dutch boards of having themselves immortalised has become part of the genetics of the culture. I still remember a professional photographer being invited to my secondary school annually to protect the composition of the school club board from obscurity. In Leiden in the nineteenth century the photographer Israel David Kiek built up a flourishing business photographing student debates and boards. He positioned them imaginatively, for example up a high stepladder, making his relaxed group portraits popular far beyond the university city, and winning him great fame and a place in Dutch photographic history. A 'kiek' or rather the diminutive 'kiekje' came to mean an informal snapshot, although the term is now dated, as is bringing in a professional photographer to grant a board visual perpetuity. Nowadays, after all, one does that oneself, and not just once but regularly. One does not only take photos of people, either, but also of eye-catching biscuits or tasty sandwiches; and no longer with tripod and camera, but with telephone and sometimes a selfie stick.

Consequently it is now a sign of originality when a true photographer devotes himself to a boardroom portrait of his own volition, and all the more so when he does this in the form of a conceptually driven documentary project: a good cross-section of a diverse range of boards, photographed on the basis of a limited set of rules. The photographer made the visits between 2009 and 2014. Leo Anema selected 85 boards from all classes and demographic groups in the Netherlands. He captured them in colour in their regular meeting rooms. With the exception of the members in the foreground, who have stood up, the photographer pictures the groups in their ordinary meeting positions, including coffee pots and refreshments. People have set aside their papers for the photo moment, put down their coffee cups and fixed their gazes on the lens. The sharp precision with which Taco Anema then portrays the board members underlines the seriousness of their task. The ideal tool for the surprising candour of the photograph is the technical camera, a digital equivalent of the classic 4x5 inch device. 'All objects and people you find within the square of the frame have equal value,' Anema believes. He puts that down to Dutch cultural identity, which insists that everything is equal. His work does not place a chairperson at the head of the table; everyone receives the same attention. 'If the essence of the polder model is consultation among equals with the ultimate aim of reaching a compromise, then that equality must also be expressed in the photo. So who you are and where you sit really does not come into it,' the photographer explains.

That point of departure is the only factor which determines the composition, a composition which appears natural, but which, in all honesty, is occasionally preceded by some shuffling, for instance where someone of substantial stature in the corner would unbalance the composition. In that case someone of a more delicate frame is asked to take the corner position. One might thus conclude that physical weight corresponds to specific gravity.

Overleg Nederland

Taco Anema was born in 1950 and boasts a successful career in the Netherlands. He has won various prizes and been commissioned for good jobs, his work exhibited in museum collections. Usefully for this project, he has also sat on various boards himself. It is funny to think that he started at the other end of the social spectrum, as an activist observer of the Amsterdam squatter riots in 1980. That was the heyday of anarchy, a model designed by squatters occupying large properties. Just two years previously he had followed a course in photography at the student cultural organisation of the University of Amsterdam, CREA, and his photos of the squatter protests were almost immediately placed in the weekly newspapers. His preference for the social documentary side of photography is undoubtedly connected with his background as a sociologist. Anema graduated with a dissertation about the Netherlands Institute for Social Research, the prominent research institute which advises the Dutch government departments. The topic reveals his interest in the underlying mechanisms of society and his project *Overleg Nederland* is an ambitious result of that.

So this time the initiative came from the photographer himself, as he created a genre which had long existed but which was brand new to photography. In 2015 the project was exhibited at Amsterdam's Huis Marseille. Initially the large prints bring the visitor close, really close, to the individual board members, whose facial expressions in general are fairly neutral and reserved. Only afterwards does one notice the space around the company, a meeting room which is rarely obvious or suited to the aims of the board, sometimes appearing to be nothing more than a hired venue. The viewing order is reversed in the project book, *Taco Anema Overleg Nederland*. Unlike seeing the works in the museum, on the page one often looks from the table to the little figures behind; it even puts the viewer in mind of a bowling alley, an impression which disappears, however, in the face of the many close-ups and cropped pictures with which the book's graphic designer Irma Boom – to put it nicely – seeks to ensure liveliness and incidentally honours the flawless photography. This is blatant cheating with respect to the rules of the project, though, as no individual is permitted extra attention. Boom, whose reputation is built on obstinacy, makes up for this with her lists of statistics and information-rich taxonomies at the back of the book, a wonderful passion of the Netherlands' best-known graphic artist.

Suit and headscarf

The best thing about Anema's project is the connection between the formal group and the aim of the charity or association. Sometimes expectations are fulfilled. For example, one would never suspect that an image of four magnificently dressed black ladies represented the board of life insurance company 'De onderlinge van 1719 U.A.' (the Netherlands' oldest independent life insurance company). The captions could not possibly be switched; the board of the Nigerian Women Association is worlds apart from the seventeen gentlemen in their immaculate suits and classic silk ties, gathered under a chandelier, in front of an eighteenth-century cabinet adorned with a Delft blue garniture. Such gentlemen appear to come from a different era, and they are not the only ones in this parade of diversity. Equally refined ladies feature regularly too; the conspicuous blonde on the board of the Royal Industrieele Groote Club is clearly particularly at ease with the camera, as are the former politicians, who evidently like to appear in cultural or other prestigious contexts. The board

'De onderlinge van 1719 U.A.', the Netherlands' oldest independent life insurance company

of the Anne Frank Foundation is an old boys' network of this kind. Since the composition of boards generally takes place on the basis of co-option, a certain uniformity is only natural, even if people express the intention of getting someone younger in next time, a woman or someone from a different background from the prevailing white. In fact the project includes plenty of specific ethnic boards. The Stichting Moskee Badr en Scholen, a foundation for a mosque and schools, is populated by bearded men in kaftans; the National Federation of Chinese Women's Associations is managed by fashionably dressed ladies, one of whom breaks Anema's rules by posing coquettishly. The gentlemen of football club VVU Ardahanspor sit importantly, with a gigantic gold cup in the background, and yet in obscurity, as the only club not to submit names. The board of the 'Nationaal Comité 4 en 5 mei', a war commemoration association in Amsterdam Zuidoost, is of mixed composition and the Landelijk Aktie Komitee Scholieren LAKS, an organisation for school pupils, features a suited young man beside a Muslim girl in a headscarf.

The board project contains all the ingredients to enable us to act as voyeurs, gazing freely at what goes on behind closed doors on administrative boards and at the people who devote themselves to their officially stated aims. The

'Nationaal Comité 4 en 5 mei', a war commemoration association in Amsterdam Zuidoost

Landelijk Aktie Komitee Scholieren LAKS, an organisation for school pupils

astonishing focus allows viewers to lose themselves in every detail or face. Everyone certainly exudes ambition and to a greater or lesser extent an eagerness for membership of the advisory board to which they have been invited. Do I detect greater than average alacrity among the board members of the Rembrandt Association? It is certainly a dynamic and extraordinarily assertive association which has helped to enable museum purchases since as far back as 1883, with an impressive set of awards to its name. Much more modest and less worldly are the people behind the Johan Messchaert concert foundation. No business suits here; the foreground features the kind of gentleman who does not care all that much about good presentation, and in trying to avoid it stands out with his pink trousers and colourful jumper. There are boards which have effectively been dormant for years, decades even, when suddenly a single decision finds them dominating a Dutch news media flurry, as in the case of the Koninklijke Vereniging De Friesche Elfsteden, the organising committee of the beloved Elfstedentocht. The ice-skating marathon which visits eleven cities in Friesland can only go ahead when the ice on the canals and lakes is strong enough to support large numbers of people, which rarely happens now in times of climate change; the last competition took place on 4 January 1997.

Polderen

All these diverse boards exposed by Anema embody the search for consensus in their own different ways. Taking the trouble to agree on a single line of action, something which can sometimes turn out to be terribly awkward, is perhaps the major stamp of the Dutch temperament. Good meetings do not overrun and they end with a practical to-do list of decisions. The path to unanimity is known as *polderen* in Dutch, after the need to keep the polder dry. The word is unknown in other parts of Europe, not only for geological reasons, but also because in countries such as France strikers and other protest groups prefer to take to the streets rather than remain seated at the meeting table. Anema's boardroom portraits provide insight into the close-knit system of civil self-government which has characterised the Netherlands since time immemorial and which also appears to have an infectious influence on immigrant compatriots. The photographer came up with the idea for this study from questions arising after a previous project, *A Hundred Dutch Households*, in 2009 (also exhibited at Huis Marseille), where he photographed families in their living rooms. Then too he opted for a multicultural approach. Visitors were surprised to discover that a family of Indian origin also lived in an Ikea interior.

Photographers of a slightly younger generation often choose a more intimate viewpoint and shrink from group portraits. Dana Lixenberg, Rineke Dijkstra and Koos Breukel exhibit a preference for the individual portrait and limit themselves to groups of two or three people. Jacqueline Hassink has made the boardroom table of large international enterprises her specific subject, but excludes all traces of humanity from her work. The reductionist character gives her photos more artistic potential than the social engagement of *Overleg Nederland*. The heart of this project is not the composition, which is minimally staged, at most based on a certain symmetry in the set-up, sometimes involving a gently triangular structure with one person standing behind those sitting (an effect which is lost in the book when the photo is spread over two pages and the standing figure is left hanging in the split of the binding). The heart here lies purely in rendering a social structure visible where it would otherwise 'rule' from behind closed doors. Bringing something into the light which normally remains hidden; is that not the core mission of a photographer?

The Delft Student Corps

A world-famous provincial board table

To ask whether it is a shame that this project is limited to the Netherlands would be posing the wrong question. A sharply delineated project programme benefits from local and of course conceptual precision. In any case, no one would level an accusation of provincialism at what is undoubtedly the most renowned board table in the world, that of the Amsterdam committee which once judged the quality of textiles, *The Sampling Officials*. Rembrandt's painting is one of the jewels of the Rijksmuseum and is ever present behind the perception of Anema's photos. When museum director Taco Dibbits explains the liveliness of this group on television, he describes how someone has accidentally opened the door, causing the men to look up and one of them to half stand up to tell the intruder to leave. Rembrandt was a keen observer when he painted this picture in 1662 and good at snap-shot-style details. The portrait of Jan Six also derives its modern effect from the movement of the body. Jan Six is putting on his glove while stepping out of the door, giving the portrait of the Amsterdam mayor, with whom Rembrandt was sufficiently friendly to be permitted to experiment, an unparalleled casual quality.

The project book mentions that Taco Anema knows his art history, but he also seems keenly aware of the deep differences between painting and photography. Rembrandt plunges the viewer into splendid doubt now and again, as in the secretive psychology of the *Jewish Bride* and the movement of that one rising sampling official, which leads one to wonder, is he standing up or sitting down? The photographer, by contrast, opts for extreme clarity, a clarity with which he lends reality – with its own hazy side – the utmost trustworthiness.

The fact that people and objects, as well as the space around them, are set down in such detail seduces the attentive viewer into secondary narratives which can sometimes be very funny. For instance, the Delft students have pulled their jackets straight, but left the candles higgledy-piggledy in the holders. Some interiors date back to the seventeenth century and fit with the boardroom culture of the day, but others are so paradoxical that they make us laugh. The good men of the Johan Messchaert concert foundation mentioned above meet in an attic with attributes reminiscent of the 1970s and weed-smoking youths. The brightly coloured bedside lamp on one of the beams above the heads of those in the meeting looks equally out of place.

Taco Anema spent many years on the administrative board project, capturing a cross section of a specific Dutch phenomenon in a particular period. It is fascinating to consider how that cross section will look in twenty years' time. Will some issues have become redundant, and what kind of progress can we expect from organisations such as Assadaaka, a multicultural association in Amsterdam which works towards social cohesion? One wonders what new consultation will be needed and what new situations will require people to put their heads together. The accents might change, but the polders must be permanently guarded. The urgency only increases: as the water level rises, the dykes must be built higher. That is the best guarantee for the survival of *polderen*.

Finally, as for the *Sampling Officials*, was the painting the inspiration for *Overleg Nederland*? No, says Anema, it was not the point of departure, but 'If you strive to give everyone equal value, you soon arrive at the same composition.' Anema shows that equality in the Netherlands does not need to be imposed by revolution. On the contrary, for centuries equality has defined our national DNA. ∎

© All photos by Taco Anema

Translated by Anna Asbury

The Nigerian Women
Association

Flanders Fields, 1917 – A Crucial Year

If we consider the history of the First World War from the perspective of its enduring legacy, we see that 1917 was certainly a crucial year, if not the most crucial year of all. After almost three years of heavy fighting, Europe was already significantly weakened and the new future world powers were entering the theatre of war for the first time. In April 1917, the United States declared war on Germany. At around the same time, the young republic of China joined the ranks of the Allies and permitted around 125,000 labourers to be recruited for the logistical support of the British and French armies on the Western Front. In October 1917, tsarist Russia was defeated by the Bolshevik Revolution, which led eventually to the foundation of the Soviet Union, and almost immediately to the dissolution of the Eastern Front, in January 1918. In May 1916, Great Britain and France shaped their colonial policy for the Middle East in the secret Sykes-Picot Agreement. This was followed at the beginning of November 1917 by the Balfour Declaration, which triggered the Palestinian issue. In short, anyone who wants to learn more about the current balance of power in the world, or about the Middle East, cannot disregard the crucial year of 1917.

That year was also of particularly great importance for the front in Flanders, or Flanders Fields, as in the poem by John McCrae. Three major events that occurred in 1917 have significant repercussions even today.

The Third Battle of Ypres

The biggest event at the front in Flanders was the Third Battle of Ypres, known by the name of its final phase, the Battle of Passchendaele. With a death toll of at least 150,000[1] between 7 June and 17 November 1917 (perhaps as many as 175,000 – the counting still continues), it is the largest massacre ever to have taken place on Belgian soil. This elevated Passchendaele (literally 'Passiondale') to the ultimate symbol of WWI warfare: a ruthless and tragic conflict in which human lives counted for little or nothing. For the armies of the European nations, it was almost the last time this would happen on such a scale. Only the Battle of Stalingrad, when Russia fought against Nazi Germany, employed the same relentless strategy, which inevitably resulted in a catastrophic conclu-

sion. It is astounding that Passchendaele could still happen in 1917, after the bloodbaths of Verdun and the Somme in the previous year. When we consider the battle in detail, it becomes only more obvious that the aim was a Pyrrhic victory pursued at the expense of unprecedented sacrifices (at least Stalingrad, in contrast, involved an actual victory). This lends the war a real sense of tragedy through human failing.

The 1917 military campaign in Flanders was sadly inspired by the French debacle of the springtime Nivelle Offensive on the Aisne. Following the failure of the attack on the Chemin des Dames and the threat of strike within the French army, it fell to the British to take up every new Allied initiative. The British commander Douglas Haig seized the opportunity to carry out an old plan: a massive assault at Ypres. This was partly out of revenge for both the First and Second Battles of Ypres, which had been particularly difficult and embarrassing for the British. The terrain, however, did not favour them. The Germans were positioned at the highest and driest parts of the front. They had also built up solid layers of defence, even more so than at the Somme, which made the chances of a breakthrough very unlikely. The boggy Flemish ground was difficult terrain for an attack, and the new British offensive weapon, the tank, would bring scarcely any advantage. When the weather turned against

Battle of Pilkem Ridge, August 1st, 1917. Pack horses on a road North of Ypres them, too, the Flemish mud became just one more enemy. But the argument was that the battle was necessary in order to shut down the German submarine bases at Zeebrugge and Ostend. They had done a great deal of damage to British supplies from overseas at the end of 1916, but by the summer of 1917 that threat had lessened. As soon as supply was organized in convoys, under the protection of Navy warships, and the bases were increasingly targeted by British air raids, the damage was significantly reduced. Haig, however, had obtained permission to attack, on the condition that he did not turn it into another Somme – and he would not be stopped. The Americans might soon be playing a significant role, and the Russians might not remain at the Allies' side for much longer, so he was in a hurry.

7 June, The Battle of Messines

The first part of the plan went rather well. Anyone who wanted to attack in a northerly direction at Ypres had to ensure that the salient in the south was at least straightened. The attack of Herbert Plumer's Second British Army, supported by an unprecedented arsenal of artillery and initially aided by the detonation of mines tunnelled beneath the German frontline, was a great success. The southern salient around Wytschaete and Messines was straightened, with relatively few losses. A little over 6,000 deaths in return for capturing over 4 km at the centre of a front that was 12 km wide.

10 July, Operation Hush/Strandfest

Maintaining this new frontline proved more difficult than the assault itself, however, and in the north, on the Gheluvelt Plateau, the German threat had not been neutralized. On 10 July, a German attack in the dunes of Lombardsijde put an unexpected end to the planned British Operation Hush, which involved an assault along the coast towards Ostend and should have been followed by a landing with amphibious vehicles. The German Operation Strandfest scuppered this plan by driving the British Fourth Army back onto the left bank of the Yser, where it was to remain.

Colossal loss and little gain

Two days later, at Ypres, the largest British bombardment of the German frontline began. Within three weeks, the frontline had been blown to shreds. The major assault followed on 31 July, involving 13 British, 2 French, 1 Australian and New Zealand divisions across a front of 24 km. This display of power, unprecedented in Flanders, cost 7,600 lives over two days on the Allied side alone. On Pilckem Ridge, 3.5 km of ground was captured. The greatest losses occurred at the centre of the assault, towards Zonnebeke and Gheluvelt, where progress was less than a kilometre and only a small foothold could be established on the plateau. The tanks became stuck in the mud and remained so for the whole of that wet summer, in spite of a few small successes. On 3 August,

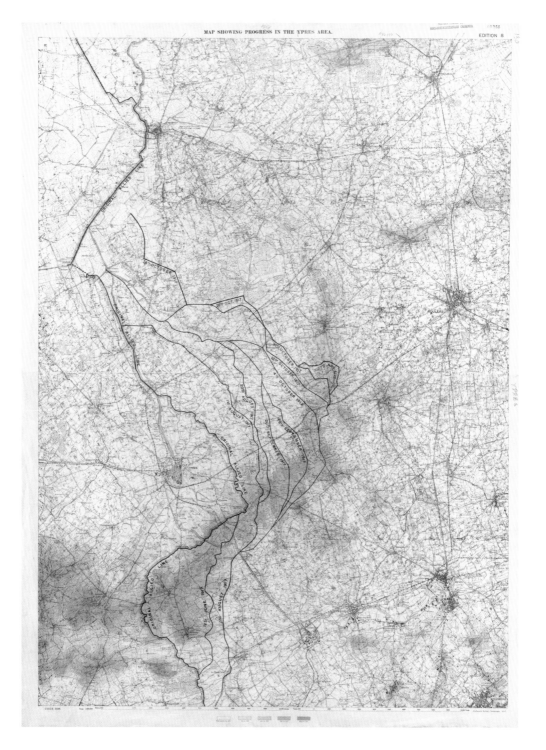

Map of the military events at the front at Ypres, with first the straightening of the salient at
Wytschaete and Messines (6-12 June 1917), followed by the Third Battle of Ypres, in eight different phases.
The newly achieved salient narrowed until it finally became an indefensible trap at Passchendaele
(Source: IFFM)

Captured German trench
during the Battle of Messines,
7 June 1917

Third Battle of Ypres.
20 September 1917.
German prisoners are being
led back through the ruins
of Ypres

the Tank Corps had already informed its commander: 'From a tank point of view, the Third Battle of Ypres may be considered dead. From an infantry point of view, the Third Battle of Ypres may be considered comatose. It can only be continued at colossal loss and little gain...' (Report from Tank Corps Headquarters, 3 August 1917).

This prediction proved accurate. In seven subsequent battles, the British army, fully supported by its Dominions, continued to attack for one hundred days. Passchendaele was eventually reached in mid-November, a target that, according to the plan, should have been achieved after the first 72 hours. With the exception of the battle of 4 October (The Battle of Broodseinde), no further significant progress was made, and the British death toll was consistently high, far higher than that of the Germans, as far as we can tell (it is hard to trace the missing German soldiers, as their names were not recorded in commemoration). The British army ultimately suffered a death toll of 60,000, the Australians 10,000, Canada 4,750, New Zealand almost 2,500, and South Africa 510. The French at the north of the attack, with the Belgians joining in behind them, lost relatively fewer men, with 2,700 French and 1,250 Belgian deaths. Every British attack took place on an increasingly narrow front, and so the final point at Passchendaele was ultimately a small and indefensible salient, which was voluntarily evacuated the following year at the beginning of the German spring offensive. Never was the futility of this war demonstrated more clearly.

Tucked in where they fell

What remained were the countless bodies, buried and unburied, of tens and thousands of men. The Imperial War Graves Commission, founded in May 1917, sent a number of representatives, including the architect Edwin Lutyens, to northern France and Flanders in July to investigate how the dead might best be commemorated after the war. Lutyens wrote to his wife: 'The graveyards, haphazard from the needs of much to do and little time for thought. And then a ribbon of isolated graves like a milky way across miles of country where men were tucked in where they fell. Ribbons of little crosses each touching each across a cemetery, set in a wilderness of annuals (...) One thinks for the moment no other monument is needed.' Eventually the commission had to accept that it was practically impossible to leave every grave in its original location, and Sir Edwin Lutyens succeeded in coming up with other monuments, which included recording the names of the missing, but the principle that each group of at least forty graves would become a cemetery determined the face of the Westhoek region as a landscape of memory. With more than 140 cemeteries, large and small, spread all over the countryside, on their original sites, it is not only the graves that have been preserved, but also the history of the war that caused them. Lutyens's simple and stunning insight has, to this day, lent the battlefields of Flanders and northern France a genius loci, a sense of place, that is unparalleled elsewhere. King George V, who made a pilgrimage to the region in the spring of 1922, stated that in his view there were no 'more potent advocates of peace upon earth' than these war graves.

Open letters

The third event of 1917 that left a legacy still felt today has never received a great deal of international attention, but then it had no direct effect on the course of the war. It did, however, make an impact on the region where this part of the war took place and where it continues to be commemorated to this day. The issue of the Flemish language (as it was then called) within the new Belgian state dated from long before the First World War. Ever since the twenty-fifth anniversary of the Belgian revolution of 1830, Flemish intellectuals had voiced their grievances about the absence of Flemish or Dutch in public life. They had to wait a further twenty-five years for the first important laws to be

Field-grave of the French marine 2nd class
Pierre Marcoux who died during the French
offensive near Merkem on 28 October 1917.
The French marines had arrived with a
full brigade in October 1914.
By the summer of 1917 their number
was reduced to a mere battalion

A British tank stuck in the mud near the Steenbeek

passed regarding the use of Dutch in legal situations and public administration
in Flanders. There were still years to go before language legislation was applied within the education system. It took the general military reform of 1913
for Dutch to receive equal status in the army. The official equality of Dutch did
not, however, mean that this was already a fact for the army on the Yser. The
French-speaking officers had obviously not yet adapted to the new situation,
and there was little enthusiasm for this change. The first Belgian chief of staff,
General Wielemans, was a moderate supporter of Flemish demands, but when
he died, on 5 January 1917, there was still a long way to go. His successor, the
Walloon General Ruquoy, was more suspicious about the burgeoning Flemish
consciousness in the Flemish part of the army. Shortly after that, in February
1917, when collaborationist Flemish militants in occupied Belgium decided to
establish a Council of Flanders as an executive body, effectively creating Flemish self-rule under the authority of the German occupier, his suspicion gave
way to the fear that any form of sympathy for the Flemish Movement in the
army verged on betrayal of the Belgian struggle against Germany. All support

for or dissemination of Flemish demands was forbidden in the Belgian army, and any suspicion of such dissidence was punished. This forced the emerging Front Movement, which propagated Flemish demands and had an increasingly political character, to go underground. In this climate of suspicion and prohibition, a series of open letters and pamphlets was circulated in the army to publicize the Flemish cause. These letters were far from perfect, but from July 1917 a growing number of Flemish soldiers in the army became aware of Flemish rights. Every frustration of this long and bloody war increasingly became part of their perception of the injustice that they were suffering as Flemish soldiers. Their leaders' attempts to suppress these developments only encouraged their feelings. When during – and particularly immediately after – the war, the commemoration of fallen Flemish soldiers was also opposed and, in some cases, even prohibited by the Belgian authorities, the battle for the language suddenly took on a new dimension. What the Flemish popular movement had not managed to do for seventy years now became reality. The Front Movement, which had created the open letters, became a Front Party, which, after the war, succeeded in placing Flemish grievances at the top of the political agenda. Partly because of the Belgian authorities' reluctance to implement the promised reforms rapidly, what had been a modest political movement became a mass movement, which to this day continues to influence the political landscape of the strongly regionalized country of Belgium. The First World War, which had a unifying effect in Belgium in 1914, was to achieve the opposite from 1917 onwards. That tendency continues today. Neither faction, however, is capable of appropriating the entire legacy of the war. The differing interpretations in both parts of the country, particularly regarding collaboration in the First and Second World Wars, continue to determine a significant amount of the political discourse though, even if they are historically inaccurate. As a result, to this day, the significance of the First World War, even as we commemorate its centenary, has a different character in the two parts of the country, particularly from a political point of view.

These issues have less impact in the area of the former front itself, as its wartime landscape of memory is determined first and foremost by the omnipresence of the tragedy that marked this region, particularly in that crucial year of 1917. ■

Translated by Laura Watkinson

NOTES

1   150,000 deaths. This figure is based on the current records of the In Flanders Fields Museum in Ypres. In the *Namenlijst*, the list of names of all the victims who died on Belgian soil as a result of the First World War, for the period from 6 June (the evening before the Battle of Messines) to 17 November (the end of the Battle of Passchendaele), the death toll is 149,225. As many missing Germans are not included in this count, along with several thousand Belgian forced labourers, who performed such functions as installing German defences, an estimate of 175,000 deaths is not excessive. The proportion of deaths to total military losses (the dead, the wounded, and the missing) is 1:5 or, in some exceptional cases, a quarter of the total number. So the losses at the front in Flanders in summer 1917 numbered at least 580,000. The counting continues …

'Making the Personal Political'

Art by Hans van Houwelingen in the Public Domain

[DAVID STROBAND]

Forty bronze lizards play the leading part in an early work, from 1994, by the artist Hans van Houwelingen (Harlingen, 1957). This now familiar work is called *Blauw Jan* (Blue John) and refers to the fine collection of animals and birds owned by Jan Westerhof in seventeenth-century Amsterdam; it is located on Kleine Gartmanplantsoen, a green extension of Leidseplein in Amsterdam. These forty creatures, near the renowned municipal theatre, the De Balie debating centre and countless shops and hotel and catering businesses, seem to have been frozen in mid-movement and, scattered amongst the greenery, look at passers-by with curiosity. A pit amongst the vegetation most likely refers to the way they came to the surface and to their possible escape route.

Blauw Jan (Blue John) is characteristic of Van Houwelingen's work. The alienating presence of these creatures adds a tension to this public space. They give the impression of having thoroughly churned up the solid ground beneath this public garden. Van Houwelingen trained as a sculptor at the Minerva Academy in Groningen and the State Academy of Fine Art in Amsterdam; he is an artist who always questions public space and, more specifically, the way we think about it, thereby putting it into sharper focus. Max Bruinsma has come up with several definitions concerning Van Houwelingen's work:

> 'Since time immemorial, art has been seen as a means of "uplifting" people, making them better. So the idea is that art starts you thinking about the meaning of the work of art; about the relationship between it and yourself; about how you and the work relate to the space you both occupy'.[1]

Van Houwelingen mainly operates in the public domain and whenever he is invited to make a work he makes it clear that art cannot function in isolation, but must actually be a relevant element in our society. Art cannot exist without historical awareness, politics, economics, philosophy and ethics. It is connected to all these things and must relate to them critically. The artist and society are able to establish a meaningful relationship when both are, or become, aware of historical, political and/or ethical contexts.

Blue John, Leidseplein,
Amsterdam, 1994

A Roman triumphal column

In the early 1990s, there were varying social and cultural tensions between
original and immigrant inhabitants in the district of Utrecht where the Amerhof square is located. The responsibility the inhabitants felt for public space
also turned out to be in increasing decline. Van Houwelingen tried to create
social awareness on the basis of a varied historical-cultural perspective. He
asked the Moroccan artist Hamid Oujaha to create a paving design for an Islamic (Persian) tapestry 'to be laid out on Dutch territory'. This carpet, with its
repetitive pattern in Dutch brick of three colours, has since 1994 lain diagonally
opposite the longitudinal axis of the Amerhof. It incorporates street furniture
and, on the playground of an adjacent nursery school, which is also part of
the carpet, seven bronze Christian lambs by Van Houwelingen function as play

The Tapestry, Amerhof,
Utrecht, 1994

objects. He observes that countless Dutch people have a Persian rug in their homes without knowing anything about its cultural origins. The tension between public space and the private domain, which in recent decades has been increasing in complexity, is one of Van Houwelingen's main points of focus.

Lelystad was designed in the 1960s by the Dutch modernist architect Cornelis van Eesteren. It was designed on the basis of a highly rational grid; functionality to the fore. In the 1990s, Adriaan Geuze's West 8 firm developed plans to restructure the town, which had a great many socio-economic problems and would benefit from a new identity. Van Houwelingen was asked to contribute and proposed giving a more radical status to an existing monument created by Piet Esser (1914-2004) in 1984. Esser had made a sculpted portrait of the engineer Cornelius Lely based on classical principles. Lely was the brain behind the draining of part of the Zuiderzee (now the IJsselmeer) and so was at the genesis of the reclaimed land and therefore of Lelystad too. Van Houwelingen designed a 32-metre basalt column, one metre for every kilometre of the Afsluitdijk – the dam enclosing the Ijsselmeer – whose form further referenced Roman triumphal columns such as those of emperors Trajan and Marcus Aurelius in Rome. The three-metre-high sculpture of the man who had made the creation of Lelystad possible, and who had also given it its name, deserved a truly high-placed monumental location on the pillar and would be able to look out over the town and the surrounding countryside from a square in the centre. The inhabitants would able to look up to and at him. By means of this work (2002), Van Houwelingen put the notion of the 'monument' into an historical perspective. Many twentieth-century monuments are modern in nature; they use an abstract visual idiom and in this sense do not tell a story in the traditional sense. What they do present, rather, is a 'meaningful' void into which every individual can project what he wishes. By contrast, Van Houwelingen considers the monument important as an object that generates meaning and awareness and believes in its traditional narrative function. At the same time, he would like to awaken Lelystad from its modern, functionalist slumber and grant it the identity of a true metropolis. And the traditional metropolis possesses monuments that are able to condition the public space, public in both the physical and the mental sense. However, Piet Esser's sculpture only remained on its column for half a year. The sculptor was not happy with the changed status of his work. A number of parties discussed the matter in an open correspondence, and this controversy came to form a substantial part of Van Houwelingen's project. Lelystad town council gave him the freedom to examine other possible ways of installing the monument and he was given permission to make a recast of the sculpture of Lely located at the southern end of the Afsluitdijk made by Mari Andriessen (1897-1979) in the 1950s and to put this new version on top of his column. With *De Zuil van Lely* (Lely's Column) Van Houwelingen raises interesting questions about the position of 'iconic' items of cultural expression in our secularised and individualised society.

In 2009, Van Houwelingen made another interesting proposal, this time to Rotterdam city council. He and the writer Mohammed Benzakour were given the task of thinking about the creation of a monument to the first generation

Lely's Column,
Lelystad, 2002

'National Monument to the
Guest Worker', Rotterdam,
2010

of guest workers to arrive in the Netherlands in the mid-1950s, who came in particular to Rotterdam. Next to the De Bijenkorf department store, there is a large sculpture by the Russian constructivist artist Naum Gabo (1890-1977), which he made on commission to the store in 1956-57. It has no title. Gabo wanted to express the reconstruction of the city from the rubble of war, and the energy of its inhabitants, but deliberately employed a non-figurative, organic idiom that was intended to leave room for free interpretation. The inhabitants of Rotterdam have never wanted to attach any significance to the work and so by 2009 it was in a lamentable state. Van Houwelingen and Benzakour propose having Gabo's work restored by craftsmen of ethnic minority background (descendants of the first generation of guest workers). And then it would be proclaimed as the *Nationaal Gastarbeidermonument* (National Monument to the Guest Worker). Since the 1950s, guest workers have made a substantial contribution to the development of the Dutch welfare state, but this has so far been barely acknowledged. The monument would be the location for a symbolic annual reception for guest workers, with speeches by politicians and thinkers. These plans led to much heated debate. There were many supporters and opponents both in the political and art worlds. In the end, the 'National Monument to the Guest Worker' was not carried out. One argument against, from the Rotterdam art world, was that it was not wise to attach new meaning to a work of art that was conceived with no specific interpretation. So the monument was not created.

Allegories of good and bad government

Van Houwelingen continues to take a committed view of relations between politics and art. In 1848, King William II commissioned the liberal politician Johan Rudolf Thorbecke (1798-1872) to write a new Dutch constitution.[2] Power was removed from the king and given to parliament. This is still the basis of the present Dutch constitution. This constitution also laid down that politics should never interfere in the arts. Thorbecke's idea was that the arts had to fulfil an independent role in Dutch society and if politics were to become involved, it would have a corrupting effect. This notion remained in force until very recently and was a guiding principle in Dutch political and cultural debate. Politics and art respected each other and their complementary but opposing values. However, since populist powers gained ground in politics at the start of the twenty-first century, these distinct positions have become decreasingly easy to maintain. The cabinet in office in the Netherlands from 2010 and 2012 received parliamentary support from the populist Party for Freedom (PVV). The consequence was serious cuts in art and culture, and people did not shrink from calling them senseless hobbies that cost a great deal of money. Van Houwelingen has always been critical of what in his view is an artificial separation of politics and art. He considers that the two should come into contact with each other more often, whereby art would become much less divorced from society thus more interwoven with the organisation of that society. From 1 to 4 May 2011 inclusive, together with the artist Jonas Staal (also an ardent advocate of the political role the artist can play) and Carolien Gehrels, the then councillor responsible for culture in Amsterdam, he organised a marathon debate lasting three days and nights at the W139 artists' initiative in that city. Four artists and four politicians from different sides of politics tried to re-inject meaning and substance into the worn-out relationship between politics and the arts. They made an inventory of the past, but also looked ahead to see how politics and the arts could once again move on together in order to continue giving meaningful form to free and democratic values. The title of this marathon debate was 'Allegories of Good and Bad Government'. This refers to the series of expressive frescoes created by the Italian painter Ambrogio Lorenzetti (1290-1348) in the Palazzo Pubblico in Siena.[3]

Tough but vulnerable Friesland

Between 2010 and 2012, Van Houwelingen worked on a triptych for the new extension to the administrative centre of the province of Friesland in Leeuwarden under the title *Mecenaat Provinsje Fryslân* (Patronage Provinsje Fryslân). The triptych was unveiled when the renovated and extended building was inaugurated. In the Netherlands, the 'province' is an intermediate administrative layer that, although it does have a number of administrative responsibilities, actually

Allegories of Good and Bad Government,
Amsterdam, 2011

plays a more or less symbolic role. As part of the Netherlands, the province of Friesland occupies a very specific position because it has its own language and thereby also a slightly more distinct culture compared with many other provinces. In a certain sense, the middle panel of the triptych, with its subtitle *Archief Mecenaat Provinsje Fryslân* (Archive Patronage Provinsje Fryslân) embroiders on the content of 'Allegories of Good and Bad Government' and offers suggestions for a new relationship between politics and art that gives priority not to pragmatism but to merit. Van Houwelingen points out the rich cultural tradition of Friesland and a big-hearted citizenship that has always been found there. In light of the abovementioned substantial cuts in art and culture implemented by the government in 2011 and the increasing role it proposed that private patronage should play, politics and art appear to be moving further apart than was already the case in previous decades. It seems that the main reason politics wants to introduce private patronage is to be freed from the funding of and the accompanying responsibility for the arts. But the American style of patronage that is so much commended in this context does not imply that politics can simply set aside its responsibility for art and culture. Van Houwelingen describes it as follows in his concept:

'To make patronage a workable new model, it is essential to give shape to the political meaning of private merit in the cultural field. A model that revolves around cultural and political morality, which stimulate each other and become a source for a richer culture. A political signal has to be given that stimulates private cultural enterprise, but also clearly appreciates it. To use the words of the philosopher Peter Sloterdijk, a natural climate should take shape for "homo politicus" in which one can present oneself in a Thymotic setting as a being that wants to give what he has or thinks he has. ... Anyone who is well disposed towards urban cultures must want towns and cities to continue functioning as platforms for an open-hearted citizenship'.[4]

Political recognition and appreciation is an essential part of this. Van Houwelingen presents the sixteenth-century Leeuwarden tower (Oldehove) as a meaningful symbol of the determination, obstinacy, overconfidence and disappointment of the Frisians. In the sixteenth century, they wanted to express their pride in their culture by building a tower higher than the Martinitoren (Martini Tower) that had just been completed in the city of Groningen, sixty kilometres away. To fund the construction, an appeal was made to the public, who then donated generously so as to make it possible. However, when the tower was only ten metres high it started to sag and, as a leaning stump, never reached higher than forty metres. It is however still a visual landmark in Leeuwarden. Van Houwelingen considers that the Oldehove outdid the Martini Tower brilliantly. 'Not in height, but in its soul':

'With each glance at the Oldehove, the tragedy of this cultural epic takes place all over again, an absolute beauty that would have been completely lacking from a straight and completed tower. Thus, taking this view of the Oldehove, the rest of the world, including the Martini tower, is at an angle. My principle is to make use of this Frisian character to constantly continue setting the world straight'.[5]

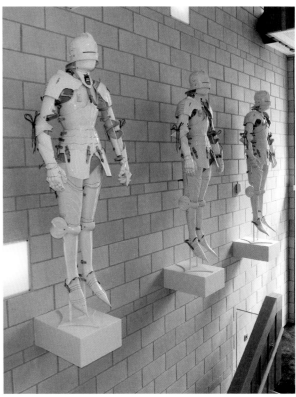

Patronage Provinsje Fryslân, Leeuwarden, 2012

The artist had a monumental oak cabinet made which, on the fifth floor of the Leeuwarden Provinciehuis, stands 2 degrees off the vertical on a console projecting from the wall. The oval frame on the front contains an illustration of the Oldehove in which it stands proudly vertical. *Mecenaat Provinsje Fryslân* is intended to put art and culture on the agenda of the Friesland Provincial Council every year for the next century. The cabinet is meant to act as an archive for the next 100 years and so the Provincial Council will have to take the responsibility of devoting an annual meeting to relations between art and politics at that moment in time. Effective Frisian patronage can only thrive in the provincial administration when the council feels it is a true ambassador, approaches businesses and sponsors or establishes links between art and the business world. Van Houwelingen also made two other works as part of this same assignment. The 'left-hand panel' of the *Mecenaat Provinsje Fryslân* triptych, which has the subtitle *Âlvestêden* (Eleven Towns) is in the new section of the Provinciehuis and is historically oriented. On eleven consoles high up on the wall in the new public area stand eleven white porcelain suits of armour with closed visors. Van Houwelingen describes these eleven monumental figures as follows: 'Stately, conservative, overconfident and fragile – each has the coat of arms of a Frisian town on its cuirass'.[6] These porcelain suits of armour are like Frisian tradition: both sturdy and fragile. Tradition can on the one hand be a protection, but it can also be a society's Achilles heel. At such times, conservatism and rigidity are not far off. The 'right-hand panel' with its subtitle *Vista Fryslân* (View of Friesland) is future-oriented and is in the provincial council chamber in the historical part of the building. Van Houwelingen commissioned the young Chinese artist Mu Xue to do six large drawings that will replace six baroque paintings in the eighteenth-century frames that form part of the wall cladding. Mu Xue's drawings consist of irregular patterns of lines that occur in an indefinable empty space. These works are intended to give the province of Friesland the room to open its windows and let the future blow in.

Mecenaat Provinsje Fryslân can be interpreted as a meaningful work, but now, in 2016, it seems that its 'middle panel' is in danger of being amputated. Van Houwelingen has had many conversations with the provincial authorities to arrive at an agreement in principle regarding the implementation of the annual meeting where culture and politics will be linked and which will provide the material to fill the monumental cabinet. Unfortunately, at a certain moment the provincial authorities ended the discussions and, with pain in his heart, Van Houwelingen found he was compelled to cancel the completion of his project. In 2018, Friesland's capital city, Leeuwarden, will be a Cultural Capital of Europe. A position that should lead to reflection, contemplation and visionary ideas. This makes it so incomprehensible and shameful that the provincial authorities should be so indifferent to the meaningful body of ideas contained in a work of art.

At the service of the public interest

Van Houwelingen continues to put forward proposals that focus our perceptions of history, freedom and other values. He was commissioned to create a work of art for the 2015 Airborne walk; it involves about thirty thousand participants and has taken place near Arnhem every year since 1944 to commem-

Death or the Gladioli, Arnhem, 2015

orate the bloody 'Battle of Arnhem' in that year. The walk calls attention to the freedom that was won at that time. Van Houwelingen takes this opportunity to examine the notion of 'freedom'. In 1944, troops came from far and wide to liberate the Netherlands from the Nazis in the name of freedom. At that time, the notion of freedom appeared to lead to little misunderstanding. Now, in 2016, it is very much open to question and is a matter of debate. Such familiar rights as freedom of expression and freedom of religion are no longer perceived unequivocally. This is something that Van Houwelingen wanted to bring up in his proposal for the work *De Dood of de Gladioli* (Death or the Gladioli); the title refers to classical antiquity, when a victorious gladiator received gladioli and the loser had to die. He proposed inviting seventy-two Muslim women to hand out gladioli to the walkers during the trip. This had the potential to be a moment when many of the participants had to rethink their familiar assumptions concerning the notion of 'freedom'. Van Houwelingen's proposal was not implemented, and this is the fate that many more of his proposals have met. But in the meantime, the debate that is regularly prompted by his plans and ideas makes the familiar ground beneath our feet briefly crumble. Max Bruinsma, already mentioned in this article, attributes to the artist in public space an awareness of being 'a medium at the service of the public cultural interest'. In addition, 'the quality of his work is determined essentially by the degree to which he succeeds in recalling that slogan of the 1960s that has fallen into disuse: "making the personal political"'.[7] May Hans Van Houwelingen long remain capable of doing so. ∎

Translated by Gregory Ball

NOTES

1   Max Bruinsma, 'Kunst Openbaar Ruimte; Enkele begripsbepalingen bij het werk van Hans Van Houwelingen' (p. 11) in *Stiff; Hans van Houwelingen vs Public Art* (ed. Max Bruinsma). Amsterdam: Artimo, 2004.

2   Van Houwelingen made two separate proposals for the installation of a monument to Thorbecke in The Hague. See www.hansvanhouwelingen.nl: 'Gedane zaken nemen geen keer / The Hague / 2008' and 'Thorbecke Monument / The Hague / 2011'.

3   Ambrogio Lorenzetti's *Allegories of Good and Bad Government* consists of three parts and six scenes: *The Allegory of Good Government, The Effects of Good Government in the City and in the Country*, and *The Allegory of Bad Government*.

4   See www.hansvanhouwelingen.nl: Mecenaat Fryslân. Van Houwelingen quotes from Peter Sloterdijk's piece *Samenlevingsdesign in de open stad/Opmerkingen over de urbane antropologie*, 2009.

5   Ibid.

6   Ibid.

7   See note 1: p. 15.

The Measure of Our Exile

On the City Essays of Guy Vaes

[PHILIP MOSLEY]

Guy Vaes (b. 1927) was a Belgian author whose magic realist fiction also drew on modernist psychological investigations and ideas of alienation. Vaes, who made his name with *October Long Sunday* (1956), returned to writing novels later in his career between 1983 and 2002. An accomplished photographer, he was also a film critic for the Brussels magazine *Spécial*, and his collected reviews were published in 2007.

His death aged eighty-five in his native city of Antwerp in February 2012 marked a broader passing, that of the francophone Flemish author. Along with Paul Willems, who died in 1997, Vaes was the last major resident representative of this curious and anachronistic line. As it gradually faded, it wove a valedictory narrative of a kind that haunts present-day Belgium. In the last half-century, while francophone Brussels and Walloon authors forged new cultural identities from their changing status as imminent citizens of independent Belgian regions, the francophone Flemings grew increasingly isolated in a thrusting Dutch-speaking region that benefited from further language laws in the 1960s and from constitutional reforms in the following two decades. Unlike other francophone Flemish writers who opted for exile from their native region, Willems and Vaes remained to face the gradual withering away of their cultural and institutional support in the wake of Flemish resurgence.

In its constant play of doubles, dreams and apparitions, Willems's work, especially his plays, repeatedly expresses the fractured identity of the francophone Fleming. Writing in 1978, Willems confessed to being troubled by the task of setting a play in the port of Antwerp: 'I see my characters, I hear them speak: they speak Flemish. It's therefore impossible for a Flemish francophone author to write "live" about a specific place located in Flanders'.

A dedicated flâneur

Vaes shared this sense of dispossession and loss, but chose not to associate it openly with Flanders. In *October Long Sunday*, set in an unidentified Antwerp, Laurent Carteras, the inheritor of a country estate, finds himself unrecognized by those around him and so assumes the identity of a gardener on the property that his cousin has acquired by default. His second novel, *The Other Side* (1983), is set in London in the torrid August of 1934. A young Fleming, Bruno, becomes the confidant of Broderick, an older friend gravely injured while vacationing on the Isle of Skye and who, like Lazarus in Eliot's *The Love Song of J. Alfred Prufrock*, has 'come from the dead/Come back to tell you all' before 'dying' for a second time. Broderick's revelations of 'the other side' turn Bruno's life upside down; he is *dépaysé* in more ways than one. And London is a perfect location, as its indecipherable vastness sets the disorientating mood of the novel.

In this way, Vaes consistently dislocated his identification with Antwerp as well as with Paris or Amsterdam, the traditional magnets for French- or Dutch-language Belgian authors respectively. Influenced greatly by British literature, Vaes's greatest affinities were for cities in the British Isles: Dublin, Edinburgh, and above all London, which he describes as an 'Eldorado for the enthusiast of unlimited epiphanies and of strangeness'. His various essays on Edinburgh and London reveal the twin paradoxes of an intimate vastness and a strange familiarity; the title of his major essay on the English capital (1963), paraphrased from Jorge Luis Borges, is *London, or the Broken Labyrinth*. 'I love labyrinths', he writes, 'and London is a maze that only gives itself up to the attentive walker'. His essay on *The Cemeteries of London* (1978) reinforces this passion by serving as the introduction to an eponymous book of his own photographs. Wandering in wonder, and invoking a range of literary and art works, Vaes offers an aesthetic and historical meditation on the distinctive atmosphere and special character of these remarkable Victorian burial grounds.

A dedicated *flâneur*, in a tradition running from Baudelaire through modernism to the 'drifting' of the Situationists and beyond, Vaes moved through cities on foot, always on his own terms, and with a boundless enthusiasm for their quirkier, less evident sides. In the essay *Poetics of Cities* (1997), based on his own experiences of London and Singapore (having written an essay on the latter at the end of the 1970s), and of others writing about London, he investigates how language may unlock the secrets and essence of cities perceived by imaginative minds. All of his city essays thus demonstrate the subtle art of a psychogeographer, one whose refined sensibility, ever open to unusual detail, combines 'attentive' walking with aesthetic, emotional, and intellectual insights in a quest for the meaning of places and of our often complex relation to them.

Guy Vaes (1927-2012)
© Erven/les ayants droit
Guy Vaes

Vieil Anvers
(Old Antwerp), ca. 1965
© Erven/les ayants droit
Guy Vaes

Born twice

In the Edinburgh essay, *The City of Interrupted Time* (1990, its title borrowed from Henri Michaux), he claims of the English and Scottish capitals, and the Irish one to a lesser extent, that he is of them rather than of elsewhere, other cities being mere passing fancies of strictly localized interest. His sense of his own dual identity further emerges in his assertion that he was born twice: once in Antwerp in 1927 and again in London on his first visit in 1958. Writing to critic Jacques De Decker in 1983, Vaes acknowledges that 'being a franco-phone writer living in Antwerp doesn't trouble me at all. On the contrary, I've always enjoyed living in a city whose language, fully familiar to me, did not belong to me at all. I felt more at ease in London, I had more room to move'. As Vaes walked through Edinburgh and London, he discovered a profound sense of identification with them, giving rise to a feeling that he belonged not only to his native land, region, and city, and to francophone literature, but to an inter-cultural continuum. This discovery permitted him to resolve certain aspects of the problem of identity he experienced as a minority writer in a Dutch-speaking region. For Vaes, Belgium is 'a kaleidoscope that offers fragments of reality but whose totality resides elsewhere'.

The interrelated strategies of walking and writing demonstrated in Vaes's essays may be productively read in light of some of Michel de Certeau's ideas in 'Walking in the City', one chapter of *The Practice of Everyday Life* (1980). De Certeau's urban walker employs a 'rhetoric' that undermines the 'legible or-der of planners' in its 'turns and detours'. In this rhetoric, 'the art of "turning" phrases finds an equivalent in the art of composing a path'. This equivalence works as easily in reverse: the twists and turns of a path correspond to the art of composing a phrase, a sentence, or a paragraph. In the process, Vaes understands with a mixture of joy and apprehension what de Certeau calls the 'disquieting familiarity' of the city, and from these revelations springs the tex-tual expression of a 'poetic geography on top of the geography of the literal, forbidden or permitted meaning'.

We may see that Vaes was deeply attached to Antwerp but resisted an easy identification with it and especially with all standard accounts of it. How then may we see the perception of his native city in *An Antwerp Palimpsest*? This essay was first published in magazine form as part of a collectively written 'new synthesis of Antwerp' for a civic celebration in 1993. Maintaining his practice of a dislocated and (in the best sense of the word) eccentric identity, he explores the ambivalent idea of a presence in yet an absence from his own birthplace. The essay leads the reader on a typically idiosyncratic series of perambulations through areas of greater Antwerp that the tourist might completely ignore. Through the eyes of an unorthodox walker, Vaes discovers a city that, in de Certeau's words, 'is left prey to contradictory movements that counterbalance and combine themselves outside the reach of panoptic power'. He reads against the grain of the city's geography, history, and architecture. For instance, he describes walking out of Antwerp along the Engelselei at nightfall on a drizzly summer evening. The space he finds himself entering seems to exist in another dimension, 'attached to which are the powerfully vague terrain, the outskirts that strike urban planners impotent, and the overgrown path that circles the old fortresses guarded only by rats and valerian—in short, all that breaks the mould and sends history back to its manuals'.

Every city can contain other cities

Another section, on Rue de Marbaix, a street marked by 'high, stern facades dating from the beginning of the twentieth century', exemplifies Vaes's eye for detail, his association of ideas, and his insistence on unhurried appreciation of a place: 'You contemplate the facades as if they were titles on the spine of books in a library. And those dusty, thick spines, a little grainy from wear, have titles smelling of ill-disguised violence and promising secrets. And, just as you

Schrijnwerkersstraat,
Antwerp, ca. 1960
© Erven/les ayants droit
Guy Vaes

Royal Museum of Fine Arts,
Antwerp, ca. 1960
© Erven/les ayants droit
Guy Vaes

find book bindings bearing vignettes or ex-libris plates, so there are facades in this street decorated with little paintings of cherubs' heads, stone gargoyles spouting wrought-iron lianas, mosaic friezes with a floral motif, and even a balcony supported by miniature columns, superbly dramatized by its stained surface'.

These often ordinary streets and districts reveal to Vaes a personal vision of the city that has little or nothing to do with its official status as the centre of contemporary Flemish cultural, economic, and political power. Instead, it has everything to do with the veiled presence of a different reality and with a set of peculiar affinities to other cities. Believing that 'every city can contain other cities' or 'at least ... indicate their presence', he tells how as a young man in Antwerp he had sensed certain aspects of London and Edinburgh before ever visiting those cities. 'It thus happens', he continues, 'that a place, because of its resemblances, confirms our roots elsewhere and allows us to measure our exile. [...] Osmosis arises between reality, literature, and iconography, a phantom identity, a visitation that lasts only a second beyond the initial surprise. [...] It is a phenomenon sparked by the unforeseen'.

Since a palimpsest is a manuscript on which more than one text has been written with the earlier writing incompletely erased, Vaes duly overlays conventional or formulaic accounts of Antwerp with his own original itinerary and thereby reinforces his eccentric identification with his native city. Though marked by episodes of anxiety and doubt, his physical and then textual traces bear witness to a heightened response to Antwerp comparable to his transcendent experiences of Edinburgh and London. That this response somewhat ironically privileges undifferentiated, hidden, and forgotten places only serves to intensify the enigma of this reality. It is the reality of what Michel Foucault calls 'heterotopias, those singular spaces to be found in some given social spaces whose functions are different or even the opposite of others'.

At the end of his essay, he finds himself veering off the beaten track in a nondescript, elevated open area called *Little Switzerland*, within the village of Mortsel, where 'like an ascetic gives up his Self in the contemplation of emptiness, Antwerp has renounced itself'. Here is no officially recognized part of the city, no district defined by public image or by developmental vision. Vaes explains that 'Little Switzerland' bears 'no traces ... of the past, no signs of the future. Of the present, you only see what unrestrained nature renews'. But we are still in metropolitan Antwerp, and Vaes persuades us eloquently that his experience here, as in other parts of the city where he chooses to walk, or as in other cities, is available to anyone in the right frame of body and mind.

Extracts from An Antwerp Palimpsest
By Guy Vaes

Every city can contain other cities. At least it can indicate their presence.

Having been moulded by the urban imbroglios of Robert Louis Stevenson, that brother of Scheherazade, and by Gustave Doré's meticulous nightmares, I happened to recognize certain aspects of London during a bus ride one day through the outskirts of Antwerp. And at that time, near the harbour, I even identified an Edinburgh 'close' in a carriage-gate left ajar. Yet at that time I hadn't set foot in the United Kingdom. These imprints of other native cities in Antwerp, during my lifetime, have always puzzled me.

Edinburgh—an introverted and aggressive city carved from rock—revealed itself one winter afternoon (1947 or 1948?) in the opening of a carriage-gate with gigantic panels. It permitted a view of an off-putting courtyard, the remains of a cul-de-sac, where barrels, barrows, and handcarts were stored. It was in the Lange Koepoortstraat, between the old Bourse and the Zirkstraat. As for the arched passage diving beneath the Boucherie, with its rather brutal overtone due to echoing voices, it announced, with immense modesty, the Cowgate along which I didn't make my way until 1959.

Very recently, in 1991, in the architectural chaos of Huy, I wandered through an alley that seemed to be a brick-by-brick 'quotation' of Edinburgh. It thus happens that a place, because of its resemblances, confirms our roots elsewhere and allows us to measure our exile. This phenomenon isn't exceptional in its own right, but it offers, for my part, a corollary that most will recognize.

Osmosis arises between reality, literature, and iconography, a phantom identity, a visitation that lasts only a second beyond the initial surprise. The critical mind, quickly regaining its hold, considers every image of Edinburgh as a projection of the Elsewhere, an immature desire, a reference—you linger over a text or a photograph—to that which hasn't yet come but will surely have to. Romantic feelings are not, or barely, involved here, especially since the experience of the Elsewhere, which usually passes in a flash, isn't contrived—it couldn't be without sinking into artifice. It is a phenomenon sparked by the unforeseen and, apart from being amenable to description, it is absolutely useless. I will not dwell on the origin of the affinities connecting me with faraway cities. It would mean entering the domain of hypotheses in which one generally may only drown.

As London has its Little Venice, which is situated by the Regent's Canal in Paddington, so Antwerp has its Little Switzerland. Its access within the village of Mortsel seems to want to avoid the gaze of non-initiates. The advantage of this helvetic plot—due to the steep slope, the roofs of villas, and the walls of warehouses hiding it, you could easily miss it—is that you get a worker airing his dog instead of a parvenu of the jet set, a wild cat instead of a star bogged down by her cellulite and her revenue, a mother with a stroller instead of a gambler, and a little boy hacking a ball instead of a vacationing diplomat. Normally, you do not suffocate here, as human presence is kept to a bare minimum. It limits itself to a small-scale representation.

Let us take the entrance at the end of the Osylei, past the playground. It combines what is visible with what is hidden. In an area set back, a narrow footpath, barely visible at first sight, broaches what you hardly dare call 'the heights'. On one side, discreet as a wink, a small notice board announces the

Promenoir le long de l'Escaut (Promenade walk along the Scheldt), ca. 1960
© Erven/les ayants droit Guy Vaes

Docks Escaut, ca. 1960
© Erven/les ayants droit
Guy Vaes

border of Little Switzerland (Klein Zwitserland). Seven or eight steps ahead and the horizon is within reach on this high, wide, and solitary ramp of a former railway track. Between the swelling of luxurious weeds, bushes, poppies, and fragrant thistles (it is June), you will see a path, if you can call it that, venturing upward. Is this what they call a veldt in South Africa? Where the path turns, you can look down to another rustic railway line and see the railcar from Turnhout to Mechelen passing by. Our path follows this bend to the right and runs through the domain of the adjacent yet invisible Château de Cantecroy. A gaggle of geese protects it. Any suspicious noises? A deafening clamour suddenly arises. In the middle of Little Switzerland, there is a green hollow, quite open, a kind of valley with bushes, toward which hints of footpaths descend. The ground, without any doubt ancient sediment from the Scheldt, is still covered with broken shells. People have even dug up sharks' teeth here. Due to a lack of alpine pasture, you discover slopes full of motley cats and hares instead of rams and cows. Finally, in an area only slightly lower, a path overlooked by the very long wall of a warehouse and completely overgrown by bushes heads for the corner of the Krijgsbaan and the Amadeus Stockmanslei. There, it coughs up the wanderer.

Like an ascetic gives up his Self in the contemplation of emptiness, Antwerp has renounced itself. Ah! The luxury of no longer being houses, harbour, cathedral, and museums; of having said goodbye even to the collective nonchalance of its parks! Thanks be given to the indistinct lands of which Little Switzerland is the queen. No traces therefore of the past, no signs of the future. Of the present, you only see what unrestrained nature renews. It is quite possible that Antwerp is yet to be born . . . Unless we are reaching the end of its history here. All that remains is my stream of consciousness.

In this Switzerland the gold of forgetfulness needs no banks. ■

From *Un Palimpseste anversois*, first published in *Colophon*, Antwerp, 1993. Definitive version in André Sempoux, *Guy Vaes: l'effroi et l'extase*, Éditions Luce Wilquin, Avin (B), 2006.

Translated by Philip Mosley

Choreographer of Letters, Servant of Text, Illustrator

Gert Dooreman Fights Banality

[DIRK LEYMAN]

Crowned with a Henry Van de Velde Award in 2015 for his entire career, a string of exhibitions to his name revealing his oeuvre in its full glory, set down in a monumental reprinted and revised book with the simple, proud title *Dooreman* (Lannoo, Tielt, 2015): this might put one in mind of a career end, but Dooreman abhors the idea, along with the feeling that he has been placed in a velvet pantheon. He still has so much to do.

So many accolades and laurel wreaths for a graphic designer in Flanders cannot be taken for granted, though. The craft still has a lower profile here than in places such as the Netherlands or Switzerland. In the 1980s and 1990s aesthete Gert Dooreman dealt a firm blow to the Flemish world of graphic design and typography, more or less singlehandedly, then patched up his victim himself and sent it off in a completely different direction, declaring war on banality and mediocrity, or at least what he saw as such. That was quite something. Infamous for being difficult and headstrong – as well as for his self-doubt – he rarely compromised, which sometimes caused friction.

Nonetheless, in many ways Dooreman prefers the sidelines. Designing books, posters and other printed materials is, after all, hardly a job for a crowd pleaser. 'Adaptor of text, image, texture and colour, in service of the message of others,' as Jan Middendorp describes Gert Dooreman in the monograph dedicated to him. Is Dooreman's primary ambition to polish up and take pride in the creations of others? Yes and no. Yes, of course, letters must support the content, but no, it's not just craftsmanship. It is much more than that. 'From the start Dooreman would come up with a concept for himself, then endure sweat and tears to fulfil that self-inflicted expectation. The short circuit of this apparent contradiction supplied the nuclear energy for a production of unbridled high quality, with no equal in Flanders at the time,' writer Tom Lanoye fittingly notes. Dooreman sees himself as an artist pur sang. Initially he wanted to become an illustrator, and that influence has stayed with him. 'People tend to see my illustrations as a kind of youthful lapse and I have to keep on telling them it's not true, that I'm really an illustrator who happens to design, not a designer who used to draw as a hobby,' he has already let slip, slightly irritably.

Things have worked out somewhat differently. The drawing and illustrating gradually faded into the background. Dooreman in fact acquired fame bit by bit with his posters and the house styles he developed for theatre companies and museums such as NT Gent or the Nieuwpoorttheater, Theater Antigone (Kortrijk), the Dr Guislain Museum in Ghent, the Beursschouwburg theatre in Brussels, the Blauwe Maandag theatre company (herald of the theatre revival in Flanders in the 1980s and '90s) or the Toneelhuis in Antwerp. He grew to be one of Flanders' most famous designers of book covers, with designs for Tom Lanoye, followed by countless other authors (from Saskia De Coster and Jeroen Olyslaegers to JMH Berckmans and Koen Peeters) and publishers (from Kritak, Prometheus and Meulenhoff/Manteau to Het Balanseer and Polis), in turn acquiring imitators and disciples. They copied him, only to wrench themselves free or cautiously push him off his throne.

His teacher Ever Meulen sums it up succinctly in *Dooreman*: 'He had an innate feel for the right spacing, between the lines too. He picked out the most elegant lower case letters and combined them with strong capitals. His page layouts were the most beautiful in the country.' This may well have been music to Dooreman's ears, as he recently decreed in *de Volkskrant*, 'A strong typographical image on the cover of a collection of poetry says so much more than some atmospheric snapshot or other.' Dooreman has designed around 1,500 book covers so far.

Frivolity

Gert Dooreman (b. 1958) originally comes from the region of Kempen. Born in Herentals, in 1958, he ended up studying in Ghent, which became his definitive biotope, the great sprawling provincial city to which he took like a duck to water. Artistically, too, he put down roots in Ghent, albeit preferring to take cover in his studio after a while.

Dooreman's parents initially wanted him to study architecture, so he followed a 3-year preparatory course at art school, after which he spent a year studying animation and three years studying graphic design. Ghent was a cultural melting pot at the time and Dooreman found himself in exactly the right circles. The artists' café De Groene Kikker turned out to be an ideal breeding ground, with an inner circle including figures such as author Tom Lanoye, photographer Michiel Hendryckx, musician Peter Vermeersch, theatre producer Arne Sierens and architect Maarten Van Severen. 'We started up music groups and a magazine... It was all very boyish. ...In the early 1980s, Ghent's cultural life was booming. The Vooruit Arts Centre opened, we organised exhibitions, it was unstoppable. The presence of Jan Hoet was an important part of that. There was a great deal going on. Much of it dreadfully ugly, to be honest. The 1980s were a dramatic time for design, a terrible time, but I don't think what we did was dreadfully ugly.' (Magazine Knack)

Dooreman hastily formed a long-term duo with photographer Michiel Hendryckx, producing work which included book covers for André van Halewyck's publishing company Kritak. He no longer needed to sign on, as he was earning money 'respectably'. Soon it became clear that a drawing was not the solution to every cover, so photos were added to the mix and before he knew it he was a graphic designer, although typographical 'jazzing up' of photos was never really his thing; he was better with drawings.

Tom Lanoye's collection of 'satirical critiques' *Rozegeur en maneschijn* (Rose Scent and Moonshine, 1983) can be considered Dooreman's first 'official' cover. It led to a continuous collaboration with the writer, whom Dooreman already immensely admired, a cooperative process only briefly interrupted since then. Dooreman created Lanoye's house style, designed in close consultation with the author, forever etched into the collective graphical memory. The two began by creating a cartoon strip together based on the police inspector Gino Spatelli, but this ran aground in the embryonic phase, something which continues to niggle at both of them. Highlights of their collaboration are the striking posters for the cycle of plays 'Ten Oorlog' (To War) produced by the Blauwe Maandag theatre company (also presented in book form), the spectacular banner for Antwerp World Book Capital on the Boerentoren skyscraper (2004, a poem by Lanoye as city poet), the book collection 'Lanoye Hard Gemaakt' (hardbacks of Lanoye's early work) and the cover of the novel *Sprakeloos* (Speechless, 2009).

Dooreman also produced bold work for Bert Bakker in Amsterdam. In the 1980s publishers still often imposed a straitjacket on the designer, leaving little room for divergence, but Dooreman gradually wriggled out of that and might be credited with designers subsequently receiving carte blanche. At the same time, he initially continued to produce his illustration work, with a range of clients including the newspapers *De Morgen* and *De Standaard*, as well as *Playboy*, sometimes in collaboration with Erik Meynen. He continued with that combination for fifteen years, until 1997, when – after a couple of disillusioning experiences – he abruptly stopped drawing.

Meanwhile he had long become better known as a graphic designer. Posters for the Blauwe Maandag company and the Beursschouwburg theatre broadened his horizons. 'The Blauwe Maandag posters often presented strik-

BLAUWE MAANDAG COMPAGNIE

TEN OORLOG

IN CO-PRODUCTIE MET VOORUIT, DESINGEL, ROTTERDAMSE SCHOUWBURG

AFLEVERING
I { **IN DE NAAM VAN DE VADER EN DE ZOON**
RICHAAR DEUZIÈME + HENDRIK VIER

AFLEVERING
II { **ZIE DE DIENSTMAAGD DES HEREN**
HENDRIK DE VIJFDEN + MARGARETHA DI NAPOLI

AFLEVERING
III { **EN VERLOS ONS VAN HET KWADE**
EDWAAR THE KING + RISJAAR MODDERFOKKER DEN DERDE

LANOYE & PERCEVAL NAAR SHAKESPEARE / THE WARS OF THE ROSES
SCENOGRAFIE: BRACK LICHT: BAGNOLI KOSTUUMS: VANDENBUSSCHE
MET: BEKS, DE WACHTER, DECLEIR, DECLEIR, DOTTERMANS,
HELDENBERGH, LÖW, OPBROUCK, PEETERS, SEYNAEVE,
SMITS, VAN DEN EYNDE, VAN KAAM, VAN VLIET

VOORUIT GENT
9 T/M 22 NOVEMBER 97
28 JANUARI T/M 1 MAART 98 TEL: 09/2672828

DESINGEL ANTWERPEN
27 NOVEMBER T/M 20 DECEMBER 97 TEL: 03/2482828

ROTTERDAMSE SCHOUWBURG
7 JANUARI T/M 24 JANUARI 98 TEL: 010/4118110

WEEKDAGEN: 1 AFLEVERING PER AVOND
WEEKEND: ALLE AFLEVERINGEN OP 1 DAG

MET DE STEUN VAN DE VLAAMSE GEMEENSCHAP, DE PROVINCIE OOST-VLAANDEREN EN DE NATIONALE LOTERIJ
AFFICHE: FRED EERDEKENS / TOYO HORNBERG / V.U.: STEFAAN DE BRYNE, ST. PIETERSNIEUWSTRAAT 23 – 9000 GENT / V.V.C.: OSL FONDEL DOEL

---

ing photos for which I devised letters, but with some hesitation so as not to obscure the image,' he commented in *Het Nieuwsblad*. Later he took the bull by the horns, resolutely producing overwhelming typographical masterpieces. Eventually 'Dooremans' could be found everywhere in the cultural world and in bookshops, yes even on postage stamps (for instance for a series commemorating Expo 58). Ever more flamboyant, he left his graphical mark, with inventive lettering, perfect line spacing and designs which exuded balance and a light frivolity, in spite of resulting from painstaking measuring and fitting work. When everything falls into place after lots of shifting about (or indeed the lack thereof), he sees it as a gift. 'You recognise a Dooreman when you see it, even if those from the 1980s are completely different from those from the 1990s or the twenty-first century. Dooreman is a chameleon', says Sam De Graeve in *Dooreman*.

The poetry of measurement

So does Dooreman transform so often? What is the key to the persuasive power of his designs? An important clue must lie in the fact that the graphic designer labels himself an 'autodidact'. From the start of his career, he wanted to know all the ins and outs of letters and the finishing touches of the craft. Pushing typography to the max – that was Dooreman's ultimate goal. He has always documented his work frenetically. Jan Middendorp recognises this: 'Self-taught graphic designers seem to feel more of a drive to support their creative work with historical and theoretical studies, to document their work in detail, than their certified colleagues. Dooreman takes this to the extreme. He is constantly in the process of self-study; every step is shored up with new knowledge and skill.' Dooreman toiled away in Ghent University Library, or busily collected old magazines and journals such as *Simplicissimus*, the German satirical magazine published between 1896 and 1944. His studio, where he sees himself as a 'lab technician', is a treasure trove of endless paper paraphernalia. Dooreman's designs emanate the entirety of printing history. Somehow typesetting must have been in his blood: his grandfather had a printing business, where Dooreman was allowed to nose around as a small child. Dooreman has gradually promoted letters to ingenious chess pieces, expressive elements, *much* more than a set of tools. To him good, precise lettering is no less than 'the poetry of measurement', hence the exceptional importance he attaches to spacing. He has rehabilitated fonts such as Gill Sans and Perpetua and worked miracles with Prague designer František Štorm's fonts. He makes the lettering his own, presenting a new take on the nineteenth-century wooden characters and greedily mining the period of the industrial revolution. Not surprisingly, Dooreman felt a certain aversion to the arrival of the computer, which completely turned the design industry on its head, although it later turned out to be his 'true instrument', as Tom Lanoye put it, 'his real biotope, his palette, his mastery'.

Focused doubt

Dooreman is well known among his entourage for his doubts, as is his life partner, children's writer and illustrator Gerda Dendooven. Perhaps that is what makes her the perfect witness of his sometimes turbulent thinking process, as he has also concocted countless book designs and covers for her work. 'Working with Dooreman is an extremely professional process but it's also exhausting: the man has a faster-than-average brain and is more demanding than your

everyday perfectionist. He is also a master at coming up with relevant issues, only to declare them irrelevant again with the same certainty.' Dooreman tends to deny this tortuous process, pointing to his rapid work pace: 'If I were a compulsive doubter, I would never have worked so much. Adrenaline works fast and my pace is rapid. I can design a book cover, an advert and two illustrations in a day. When I have my doubts, I'm focused about it. But I manage to be both subjective and objective. Sometimes I take a turning into the woods and follow a path. Sometimes I end up in a swamp, but I've always left a path of pebbles behind on my computer. I can always get back,' he said in an interview in *De Morgen*. 'Fundamental doubt alongside unshakeable self-confidence,' was how Tom Lanoye summed up his attitude.

It is also worth noting that Dooreman is colour blind. That means he has to keep a handle on his palette one way or another. 'His palette is on the austere side: lots of black, red, grey and off-white, plenty of earthy colours, the occasional bright but generally tasteful standout. He's no magician when it comes to colour,' says Jan Middendorp. Of course, 'In der Beschränkung zeigt sich erst der Meister,' ('The master shows himself first in confinement') as Goethe put it. After all, have there not been deaf composers and orators with speech impediments, as Dooreman pointed out in 2005 in response to the commonly asked question as to how colour blindness affected his work? 'I know how to handle colours. I'm very familiar with the grey values, so I know the characters of the colours really well. I have to work hard for it, unlike others, who are surrounded with colours like children in a sweet shop. I can't combine twelve colours. I stick to three. That's become my rule: if my design can't stand up to that, it's no good.'

It might be considered remarkable that Dooreman apparently does not read the books he designs at all – if he did, it would make his work pace well nigh impossible, of course. In that respect he differs from Dick Bruna, who claimed

that he really read every book in the Zwart Beertje series for which he designed covers. In any case, Dooreman is well aware of the tension between the discreet interior design and the attention-seeking character of the cover, which he prefers to design collaboratively. 'They're two different disciplines. The interior demands a high zen-content. It has to be balanced and harmonious, so that you barely notice it. The cover is a law unto itself. It just has to stand out.'

The illustrator seizes the moment

If you run through Dooreman's fantastic productions of the last thirty years, you see steady quality with many highs and remarkably few lows. There is an unmistakable evolution towards powerful, authoritative typography and transcendence of the Zeitgeist (more conspicuously presented in the early designs, despite the resistance to the ugliness of the 1980s). Dooreman needs less and less to achieve the desired effect. He avoids garishness; it is the architecture of his letters that has to do the work, which has also grown more timeless. You will not find gratuitous aesthetics in Dooreman's work. Letters must support the content. Craftsmanship is essential in making the leap from typographical balance to art. His colour palette might be modest, but he finds other ways of achieving contrast. In one case he opts for a modest letter, in another for extraversion and exuberance. Sometimes we find elements recycled from the Russian constructivism of the interbellum – Kazimir Malevich, Alexander Rodchenko or El Lissitzky – mainly in designs for Lanoye, especially 'De Boerentoren schrijft' ('The Boerentoren writes') and the posters of the Blauwe Maandag company. Nevertheless, it seems that Dooreman has achieved the greatest unity in his book covers for publishers Meulenhoff/Manteau and the later De Bezige Bij Antwerpen, where the designs are frivolous and inventive with a purified quality. When photos enter the mix, Dooreman clearly has a little more trouble making his mark. Which book fair poster is his most beautiful so far? Undoubtedly that of 2006, Dooreman's signature, a poster of letter building blocks.

Is Dooreman now consecrated, lionised and neatly canonised? Apparently not. But what direction will he take next? The designer has countless plans on the go and currently allows his new assistant Stijn Dams to knit extensions seamlessly onto his own style. 'The old excitement has gone, I'm done with books,' Dooreman confessed in *Knack*. 'I work seven days a week, up to sixteen hours a day. I'm gradually becoming saturated.' Perhaps the freedom of illustration is beckoning again. The revised version of the monograph about Dooreman noted the increased share of his work devoted to drawing and illustration – a small atonement, observing the unmistakable influence of Honoré Daumier, Hans Holbein and Egon Schiele, as well as the better cartoon strips. These are illustrations with a tendency towards caricature, full of pointy enlargements. As *De Standaard* once wrote, 'Dooreman is the choreographer of his characters. In every illustration there is a swirl, a twist, a flourish. The illustrator knows the precise moment to strike.' From choreographer of letters to elegant characters: it is possible to return to one's roots. He also dreams of furniture design. Well then, the ultimate Dooreman cabinet, how would that look? ■

Translated by Anna Asbury

The first collection
presentation *Full Moon* of
the Museum Voorlinden
in Wassenaar
© Museum Voorlinden

Chronicle

Cultural Policy

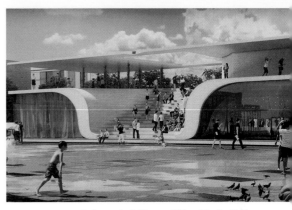

Leeuwarden's Tower of Pisa: Lân fan Taal

Leeuwarden-Fryslân 2018
An Exceptional European Capital of Culture

On 6 September 2013, the Frisian flag with its characteristic *pompeblêden* (water-lily leaves) fluttered proudly from the Westertoren in Amsterdam. This was quite exceptional, as even the Dutch national flag was seldom raised there. Why was this? The administrator of the Westerkerk had been 'bribed' with a simple Frisian sugar loaf. It heralded the outcome of the meeting of the European Capital of Culture committee, which that afternoon was to award the title for 2018 to one of the three candidate cities that remained in the running: Eindhoven, Leeuwarden and Maastricht. To the huge amazement of the whole of the Netherlands, it turned out to be Leeuwarden. It had nothing to do with the sugar loaf, only with the quality and extraordinarily ambitious nature of its bid book, which took as its title *Iepen Mienskip* and as a slogan *Criss-Crossing Communities*.

What on earth is *mienskip*, a word which the European panel was actually perfectly able to pronounce? The bid book expresses it clearly: 'The term *mienskip* is derived from times when the struggle against water led people to join forces, sharing talents with the goal of building terps and dykes for the common good. With our bid we aim to re-invent this old Frisian spirit of shared community feeling'. 'Leeuwarden 2018' is intended to bring about this renewal, establishing an *iepen mienskip* in 2018 through the medium of three major European themes: a link between Nature and Culture for a sustainable future; closing the gap between City and Countryside so as to give rise to a creative ecology; and involving Community and Diversity to enable people of differing cultural backgrounds to develop a new sense of community. With these themes at the back of their minds, 41 projects were set up, in which national, international and Frisian producers and artists cooperated closely. To be able to achieve an *iepen mienskip* in 2018.

How is Leeuwarden 2018 doing in 2017? First of all, the name has been changed to Leeuwarden-Fryslân 2018, by analogy with Marseille-Provence in 2013. It is after all not only the city, but the whole of Friesland, with its own language, literature and culture, that is taking part in 2018. After the ups and downs that all European Capitals of Culture are subject to, the organisation has for the time being entered a period of stability. A small team of steady members of staff is now carrying out the immense project very meticulously. In 2015, the Flemish Lieven Bertels took up the post of CEO and artistic director, his domestic and international experience with the Sydney Festival and Holland Festival being a real asset. A Club 2018 has been set up, which at least 300 SMEs have joined at a fee of 2018 euros. Some major sponsors have been found, such as the ING Bank and the Leeuwarden Entrepreneur Fund, though the intended budget of 65 million has not yet been amassed. The provincial authorities set up an Iepen Mienskip Fund that honours the best local initiatives with a grant of 2018 euros. The producers wrote business plans to get a realistic view of the feasibility of their projects. Some of the projects in the bid book were dropped because they were too expensive (e.g. *Floating Future*, a spa island in Frisian waterways) or too excessive (*Romantic Painters from the North* at the Fries Museum, which was already organising major exhibitions of such Frisian icons as Alma-Tadema, Mata Hari and Maurits Escher). Some new ones were added, such as *Escape*, a virtual tunnel with physical entrances in Leeuwarden and Valetta, the other European Capital of Culture in 2018. In March 2016, Lieven Bertels gave the green light to the majority of the 41 projects in the bid book. So the party could get started.

What will the domestic and international visitor encounter in Leeuwarden and Friesland in 2018? A lot! I'll give just a few examples. On the square in front of the Oldehove, Leeuwarden's Tower of Pisa, a remarkable *Lân fan Taal* is being built, an 'experience centre' for language diversity. The time-honoured *Oerol* Festival on the island of Terschelling is being expanded under the title *Sense of Place*, a large-scale landscape project with a Mondrian salt marsh in the Wadden area. In the *Grote Kerk*, the producer Jos Thie is setting up a performance with stories of 750 Frisian and foreign churches, called *Under de Toer*. The internationally renowned felt artist Claudy Jongstra, whose tapestries can be seen in the MoMA and who has dressed Lady Gaga and Madonna, among others, is turning her farm in Friesland into a *Farm of the World*. For the towns on the *Eleven Cities Skating Tour*, eleven artists have designed an artwork-with-water, called *Eleven Fountains*, among them the Frenchman Jean-Michel Otoniel (Franeker), the Spaniard Jaume Plensa (Leeuwarden) and the Fleming Johan Creten (Bolsward). For *Potatoes Go Wild*, seed-potatoes from Friesland will be sent to Malta with Frisian poems, and in March will return as mature Malta potatoes with Maltese poems. There is the literary project *The Sea! The Sea!*, co-produced by the Flemish foundation *Behoud de Begeerte*. International dance and theatre productions will be shown under the heading *Strangers on Stage*, a Polish-Dutch theatre company will perform *Lost in the Greenhouse*, a play with music, in the vegetable glasshouses of St.-Annaparochie, Opera Spanga is producing *Aida* in the open air in both Spanga and Valletta, thousands of sportspeople will be coming to the European Sports for All Games (traditional sports) in Friesland, and so on.

Let this much be clear: Leeuwarden-Fryslân 2018 will be a great European cultural feast. You have to be there!

RUDI WESTER
Translated by Gregory Ball

www.2018.nl

Film

Longing for Perfection
The Red Turtle by Michael Dudok de Wit

The life of Michael Dudok de Wit (b. 1953) was changed by a digital message from Japan. In 2007, the Dutch animator received a surprising e-mail from Studio Ghibli, the renowned Japanese animation studio responsible for such hand-drawn masterpieces as *Grave of the Fireflies* (1988) and *Spirited Away* (2001). It contained two questions: 'Your short film *Father and Daughter* is marvellous; do you have a distributor in Japan?' and 'Would you make a full-length film for us?'

Dudok de Wit, who had grown up in Laren in North Holland, studied animation in Switzerland and England and has for a long time lived in London, had never previously made a long animated film. And what's more, in interviews he had always said he never wanted to make one. But the offer from Japan could simply not be refused. At the animated film festival in Annecy he once said: 'It took me two months to get over it. I just couldn't believe it'.

However, it took another nine years after that first mail in 2007, two and a half spent in production, before the end product of this collaboration finally saw the light of day in May 2016. One of the reasons for this was Dudok de Wit's extreme perfectionism. In the documentary *The Longing of Michael Dudok de Wit* (2016),[1] which keeps track of him during the production of the film, he talks about this: 'I cannot

Michael Dudok de Wit, still from *The Red Turtle*, 2016

accept that something is finished. I go home every day with the feeling that I haven't done well enough. I work towards an ideal, though I know I can never achieve it.' However, the final result turns out to be well worth the wait: the film, called *The Red Turtle*, is an extraordinarily beautiful, philosophical and completely wordless fairy tale about a castaway washed ashore on an uninhabited tropical island. This nameless man desperately builds one raft after another, but each time he thinks he is about to escape he is thrown back into the sea by a mysterious red turtle.

The premiere of *The Red Turtle* was at the Cannes Film Festival, where it was awarded a special prize called *Un Certain Regard*. The international press also showered it with praise. *The Telegraph*, for example, called it 'a compassionate, wistfully beautiful film'. And then, in its first five days in Dutch cinemas, it drew ten thousand viewers; a record for a Ghibli film and exceptional for an animated film for adults.

Dudok de Wit, already one of the Netherlands' leading film artists for several decades, although he is little known among the general public, more than deserves this success. This feeling increases even more when one watches the abovementioned documentary. It is almost endearing to see Dudok de Wit at work in the film. For example, when he goes out on his own to study and film the surf, and then when he is viewing the images he shot, and becomes completely absorbed in how marvellous the shadow at the edge of the water is. One of the French members of his team actually describes him as 'a big child, always with his head in the clouds'.

Dudok de Wit is always looking for beauty in details. In an interview he called it 'adding a personal poetry'. 'Starting with a realistically stylised controlled movement, I add a personal signature. That is the secret of animation.'

Dudok de Wit's signature is clear to see in *The Red Turtle*. It is especially the elegance of the movements that is striking – of the animals and people, but also of the clouds and the water – and the simplicity with which it is conjured up on the screen. In *The Longing of Michael Dudok de Wit*, a Spanish animator says: 'Michael takes a very minimalist approach. He can set down the essence of what he wants to express in just a couple of perfectly drawn lines. He looks for the essence of things. But it is very hard to arrive at this essence'.

You also see this combination of simplicity and elegance in his earlier, much rougher and sometimes almost abstract short films. But *The Red Turtle* is also related to the rest of Dudok de Wit's oeuvre in terms of its theme: longing is the thread that runs through his work. For example, his Oscar-nominated short film *The Monk and the Fish* (1994), a droll comedy in watercolour style, tells of a monk who obsessively pursues a fish. Until he finally learns how to live in harmony with the creature. The Oscar-winning *Father and Daughter* (2000), until recently his best-known work, also has many points in common with *The Red Turtle*. In this eight-minute minimalist masterpiece, a daughter returns again and again to the place where she last saw her father sailing on the sea. She herself grows up, the seasons change, she grows old. And still she continues to stare hopefully at the horizon, just like the castaway in *The Red Turtle*.

Where does Dudok de Wit's fascination with the theme of longing come from? He called it 'a beautiful pain' in the same interview: 'Alongside love, I find deep longing, even though it sometimes hurts, the finest feeling you can experience'. And in this interview, regarding the inspiration for *The Red Turtle*, he says: 'I was very happy with my girlfriend, now my wife, and with my work. And yet I was aware I was looking for something else'.

But at that time he didn't know exactly what he was looking for. In the same way as it never becomes entirely clear what the man in *The Red Turtle* longs for so much. But it may be Dudok de Wit's pursuit of the ultimate beauty, combined with his perfectionism, that made him so restless. In another interview, with striking frankness, he said that 'it is a longing that every artist experiences, the longing for the ultimate beauty. But this longing has another side to it. From an early age I was very susceptible to... I don't want to call them depressions... they are more like periods when I don't feel the passion for life very strongly. What presents itself is a sense of emptiness.'

The Red Turtle is the ultimate depiction of this emptiness. And as far as the ultimate beauty is concerned, Dudok de Wit will probably feel that he didn't quite succeed in his first full-length animated film. After all, as far as he is concerned, it is an ideal he will never be able to attain. But in *The Red Turtle* he certainly came very close.

JELLE SCHOT
Translated by Gregory Ball

1   Available online at:
    www.vpro.nl/programmas/2doc/2016/het-verlangen-van-
    michael-dudok-de-wit.html

Breaking Free from Expected Patterns
Fien Troch

With *Home*, only her fourth feature film, Fien Troch (b. 1978) hit the headlines both nationally and internationally. The Film Fest Gent awarded her both the Grand Prix and the Audience Award, while famous festivals such as Venice and Toronto praised Troch for her strong author's vision. It is clear that the Flemish film-maker stands on the cusp of a definitive break-through, thanks to her stubbornness, persistence and individuality, and the determination with which she demands attention, not for herself but for her films.

Someone Else's Happiness (2005), *Unspoken* (2008), *Kid* (2012) and *Home* (2016) tell differing tales but have things in common. Troch always narrates from the general situation or the emotions and not from the story line. A second constant is the fact that drama is intertwined with communication problems. 'When I'm writing I always feel intuitively more challenged by what remains unexpressed than by what is actually said', says Troch, 'while apparently idiotic utterings always tell me more about characters than fluent dialogues.' The daughter of film editor Ludo Troch learned a love of film at her father's knee, yet on her eighteenth birthday she didn't know what she really wanted to do in life. She thought of being an actress, but when she wasn't accepted for the training she went to the Sint Lukas Art Academy in Brussels – simply because she wanted to do something connected with the arts. It was during her studies there that she discovered her passion for film, thanks to her short films *Verbrande aarde* (Burnt Earth, 1998) and *Wooww* (1999). After graduation more short films followed (*Maria*, *Cool Sam & Sweet Suzie*), but Troch didn't feel inclined to spend years continuing with such finger exercises. And she was even less inclined to get trapped in the golden cage of advertising films, although these won her prizes and provided a good income.

What took precedence was that first feature film. Irrespective of the budget. For Troch it was about the artistic freedom that fiction films need. For her film is an art form: not a vehicle for telling a tale, but an end in its own right. Her debut, *Someone Else's Happiness*, is a mosaic of a film that follows twenty or so characters and shows how a village is dislocated by a mysterious fatal accident. The driver in question remains outside the frame; by means of the reactions to the drama Troch probes the *zeitgeist* and the malaise in society. The orphaned children and the narcissistic parents reflect a countryside characterised by loneliness. The result is an atmosphere film that brings subdued emotions to life with limited dialogue.

The somewhat detached approach is exchanged for intense involvement in *Unspoken*. This muted double portrait of a married couple who have swallowed their grief for their fourteen-year-old daughter who has disappeared without trace, attempts not to unveil the mystery but to examine how those who are left behind behave towards each other. Grief and pain are not expressed but come to life via silent, claustrophobic images. Loneliness, powerlessness and isolation have a stifling effect on the protagonists and that feeling is underlined by

Fien Troch

extreme close-ups, symbolically charged images and long silences broken by moving rejoinders. Troch avoids sentimentalism and obliges the observer to seek out the emotions for him or herself.

Empathy and identification are verbs for her; pleasure entails an effort. Film may, actually must, make people squirm. It's good that afterwards the audience feel confused, rebellious or sad. It is in this spirit that in *Kid* the world is seen through the eyes of two brothers – a seven-year-old rascal and his two-year-older good brother – who don't always understand everything. The absent father, the mother who is beset by creditors, the moribund farmstead; the what and the why of everything remains vague. The only clear thing is that the happy child is being forced to grow up.

Whereas her first three films formed a triptych around children, in *Home* Troch focusses on young adults. Including the generation gap: young and old live in their own, non-communicating worlds. At the centre is a seventeen-year-old, wrestling with his own identity, who has spent a period in a closed institution and is now hoping to find a new home with his aunt. But the unhealthy home situation of a new friend brings out both the best (friendship, loyalty) and the worst (betrayal, violence) in him. By opting for a not quite square 4:3 ratio image format, Troch creates a claustrophobic universe while the intertwinement of smartphone images, home movies and observational shots cause the generations to clash visually as well. *Home* is in a more narrative mode than Troch's earlier films; it is also an illustration where the hormones go berserk more, run in a documentary, realistic film style.

This film-author's cinema remains driven more by emotion than plot. 'I want to uncouple myself from what's in common use and research how I can give cinema something extra, via music, image and narrative style', states Troch, 'I want to free myself from expected patterns. Because cinema is an art form I don't have to be bound by conventions. I would love to make films for 500,000 viewers, but if it means settling for a compromise, then no.' Fien Troch is quietly and resolutely following the path to an original, lively and individual output.

IVO DE KOCK
Translated by Sheila M. Dale

History

Before She Became Mata Hari
Newly Discovered Letters by Margaretha Zelle

The letters and photographs published in this beautiful new book cover the last two years in the life of Margaretha Zelle (1876-1917) before she left the Netherlands and began a new life in Paris, becoming famous the world over from 1905 as the oriental dancer Mata Hari, *femme fatale* and female spy during the Great War.

Written between 1902 and 1904, these newly discovered letters were unknown to Pat Shipman when she published her biography of Mata Hari, *Femme Fatale: Love, Lies and the Unknown Life of Mata Hari* in 2007. They had been lying, forgotten for more than a century, in an attic chest belonging to her in-laws, whose help she was seeking during difficult divorce proceedings against her husband, Rudolph (John) MacLeod.

It is her own story, in her own words - the often heart-breaking tale of her bad marriage, aged eighteen, to a much older, authoritarian bully of a man, a colonial officer in the Dutch East Indies, a jealous, violent and syphilitic domestic tyrant, whose abuse and control, accusations and spying eventually became unbearable and led to their separation. Though he was an officer, he certainly was no gentleman: he refused to pay the alimony that was her due, and drove her to despair by taking away her little daughter, Nonnie. The courts were unable to intervene and to force him to pay up. So all the cards were stacked against her: separated, she still was a totally dependent woman, on a slow but inexorable trajectory to debt, destitution, despair, illicit liaisons and social exclusion.

The painful story in these letters, of her social downfall in Dutch society around 1900, reminds one of the bleak and bitter naturalistic novels in Dutch literature of the period, by Arnold Aletrino and Herman Heijermans; but equally of the autobiographies of her female contemporaries, the first woman doctor of the Netherlands, Aletta Jacobs, and the Dutch-French-Belgian writer Neel Doff. As *documents humains* Zelle's letters fill an important gap in our knowledge of the life of Mata Hari, and will benefit her new biography by Jessica Voeten and Angela Dekker, which is due out in 2017.

Nonetheless, in these letters we also see how Margaretha Zelle went in search of a new future. Deciding to emigrate, she never looked back and started a new life on her own terms, a resilient, nomadic life of an imaginative kind, reinventing herself as a totally new *persona* - an exotic oriental dancer, a star of immense charm and eroticism, scoring triumph after triumph, right up to the First World War, as a star of the theatre, dancing in theatres all around Europe - projecting a beguilingly seductive image wherever she performed, in the Musée Guimet, the Trocadéro and the Folies Bergère in Paris, La Scala in Milan, the Metropol theatre in Berlin, and the Apollo theatre in Vienna, leading a life of glamour and luxury in the capitals of Europe, having scores of admirers and lovers everywhere. And yes - in all those countries, she did have a thing for members of the officer class.

In the end, though, as she was flitting from one officer in one European country to others in different countries, the Great War caught up with her, and she had to pay the ultimate price. Sentenced for espionage and high treason, she was executed, aged forty-one, by a French firing squad, at dawn on 15 October 1917 in the Bois de Vincennes.

Today, in her native Leeuwarden (which she left aged fifteen), there is not much that reminds one of her. And looking back from today, it is almost impossible to understand how she ever managed to conjure up this new and exotic image as a Javanese princess, embodying the height of European orientalist fantasy - especially when the photographs in this new book show her so very clearly as a solid Frisian woman from the north of the Netherlands.

She really did make the most of it - in the performance of her second life as Mata Hari, and living on ever after, through countless pictures, paintings, sculptures, musicals, opera, novels, and films, as an icon and a byword for *femme fatale* and female spy.

REINIER SALVERDA

Don't Think That I'm Bad - Margaretha Zelle Before Mata Hari / Denk niet dat ik slecht ben - Margaretha Zelle vóór Mata Hari, bilingual edition by Lourens Oldersma, Bornmeer - Tresoar, Gorredijk - Leeuwarden, 2016, 215 pp.

Mata Hari (1876-1917). Photo taken by the Amsterdam Studio Merkelbach in 1915

'The Only Friend of the Indians'
Restoring the Reputation of Father Pieter-Jan De Smet

On 4 December 2016, outgoing US President Barack Obama ordered work to stop on the Dakota Access Pipeline. For months, environmental activists and members of the Lakota people of the Sioux Nation in North Dakota had been protesting against the laying of this pipeline. In their protests they invoked a treaty signed by the Lakota and neighbouring Native American tribes with the US government in 1851, which grants the region crossed by the pipeline to the Lakota. This treaty also had a Belgian flavour, as one of the negotiators was the Belgian missionary Pieter-Jan De Smet (1801-1873).

De Smet (sometimes referred to in Dutch as *Grote Zwartrok* (Great Blackrobe)), was in the news in 2016 when the Museum aan de Stroom (MAS) in Antwerp and the Catholic Documentation and Research Centre in Leuven joined with the provincial executive of Oost-Vlaanderen to organise an exhibition dedicated to him (*The Call of the Rockies*) in the Caermersklooster cultural centre in Ghent. The exhibition reawakened the debate about Father De Smet, the missionaries who went to 'Christianise' America in the nineteenth century and the question of whether they were accomplices of the colonising whites, or 'protectors' of the indigenous peoples.

The controversy surrounding De Smet also coincided with the wave of paedophile scandals that has come to light in recent years. Priests and nuns in the United States, too, committed assaults on innocent (often indigenous) children. The Catholic Church has already paid out 3 billion US dollars in damages to abused children or their descendants. And although no accusations were made against De Smet himself, his status as 'friend of the Indians' was severely damaged. In May 2015, the (Jesuit) Saint Louis University removed a statue of De Smet because it was felt to be too paternalistic.

In the 1970s, Native American activists and publicists such as Vine Deloria Jr. were fiercely critical of missionaries like De Smet, arguing that they had 'facilitated' the suppression of the Indian nations.

What is certain is that De Smet left for the US in 1821 full of good intentions. His family, part of the wealthy bourgeois society in the Flemish town of Dendermonde, had hoped that he would become a priest in his own country, but the stories of Father Karel Nerinckx set his head reeling. Nerinckx was the first Catholic to be ordained as a priest in the US. He was keen to introduce the old 'reductions', founded by the Jesuits in Paraguay but disbanded at the end of the eighteenth century, into the United States. These reductions were independent Native American states which even had their own armies.

Nerinckx and De Smet believed that they could bring together the Indians in a large area to the west of the Mississippi. Here, they would spend two generations separated from the (negative) white influence and, under the supervision of missionaries, would learn how they needed to become a sedentary people (and Catholic, of course). Thereafter, the area would acquire full status as a US State.

De Smet's plan took shape in the period 1840-1860, when he established a whole series of missionary posts in Montana. For a long time it looked as though his experiment would succeed. Then came the discovery of gold in the area, and the whole dream collapsed like a house of cards. Gold prospectors and other colonists flooded onto the prairie, prompting the Indians to take up arms. Initially they were highly successful, and America accepted treaties that were fairly favourable (for the Indians). For example, the 1851 and 1868 Treaties of Fort Laramie stipulated that large tracts to the west of the Missouri could remain in the hands of the prairie tribes.

In 1868, De Smet travelled to meet the legendary Lakota leader Sitting Bull to persuade him to accept a second treaty. Sitting Bull did not sign himself, but he had so much faith in De Smet ('the only friend of the Indians') that he allowed his lieutenant to sign the treaty, rendering it binding.

Sitting Bull understood that De Smet was right when he warned the Indians about the determination of the American government. They either had to accept the treaties or they would be wiped out. An offensive by the American army which began in 1876 quickly made this clear. Following their initial victory at the Battle of Little Bighorn, the prairie tribes were eliminated one by one. De Smet had been dead for three years by this point. The Indians were driven together on small reservations which were but a fraction of the size of the Great Sioux Reservation that was established under the 1851 treaty.

Viewed through a modern lens, it is all too easy to dismiss missionaries like De Smet as paternalistic white religious zealots who regarded the Indians as inferior heathens. The Jesuits made a sincere attempt to set up an 'Indian state' in the United States, and when that attempt failed, they opted for a strategy of damage limitation. Any other choice would have been criminal.

Critics should ask themselves whether the Indians – who still defend their rights with great vigour – would stand any chance today if their forefathers (such as Sitting Bull) had not signed the treaties. Those treaties between the Indians and the US government are legally valid and enforceable in the courts. They have proved to be a thorn in the flesh for many US politicians – including Donald Trump – because, while the reservations may be unsuitable as farmland, they are chock-full of valuable commodities such as uranium and petroleum. The centuries-old hunting and fishing rights can also not simply be swept aside.

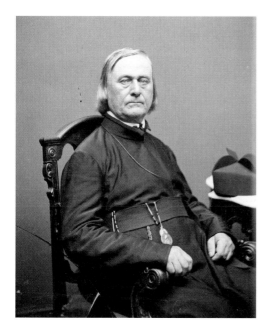

Father Pieter-Jan De Smet (1801-1873),
Library of Congress Prints and Photographs Division –
Brady-Handy Photograph Collection

Father De Smet was a man of his time. Was he a paternalist who regarded the Indians as small children? Undoubtedly. Was he a warmonger who wanted to assimilate the Indian peoples? Absolutely not; he respected their culture and their history too much for that. The fact that he was ultimately forced to watch on with chagrin as the American government shamelessly infringed all the treaties, caused him sorrow to his dying day. The fact that the descendants of Sitting Bull have today achieved an historic victory in North Dakota against the American government is however a posthumous feather in De Smet's cap.

KARL VAN DEN BROECK
Translated by Julian Ross

The author of this article published a book in 2016 entitled *Waarom ik de indianen wil redden - Op zoek naar het kruis van Sitting Bull* (Why I Want to Save the Indians. In Search of the Crucifix of Sitting Bull), Polis, Antwerp.

Language

500 Years Old
The 'Collegium Trilingue' in Leuven

Canon Hieronymus Busleyden (ca. 1470-1517), member of the Great Council of Mechelen, played host at his Mechelen residence to visits from Erasmus, Thomas More and Adriaan Boeyens, later Pope Adrianus VI. When the humanist and patron Busleyden died in 1517, he left enough money to enable an idea cherished by Erasmus finally to be turned into a reality: the founding of a school in Leuven dedicated to the study of the three classical languages Hebrew, Greek and Latin, in accordance with the philological principles of the humanists. Erasmus had published his first critical edition of the New Testament in Greek in 1516, and more importantly had produced a Latin translation which made many corrections to the 'sacred' translation by the fourth-century church father Jerome (the well-known Vulgate edition). His edition, however imperfect, marks the beginning of the scientific approach to Bible texts.

The *Collegium Trilingue* or *Collegium trium linguarum* was the first of its kind in Europe. Leuven University, and in particular the conservative Faculty of Theology and the Artes faculty, which was afraid of losing students, initially regarded the Collegium with distrust. It was not until 1519 that the Collegium, founded by will in 1517, and officially launching its teaching programme in 1518, was formally recognised by the university as a full-status institution.

Erasmus did not teach at the Collegium himself, but did recruit the best teachers and was the driving force behind the institution. A meagre remnant of the original buildings can still be seen on Busleidengang, a short alleyway leading off the Vismarkt in Leuven. King Francis I of France took inspiration from the Leuven Collegium when founding the *Collège Royal* (now the *Collège de France*) in Paris in 1530. He tried to attract Erasmus, but his invitation was turned down.

The Collegium quickly became a success. Renowned alumni included the anatomist Vesalius, the botanist Clusius, the philologist and humanist Justus Lipsius and the diplomat Ogier Ghiselin de Busbecq.

In one of his last letters from Basel (28 June 1536) to his great ally in Leuven and a teacher of Latin at the Collegium, Conrad Goclenius, Erasmus wrote about his nostalgia for Brabant, saying that this was where he would like to end his life. At this time he was still involved with his brainchild, the Collegium, where there was a problem with the Professor of Greek: Rutgerus Rescius.

He had been appointed in 1518 at a young age (around the age of 21!), and received a modest stipend in view of his limited teaching experience. Initially, as was expected of the teachers, he lived in the Trilingue. He married in around 1525 and started a large family. That prompted him to look around for additional income and to move with his family to live outside the college, thereby somewhat neglecting the Collegium. This academic neglect appeared to increase when, following the retirement of the printer Dirk Martens, he set up his own printing press in Leuven which he used mainly to print Greek works (he had lived in Dirk Martens's house in Leuven between 1515 and 1518 and assisted him with his Greek printing). The final straw came when he began giving Greek lessons in the Trilingue based on a Greek work that he himself had printed (with the obvious intention of driving up his income). This led to conflict with the Faculty of Law, which naturally claimed this work for itself.

Erasmus had welcomed the appointment of Rescius at the Trilingue, though he had opined that it might have been better to appoint someone who was a little older and with a greater reputation as a Hellenist. Erasmus had also supported Rescius later, after the latter's marriage. Gradually, however, he began to see that it was not good for the Trilingue that Rescius had been allowed to live outside the college with his family.

In his letter, Erasmus criticises the fact that Rescius uses second-rate Greek literature in his teaching. He was obviously aware that Rescius was thinking of his own profit and was in danger of sparking conflicts with the Law Faculty. Put somewhat dramatically, in doing so he was effectively destroying the Collegium.

The Collegium was not destroyed, however. It did not disappear until 1797, together with the other university colleges, when the French occupiers abolished the Catholic University of Leuven and declared its possessions forfeit.

After a gap of almost twenty years, in 1817 King William I of the Netherlands opened what was intended as a neutral state university in Leuven. At the initiative of the Belgian bishops, this institution was once again replaced in 1834 by a Catholic university. But the Collegium did not return. As an alumnus of Leuven University who studied Latin and Greek there and was taught by the great neo-Latinist Jozef IJsewijn, I wonder if it would not be a good idea to reinstate the Collegium, bringing the teaching of Latin, Greek and Hebrew back under one roof and perhaps giving these three classical languages new impetus. The shining past is still there; it could be used as a springboard for the future.

LUC DEVOLDERE
Translated by Julian Ross

Erasmus's edition of the New Testament in Greek and Latin, Basel, 1516
© Library of the Great Seminary of Bruges

Literature

Occupied City
Paul van Ostaijen on the Map of Modernism

There are some literary works written in Dutch without which the narrative of literature in Europe is incomplete. *Occupied City* by the Flemish poet Paul van Ostaijen (1896-1928) is one of them. None of the standard textbooks on modernism in European literature that I consulted[1] even mention Van Ostaijen despite the existence of anthologies of both his poetry, *The First Book of Schmoll*, and his prose, *Patriotism, Inc. and Other Tales*, in English translation. It is to be hoped that *Occupied City* in David Colmer's lively and engrossing translation will be the work to change this.

First published in 1921, *Occupied City* is a collection of poems tracking and evoking the German occupation of Antwerp during the First World War. The titles of these poems – such as 'Threatened City', 'Hollow Harbour', 'Dead Sunday', 'City of Grief', 'Music Hall', 'The Withdrawal' – give a sense of the evolving situation and shifting mood in Antwerp as seen through the poet's eyes, but not a hint as to the avant-garde character of the poems. Experimental in form, *Occupied City* is described on the back cover of the translation as 'one of the key works of the Dadaist movement' and as 'a work of "rhythmical typology"'. At the same time, many commentators see *Occupied City* as representing the loss of Van Ostaijen's earlier humanitarian ideals. It certainly depicts the many modes of human suffering involved in life under occupation.

As a twenty-first-century reader, I am struck by the distinctive multiplicity of Van Ostaijen's poetic voice. Take, for instance, its seemingly natural multilingualism or the fact that the word 'nihil' occurs thirteen times in almost as many typefaces and different layouts. He has dispensed with recognizable poetic form and diction, exchanging it for an extreme dynamic which is as visual as it is textual. The opening section sets the scene with its emphasis on film – 'Much shall be forgiven you / for / you've seen a lot of movies'. God the Father as impresario and Archangel Michael as director have reached the end of their dominion: 'all cathedrals / all prophets / all pulpits / struck dumb'.[2] The poet wants to take over, staging a burlesque performance. And in a way, the all-singing, all-dancing presentation of words on the page in the poems does just that.

Although the poems that follow the dedicatory section 'To Mr Soandso' narrate destruction, fear, looting, 'corpses strewn around the city', and 'Fleeing tykes / fleeing people / Fleeing army / the 3 ages flee', and the port of Antwerp is at a standstill, this introductory poem sounds a note of hope: 'perhaps / there will be room / for a beauty that speaks for itself'. In this way, *Occupied City* reveals a different dynamic from Dadaism, one where there is a way back from nihilism. And in the context of Van Ostaijen's work, it prefigures his last phase of 'pure' poetry.

It will be clear from this description of the poems that David Colmer's translation of *Occupied City* involved a great deal more than transferring words and metre from Dutch to English. The typographical features – words forming arcs, slopes, steps and slogans; so many different fonts or typefaces; discontinuous elements and words with multiple collocators, not to mention the use of different languages – all these call for an adaptive approach, as Colmer explains in his note on the translation. Colmer and Van Ostaijen have been wonderfully served by Smokestack Books who clearly believe that if a book is worth translating, it is worth doing the job properly. The typographer Katy Mawhood brings her expertise to bear on the visual aspect of the translation, while David Colmer exercises his creativity in producing a work of modernist literature that is exciting to read, giving this reader a taste and feel of occupied Antwerp that no historical narrative can provide.

The mood of disillusionment is brilliantly evoked in 'Sous les Ponts de Paris', a more conventional-looking poem of couplets which addresses a 'You' whose corpse and wounds have been put on display:

> Our faith is so small and so weak
> like the flame that dances at your feet
>
> You are displayed on every corner HARLEQUIN
> with your beaten attitude and Your suffering
>
> Among us again in all Your statues You are one
> with the occupied city (...)
>
> We cannot see God but as a Harlequin
> our times are so full of pain and suffering

In the second poem of 'Sous les Ponts de Paris', God and Harlequin become a deserter heading into the dance hall. This is where forgetfulness is found, in the music hall, the cinema, the bar, the dance hall, and in desire, passion or love.

Occupied City ends with the withdrawal of the German occupiers and a frenzy of celebration. The line 'everything is meaningless / now' leads not to despair but to a sense of energy and surging life, though we are left wondering where this will lead: 'maybe some day / the need will grow so great / all the dykes will break'.

JANE FENOULHET

Paul van Ostaijen, *Occupied City*, translated from the Dutch by David Colmer, Smokestack Books, Ripon, 2016.

1   For instance, M. Bradbury & J. McFarlane, *Modernism: A Guide to European Literature 1890-1930*, Harmondsworth, 1991 or P. Lewis (Ed.), *The Cambridge Companion to European Modernism*, Cambridge, 2011.

2   The spaces are part of the printed poem. Note that the absence of page references is due to the lack of pagination of *Occupied City*, a choice which is in keeping with the typographical experimentation of the text.

Start Early and Keep Going
Flanders and the Netherlands at the Frankfurt Book Fair

It sounds simple. Every year some 150,000 people in the book business travel from all over the world to the Frankfurt Book Fair. Suddenly the country or language area that can promote its literature as *Ehrengast* is on the map. But in fact it's not so simple. All these book people are in Frankfurt to work. Day in day out they run from one appointment to the next. They know there is a country that is Guest of Honour, but which is it? By no means can every regular fair visitor still remember that a few months after the *Buchmesse*.

When the Netherlands and Flanders were Guests of Honour in October 2016, the organisers had a hard job to stand out. Just sending a trainload of the new generation of writers – from Joost de Vries and Niña Weijers to Bregje Hofstede and Charlotte Van den Broek – to the capital of the book world is not enough to get them translated into the most important world languages. Let alone sticking posters on all the buses and trams in Frankfurt for a few days, as previous Guest of Honour countries had been known to do.

So Team Frankfurt, the joint project committee of the Dutch Foundation for Literature and the Flemish Literature Fund, chose not to peak just for a few days during the fair. Their Guest of Honour preparations began a long time in advance, primarily by allowing the German publishers from various disciplines to become acquainted with the Dutch publishing sector on the spot, but also by ensuring Dutch-language authors were on the programme at German festivals for an entire year. In addition, from July 2016 there was a whole bookselling campaign with author appearances and a brochure. Everyone in the *Buchmesse* homeland was already warmed up when the fair opened.

A masterstroke was the appointment of Bart Moeyaert as artistic director. This internationally renowned author, whose almost entire output has been translated into German, meant that being Guest of Honour was not just a matter of carrying out policy objectives, but that there was also a coherent vision underlying these. This was expressed in the choice (dazzling in its simplicity) of the North Sea – the sea shared by the Netherlands,

Flanders and Germany – as the underlying theme, a well-thought out design and, above all, an effective slogan.

'This is what we share' – read the Dutch-Flemish motto. That referred naturally to the common language, by means of which writers on either side of the border enrich each other through the differences in culture. Right from the opening, when very cleverly the kings of both countries (alias the heads of national marketing) made an appearance, it seemed that everyone adopted the phrase as the essence of what happens in Frankfurt: the handling of translation rights, by means of which everyone all over the world can share each other's power of ideas and imagination. So the Netherlands and Flanders became the talking point of the fair almost automatically.

Of course the big question is what being Guest of Honour has achieved. That's not easy to measure. There's the number of translations that were published in German before the *Buchmesse*: 454, of which over 300 were literary translations. An unprecedentedly high number for a Guest of Honour country. There's the number of articles, reports and reviews of the translated works in the world media. The number of German-language pieces alone that appeared online topped six thousand, according to the proud press release from the literature foundations afterwards.

But what do these statistics tell us about the impact of being Guest of Honour country? The traffic in Dutch literature can seem to be a huge flash in the pan. The German publishers of all these newly discovered writers may stop after a single translation, on account of poor sales figures or lack of recognition on the part of critics. And publishers in other languages, who have to be tempted by the Guest of Honour status, together with all these *Neuerscheiningen*, to taste what the new generation from Flanders and the Netherlands have to offer, may be disappointed and lose interest. In that case being Guest of Honour has been a failure.

Only time will tell. The first signs are favourable. Immediately after the fair, the literature foundations reported good sales results for a few titles. 8,000 copies of *Boy*, by Wytske Versteeg, had been sold in Germany, 35,000 copies of *Die Eismacher* by Ernest van der Kwast, and Joost Zwagerman's *Duell* was into a third impression, which meant the

Photo D. Van Assche

publisher wanted to translate his *Gimmick!* as well. New deals had also been struck. Milkweed Editions is bringing out an anthology of Dutch-language poetry in English and the Kalachuvadu publishing house one in Tamil.

Fine. But these are no more than first steps – no more striking than the good news the literature foundations always send out to the world after this sort of fair. So it's heartening that the Dutch and Flemish organisations have thought about the aftermath of being Guest of Honour. That's why the campaign ran all through the autumn and there's now a deliberate translation and presentation policy for the French- and English-language areas.

MAARTEN DESSING
Translated by Sheila M. Dale

An Ingenious 'Exercice de Style'
The Evenings by Gerard Reve

It is astonishing that we have had to wait till 2016 for an English translation of Gerard Reve's famous 1947 debut novel, *The Evenings*. For not only does it, and very characteristically, mark the beginning of a literary career that blended critical admiration, moral controversy and popularity in about equal, and sometimes fused, proportions, it is itself a work of palpable originality, with a distinctive atmosphere which caught the mood of a whole generation – and spoke to its successors. Its governing idea is one of impressive, galvanising simplicity. Opening on 22nd December 1946 it follows its protagonist, twenty-three-year-old Frits van Egters, through each day (with its dream-troubled attendant nights) until New Year's Eve gives way to New Year's Day 1947. The back-end of the year is dominated by colourlessness and cold. Businesses (like that which employs Frits as a clerk) are shut more often than open, and people try to cheer themselves up from the fogginess outside by forced sociability indoors – with only partial success: the aging parents with whom Frits lives run their home rather ineptly. These are circumstances to strike chords with most readers and are rendered here with a multitude of convincing details. But the author is also intent on making us perceive the strange, the inexplicable lurking behind drab familiarity.

This Pushkin edition of Reve's now classic work has been given a deserved welcome by an Anglophone public. Sam Garrett's translation flows wonderfully well. Told as the novel mostly is through dialogue (including Frits's many, mostly cynical, asides to himself) he has rendered the speech in spot-on idiom, neither too redolent of the 1940s nor of our twenty-first century. And the book's appearance is handsome, with its cover illustration by Bill Bragg of an appropriately uncompromising urban milieu, and plaudits by such eminent writers as Lydia Davis. Yet how to best read the novel presents some tough challenges. 1946 is history, we should adapt to it. But in addition, there is a problem of hindsight. Most readers with knowledge of Dutch culture will know how Reve (1923-2006) – never averse to limelight – spectacularly developed.

The people we meet, the never-named town they live in and which we get to know through numerous topographical specificities, were living with war and occupation as norms until a mere nineteen months before the novel begins. But they do not discuss this past, and only occasionally is it referred to, and that obliquely, as in the matter of Frits's broken Gymnasium education. In the present Austerity rules; everyone takes that for granted. Frits and his parents have their electricity by courtesy of a metre, and sometimes it goes off and they have to scrabble for the redeeming voucher. Heating a house adequately, providing a large or satisfying meal – these are not easy. The texture of

Gerard Reve in 1950 © Hollandse Hoogte

life that Reve's novel weaves would have been one known to all the first readers. If we of today wonder about the absence of reflections on past occurrences or of speculations about a brighter future, then attention to the text puts us in our place. This, we appreciate, is how ordinary people react; they turn imposed circumstances into normality. Reve brings his stranded society to life with infectious vividness. It is only fitting that the Netherlands rewarded him with their gratitude.

Such stark conditions beget mental attitudes, private hopes and fears. The spiritual climate of *The Evenings* is as engulfing as the physical. Frits and his friends – and his brother Joop – are infused by the kind of jocular irony, the rejection of sensitivity and seriousness, the refusal to appear defeated but, instead, the wish to greet the world with mocking faces and words (jokes, taunts, shocking stories), to which, we feel, a majority of young males might have recourse in any like situation. Frits is stuck in a dead-end job, of which we hear no memorable particulars; not for nothing is the novel named *The Evenings* since this is when he and his mates come to anything at all resembling life, however much the eponymous hours drag, however much their attempts to override the prevalent dullness is offset by disturbing dreams which don't spare victims horrible examples of *memento mori*.

Our historical sense tells us that during the recent war these young men (for the two young women do not leaven the book's dominance by males) must have heard of and even seen cruelties greater than those that fill their talk. For if Frits is the usual instigator of the many lurid anecdotes of sadism and suffering that fill this otherwise eventless book, he unfailingly finds an apt audience and lively conversational returns. Surely these exchanges are essentially a form of accommodating – in surreally humorous forms – unbearable experiences only lately endured by known real people? But hindsight makes us baulk at this explanation.

To give one example among many. Frits amuses his friend Louis by telling him of a father who tosses his eighteen-month-old child in the air, and accidentally lets it drop to its death while the mother in the bathroom inadvertently lets their other child drown. '"Didn't you tell me that one before?" "No," Frits replied, "you're confusing it with the one about the father who picked up his children by the head...." "Yes, yes," Louis said, "but this one is also very good. Wonderful stuff."'

And then one remembers how in life and in letters Reve was addicted to the sadomasochistic, how his triumphant ascent into fame was accomplished by relentless provocative self-advertisement, and one begins to suspect that Frits – forever teasing all his friends about their (incipient) baldness, and deriding his parents as they boringly stumble about their limitedly resourced home – is not so much a sympathetic representative of a bemused, deprived generation as an analogue for the author's own compulsive exhibitionism. This realisation makes us relate the novel to its times differently. Frits's impatience with ordinary movements through time and space and with the passing of the hours takes us to the newly fashionable French Existentialists' insistence on the absurdity of life. Soon it will lead to such exposures of the banalities of bourgeois quotidian living as Ionesco's Absurdist play *The Bald Prima Donna* (1949/1950).

Approached in this way *The Evenings*, for all its glimpses of an actual past, becomes above all an ingenious 'exercice de style'. For it to be hailed by the Society of Dutch Literature as 'the best Dutch novel of all time' is quite inappropriate. Have the judges forgotten Couperus's *Eline Vere*, Hella Haasse's *The Tea Lords*... ? The list is long.

PAUL BINDING

Gerard Reve, *The Evenings*, translated from the Dutch by Sam Garrett, Pushkin Press, London, 2016, 317 pp.

'Writing with Such Freshness and Agility'

A Well-Chosen Selection of Dutch Short Stories

The Penguin Book of Dutch Short Stories has a beautiful cover photo: the picture by photographer Hendrik Kerstens is an undeniably Dutch image with its references to the seventeenth-century paintings by Johannes Vermeer and Rembrandt's portraits of stately women. Kerstens's daughter Paula looks out at us with a confident stare, her pale face and white headdress contrast with the black background. What first looks like a seventeenth-century white bonnet turns out to be a plain linen napkin on her head.

I can only assume that the art-loving writer and essayist Joost Zwagerman (1963-2015) chose this image. He was the editor of this (posthumously printed) collection of beautiful short stories (Zwagerman tragically committed suicide in September 2015). In his foreword, Zwagerman discusses Dutch art versus Dutch literature. How can it be, he wonders, that Dutch art, with Rembrandt and Vermeer, 'is [so] integral to Western art history[?] Our literature likewise merits recognition as an integral part of world literary history!'

Zwagerman's selection is well chosen; the stories give a good, varied overview of Dutch literary history over, say, the last hundred years. Zwagerman's introduction, however, loses appeal because it is somewhat apologetic – as if the author himself is not so convinced the stories are worth reading. Zwagerman turns to American literary critic Harold Bloom for help, saying 'the miraculous thing about many Dutch short stories is that they combine the best of both (Chekovian and Borgesian) stories' (a genre distinction Bloom came up with). And he turns to the American editor of Dutch writer Nescio (1882-1961), explaining it often 'takes an outsider to explain to us here in the Netherlands why a particular work of art deserves its place in our national canon'. Zwagerman likes to prove his point further by quoting at length from an article in German newspaper *Die Welt*, praising the Dutch for 'writing with such freshness and agility'. I would have rather heard in Zwagerman's own words why he made the selection of short stories he has made.

There is even a tinge of *Blut und Boden* theory to the introduction, especially when Zwagerman tries to define what makes all these different stories so very 'Dutch': 'the proto-typical Dutch writer creates protagonists that are [...] contemplative arch-romantics, reserved iconoclasts'. That may be the case for Nescio's protagonist Koekebakker in *Young Titans*, who makes explicit what many other male protagonists in this collection could have said: 'The truth is we did nothing but talk, smoke, drink and read books.' But it definitely is not true for Mensje van Keulen's (b. 1946) male character in *Sand* who is raped and abused on a deserted beach, or for the female lead in Maria Dermoût's (1888-1962) story *The Sirens* who magically turns her shipmate from submissive, young man into a splendid golden tiger.

The strength of Zwagerman's choice indeed is in its variation: Manon Uphoff's story *Poop*, for instance, with its brilliant focus on social class and human cruelty, is incomparable to Remco Campert's (b. 1929) boyish display of 'party-time' in *The Kid with the Knife*.

Zwagerman's attempts to define a particular 'Dutch-ness' that would underpin all these stories contradict with his own efforts to place them in a global context. He sounds on the defence when saying, 'contrary to the old misconception that Dutch literature is inward-looking and set within our national borders, many of these stories unfold outside the Netherlands.' Ironically, he refers to Albert Alberts's (1911-1995) story *Green* as an example, which strictly speaking took place *within* national borders. *Green* is set in the Dutch East Indies (Indonesia), at the time a Dutch colony. Alberts's insightful story is a critique of Dutch colonial administration. The suicide of colonial employee Peereboom shows the violence, futility and absurdity of trying to govern people on the other side of the globe.

Green finds an interesting pendant in Frans Kellendonk's (1951-1990) *Foreign Service*, written more than thirty years later and set *within* the national borders. Kellendonk's unemployed Dutch narrator hires an illegal Egyptian cleaner. His feelings of natural entitlement towards the migrant show hierarchical power relations *post* Dutch colonialism: a very current topic.

According to Zwagerman, the Dutch language is quite different from English: 'for a child in Manchester [...] Shakespeare's writing is not nearly as

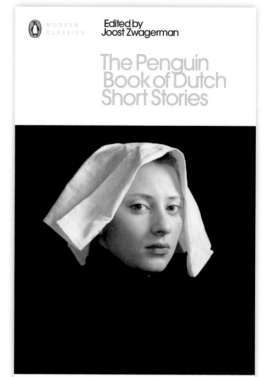

impenetrable as a book written in Hebrew'. But to Dutch readers 'eighteenth-century Dutch [...] seems almost like a foreign tongue, as exotic and indecipherable as Hindi.' This seems a far-fetched reason to explain the minor fame of Dutch literary writing. Dutch simply never was a *lingua franca*, as English is nowadays. Good stories simply need to be translated to find a global audience.

These are wonderful stories and they have been chosen well by a known name in the Dutch literary field. *The Penguin Book of Dutch Short Stories* does not necessarily need an introduction; the stories just had to be translated and put into context. And that has been done very well too.

STEFANIE VAN GEMERT

Joost Zwagerman (ed.), *The Penguin Book of Dutch Short Stories*, Modern Classics, London, 2016, 592 pp. (978 0 14 139572 2).

Media

From Weekly to Monthly
Vrij Nederland

In December 2016, the once so famous Dutch weekly magazine *Vrij Nederland* was transformed into a monthly publication, with a modernised website for more current contributions. This was a necessary move in the light of decades of steadily dwindling circulation. After reaching a peak of 120,000 in 1978, paid circulation had collapsed to 45,000 copies in 2010, before halving again over the next five years. For anyone over 50 who – to paraphrase the Dutch writer Renate Rubinstein (1929-1990) – 'used to be on the left, but has not moved to the right', that was a sobering moment; yet another confirmation that the world of their youth no longer exists.

When I became a student in Amsterdam in 1977, I took out a subscription to the *Vrij Nederland* weekly, which at the time was seen as the Valhalla of journalism and as representing the conscience of progressives in the Netherlands. I wallowed in the overblown prose of Martin van Amerongen – who by his own admission wrote mainly about old socialists, oddball vicars and dead German poets – and avidly read the interminable articles by Igor Cornelissen about the infernal arguments that had tormented the workers' movement in the past. The high point of the week was often the interview by Bibeb, who not only persuaded artists to allow a glimpse deep into their souls, but who also often tempted figures of authority to say more than they had been intending. Then there were the surprising and often provoking columns by Renate Rubinstein and Hugo Brandt Corstius, while an array of investigative journalists wrote extensively about the perfidious and underhand plans of greedy businesses, over-zealous civil servants and (right-wing) politicians. A sharp eye was also kept on international affairs, with the imperialist United States and its allies being seen as the principal villains. When the legendary cabaret duo Neerlands Hoop campaigned against Dutch participation in the 1978 World Cup in Argentina, they were given a platform in *Vrij Nederland*. The magazine had a lot to offer on the cultural front, too, as illustrated by the fact that the colour supplement, launched in 1977, dedicated its content entirely to books once a month.

I cancelled my subscription in 1986. Van Amerongen was by now editor-in-chief of the weekly magazine *De Groene Amsterdammer*, Igor Cornelissen was increasingly writing about Trotskyist philatelists or people who had shaken the hand of Willy Brandt in the 1930s, and Hugo Brandt Corstius had accused Renate Rubinstein, the daughter of a Jewish father, of 'neo-anti-Semitism'. The once so refreshing reports by Gerard van Westerloo about 'ordinary' people also seemed to me to have become fairly monotonous, while the commentary on new plans by the government of the day led by Ruud Lubbers, or about the foreign policy of the United States, had also become fairly predictable.

Looking back, it became clear that the decline of *Vrij Nederland* had already begun then. An unsavoury tribal struggle had broken out in the editorial team, in which the actions and position of star reporter and champion moonlighter Joop van Tijn were often the bone of contention. On top of that, the circulation was steadily declining; it was no longer fashionable to be 'on the left', and many baby-boomers were no longer so interested in reading about the reprehensible actions of capitalists.

Broadly speaking, the period 1965-1985 was the golden age of *Vrij Nederland*, when the magazine was regarded as the best and most important weekly publication in the Netherlands. Anyone who did not live through this period may be surprised about the moral superiority assumed by this former resistance magazine – most of the editors had experienced the Second World War as babies or toddlers. Whether the topic was a census, the policy on minorities, the debate about nature or nurture or plans to keep the welfare state affordable, the war was brought into everything. And the fact that the journalists who wrote for *Vrij Nederland* and the subscribers who read it were on the 'right side' went without saying. Sporadically, the magazine did contain criticism levelled at the ideas it espoused, for example in the form of the sociologist and political scientist Bart Tromp, who regularly lampooned the trendy left-wing ideas that were promoted in the magazine.

There is therefore no cause for too much nostalgia. During its peak years, the journalism in *Vrij Nederland* was very self-satisfied and, according to the rumours, the magazine 'floated on alcohol'. And in case anyone has forgotten: it was not just the mental hygiene that left something to be desired at that time; the same also applied for bodily care, as is apparent from a chance sentence in a report about the alternative psychiatric institution Nieuw-Dennendal, where according to the *Vrij Nederland* reporter the chaos was really not as bad as was sometimes asserted: 'In a family, too, not all the beds are always made, [...] and there's always a teenager who manages to avoid having their weekly shower.' The good old days?

ROB HARTMANS
Translated by Julian Ross

A book has recently been published on the history of *Vrij Nederland*, and specifically its glory years (1965-1985): JOHN JANSEN VAN GALEN, *De gouden jaren van het linkse levensgevoel. Het verhaal van Vrij Nederland* (The golden age of left-wing thought. The story of *Vrij Nederland*, Balans, Amsterdam, 2016, 494 pp). This publication, which draws mainly on interviews and internal communications, is not available in English.

Music

A Double Talent with a Double Personality
Jaap van Zweden

Jaap van Zweden has an illustriously unconventional career. His father was a pianist and, going by the television series dedicated to Jaap a year ago, it was abundantly clear he was 'a man of the people'. That folkish character trait was handed down from father to son, even when the son turned out to be an exceptionally talented violinist. Born in Amsterdam in 1960, by age ten he was already receiving pats on the back by such old maestros as Theo Olof, and at seventeen he won the Dutch Oskar Back Violin Competition before going to study at the Juilliard School of Music in New York. He hadn't even turned twenty when he became concertmaster of Amsterdam's Royal Concertgebouw Orchestra in 1979. Two worlds co-existed side by side – and Jaap felt it. The older, respectable orchestra members thought he was too much of a working-class lad who ought to shine his shoes more often. Not only was he soon performing the more 'received' repertoire with leading conductors, but also delving into more popular realms of classical music. He played concerts by Locatelli and Vivaldi (he did not really pay that much attention to historically informed performance), but was just as happy to perform with such musicians as Dutch flautist Berdien Sternberg (b. 1957). He was equally as fond of Gershwin arrangements as he was of Rihm and Mendelssohn. In a 1990 interview, he declared he wanted to be considered among the top fifteen living violinists in the world. And if Bernstein asks you to record his Serenade, then you are getting close.

Because of his position at the Royal Concertgebouw Orchestra, he was permanently able to work with the greatest conductors of the day. That experience awakened the desire to become a conductor himself, certainly when Bernstein once asked him to lead a rehearsal in his absence. Van Zweden was also extremely ambitious as a conductor. After several successful stints conducting various Dutch orchestras, in 1996 he became principal conductor of the Orkest van het Oosten (Netherlands Symphony Orchestra). He introduced new Dutch repertoire to the eastern part of the country along with that of such masters as Mahler and Beethoven. He set the bar high and did not hesitate being tough on orchestra members. This gradually resulted in a vast improvement in the orchestra's level of playing. That aroused interest among orchestras of greater standing. From 2000 to 2005, he was principal conductor of the Residentie Orkest (The Hague Philharmonic), followed by the Radio Philharmonic Orchestra in Hilversum and deFilharmonie (Royal Flemish Philharmonic) in Antwerp. Characteristic of his performances is the love of the grand gesture, not without pathos. The downside to this could be a certain crudeness, the upside a greater grasp of form in such long and dramatic works as Mahler's symphonies and Wagner's operas.

Van Zweden's repertoire was partly selected by the orchestra programmers. That led to him presenting a relatively higher amount of unfamiliar and new repertoire to Dutch broadcasters than with other companies. His growing number of guest performances with foreign orchestras resulted in him presenting relatively less adventurous work while at the same time raising his level of performance. The grand gesture that veered perilously close to grandstanding now vied less often with his preference for achieving quality. Being able to work more and more with orchestras of the highest quality also contributed to this. He subsequently became principal conductor of the Dallas Symphony Orchestra, the Hong Kong Symphony Orchestra, and (as of 2018) the New York Philharmonic. His growth as a conductor can clearly be heard in his recordings. In his younger years, his preference for tweaking the repertoire in the studio often clashed with his need to pull out all the stops, which often led to variable results. In the concert hall, he was increasingly able to reconcile his 'outspoken, folkish and rugged disposition' with the complexity and subtlety of his repertoire. Recent highpoints are the CDs of Wagner's *Das Rheingold* and *Die Walküre* (with the Hong Kong Symphony Orchestra), Bruckner's symphonies (with the Radio Philharmonic) and Mahler's Third Symphony (with the Dallas Symphony Orchestra). His concert schedule betrays a preference for

Jaap van Zweden

large-scale, popular classical-romantic works (since 1980 including modern Russian composers) while fortunately also allowing room for Dutch repertoire while touring abroad. Even Louis Andriessen, who avoided symphony orchestras for years, is going to compose a piece for him. He does not play the violin in public anymore.

At present, Van Zweden's double background is no longer a source of conflict, but of inspiration. As a man of this day and age he makes no bones about who he is or his biography (he is an excellent cure for the notion that classical music is solely intended for the elite). He let a television crew follow him for a year which allowed us to witness not only his occasional short-tempered outbursts during rehearsals, but also his contact with his autistic son (who now lives in a house with other autistic people set up by him and his wife). It is probably safe to say that we will never hear of any other conductor who deals not only in houses but is also cut out to make vigorous music as well as engage in the kind of intensive, direct PR that is the lifeblood of American orchestras.

EMANUEL OVERBEEKE
Translated by Scott Rollins

Jazz Legend 'Between a Smile and a Tear'

Toots Thielemans (1922-2016)

Those musicians people can recognize after only hearing a couple of notes are few and far between. Only the truly great are endowed with that power. Toots Thielemans was one of them. According to connoisseurs he was, after Jacques Brel, probably the greatest Belgian musician of the last century. 'Toots' passed away on August 22, 2016 at the age of ninety-four.

His biography reads like a succession of fortunate coincidences. He often found himself in the right place at the right time and was able to make contact with those people who were instrumental in promoting his career. The truth is that Toots was extremely talented which connoisseurs always rapidly acknowledged. That was already the case even as a young boy playing his first tunes on a children's accordion at his parents' café in Brussel's *Marolles* district. Toots later discovered the harmonica after watching a movie. He soon became a virtuoso on this unusual instrument. But since his friends still deemed it a novelty instrument, he learned to play guitar. He was especially fascinated by the repertoire of Django Reinhardt. By the end of the war Toots was playing so well he regularly performed in clubs in Brussels frequented by American soldiers. It is also the time when he was dubbed 'Toots'. Jean-Baptiste Thielemans didn't have enough swing. A colleague who played trumpet suggested he assume the name Toots. He had found it in an American magazine and it is presumably borrowed from the Italian musicians Toots Mondella and Toots Camarata.

Toots Thielemans began his career with Belgian bands. Some of his earliest musical collaborations were with Flemish composer and performer Bobbejaan Schoepen's group and such jazz musicians as Bobby Jaspar and René Thomas. Édith Piaf and Charles Trenet also requested his services when they came to play in Belgium. But Toots dreamed of a career in the United States. He travelled there for the first time in 1947 and met jazz photographer Bill Gottlieb. Gottlieb introduced him to a few New York jazz clubs where one of the many people he met was Benny Goodman's impresario. Goodman invited Toots to come and play in America in 1948, though unfortunately, Toots was unable to get a work permit. When Goodman came to tour Europe in 1950, he asked for Toots again. This time around turned out to be his real introduction to the world of professional jazz. The tour also took Toots to Stockholm, where he met Charlie Parker, one of the most influential jazz musicians of all time. Toots often played in Sweden later on in his career. He was tremendously popular there, not in the least because of his musical contribution to the 1974 animated movie *Dunderklumpen*. Reportedly, the film score he composed and on which he performed are part of the collective memory.

Toots got his green card in 1951 and emigrated to America. He would later become naturalized as an American citizen. The blind British-American pianist George Shearing hired him as his guitarist. Toots developed his own special sound. He whistled along with the melody while playing his guitar. That and his harmonica were his unique trademark.

The next six years were an extremely hectic period in which he took his seat in touring buses, often as the only white player, with the other members of the Shearing Quintet, the Count Basie Big Band, the Miles Davis Quintet, and even Billie Holiday and her chihuahua. It was also when he was introduced to trumpeter, arranger and producer Quincy Jones, who would later gain great fame and fortune as Michael Jackson's producer. Toots and Jones became friends for life. They shared composing duties on quite a few movie scores. Toots's contribution to the opening title song on *Midnight Cowboy* became world famous, but he also participated in *The Getaway* and various French films. Everyone in Flanders and the Netherlands knows his contributions to the movie *Turkish Delight* and to the detective series *Baantjer* and *Witse*. Toots was also often asked to perform on commercials. That was the easiest way to make money. He could once be heard playing in a Chrysler ad with his great idol Louis Armstrong. Still, they never actually met, since their parts were recorded separately. Toots also played the opening signature tune for the world famous children's television series *Sesame Street*. It made him hugely famous, but not a lot of money.

In 1962, Toots composed *Bleusette*. A stroke of luck, he called it, but it became a global hit covered by several other prominent musicians including Ella Fitzgerald and Ray Charles. One of the most

Toots Thielemans (1922-2016)

spectacular versions of it was the maestro's duet with Stevie Wonder, one of his greatest admirers. Toots referred to *Bleusette* as his retirement fund.

Toots suffered a stroke in 1981. That made playing the guitar increasingly difficult, so he concentrated solely on playing the harmonica, on which he became the world's number one player. Everyone wanted to make music with Toots, including pop artists with a global audience. Sting, Nick Cave, Paul Simon, Billy Joel and countless others shared the stage with him. Some critics blamed him for becoming too commercial. But in the end, he also came back to jazz. In 2009 he was duly bestowed with the Jazz Master Award, the highest American accolade in the jazz world. He was the first European to receive it. The Belgian King Albert II raised him to the peerage in 2001. In order to receive the title of Baron, he had to become a Belgian citizen again. Ever since Toots enjoyed dual citizenship.

Dual citizenship might well have suited this amiable man best. His musical inclinations were very American, though in actual fact he remained a true native of Brussels. An 'AfroAmerican *Marollien*,' as he called himself. That he had never renounced his Brussels origins was clearly most audible whenever he spoke in Dutch or French. But if you asked him where he liked situating himself most, he always replied: 'Between a smile and a tear, that's where you can find me.'

DIRK VAN ASSCHE
Translated by Scott Rollins

A Modern Troubadour
Jozef van Wissem and His Lute

Jozef van Wissem (b. 1962) is among the most celebrated lute players of this day and age. The Dutch-born, but Brooklyn-based musician is on a mission to free the lute of its stuffy image and to that end combs international stages with success.

Since 2000, Jozef van Wissem has released more than a dozen records, not including collaborations with avant-rock pioneers Gary Lucas and James Blackshaw. Moreover, he recorded three records with his friend Jim Jarmusch, who besides being a filmmaker is also known as a noise guitarist. The Dutchman's music for Jarmusch's vampire film *Only Lovers Left Alive*, starring Tilda Swinton and Tom Hiddleston, was awarded the prestigious Cannes Soundtrack Award in 2013. He could also be heard for the first time as a vocalist on the 2014 album *It Is Time for You to Return*.

Van Wissem became enthralled with the lute at the age of twelve when he saw one in the corner of his guitar teacher's room in Maastricht. 'I was especially attracted to its shape,' he recalls. 'Something mystical emanated from it.' The lute in question was so fragile he was not even allowed to touch it, but he did learn how to play pieces that were especially composed for it. The melodies compiled in the book *Music from Shakespeare's Time*, turned out not to be very intricate. Van Wissem would later use one of them, referred to in *Much Ado about Nothing*, in one of his soundtracks. Before he thoroughly immersed himself in the lute, however, he switched from classical to electric guitar, playing in punk and new wave bands.

Lute players use their thumb to produce constantly varying bass notes and the rest of their left hand to form chords, a technique similar to the one employed by harpsichordists. Jozef van Wissem considers it an advantage there is such a large repertoire for the instrument. 'What interests me is how to create something new from something old,' he says. 'I do that, for instance, by mirroring existing scores. My debut album *Retrograde* consisted mainly of lute music that was played backwards.'

Technique and discipline are crucial to any lute player aspiring to achieve a certain level. The neck of the instrument is equipped with a double row of strings that he must press in a specific way to ren-

Josef van Wissem

der a pure tone. 'Pretty complicated,' Van Wissem confesses. 'But as a composer my aim is to keep things as simple as possible. That is why I prefer playing melodies consisting of only three notes.'

He shuns frills and calls himself a minimalist. In his opinion, it is simply much harder to construct a good melody with a limited number of building bricks, than to show off with complicated runs. 'Anyone spending a few hours in a totally white room loses all sense of time. I would like my music to induce a similar effect on the listener. If you keep on repeating the same three chords, it *does* something to you. I wouldn't call it slow down music, but it is a protest against a society in which there are so much stimuli it is impossible to process it all.'

Jozef van Wissem once said that art ought to be oppositional and anti-establishment. Accordingly, the titles of his compositions refer to philosophical and political documents that advocate a specific attitude to life. He is convinced you don't need a computer screen to communicate: you can also go outside and talk to someone. His choice for such an anachronism as the lute is an act of resistance towards a technology that alienates us from ourselves. 'An artist may never forget that he has a social role to play. He is practically the only one who can go against the grain of the spirit of the age, and can protest against McDonalds, Starbucks, Coca Cola or other things that make the world uniform. There's no room anymore for something that's original, raw or real: everything's been formatted. So it's up to the artist to change our way of looking or listening.'

Van Wissem consciously cultivates the image of the outlaw: as a lutenist he leaves the beaten path and feels connected to the underground. No wonder he gets on so well with Jim Jarmusch, who is trying to come to grips with mainstream culture, but is having an increasingly difficult time finding financial backing for his films.

Van Wissem's romance with the lute coincided with his move to the United States in 1994. He had been burning the candle at both ends in Groningen, in the punk bar he ran at the time. So he fled to New York, where for the first year he led an entirely spiritual life, virtually cutting off all contact with the outside world. One day he read an advertisement by a certain Pat O'Brien, an experienced lute teacher who once began as a guitarist and had been a student of the legendary bluesman Reverend Gary Davis. Van Wissem had ventured taking lute lessons once before at The Hague Conservatory, but it had not been a success.

When he took up the lute, Van Wissem was considered a village idiot. His instrument was so unhip, many people looked down their noses at it. Hollywood associated the lute with Robin Hood, academics considered it somewhat elitist. 'Just as I was making a concerted effort to boost its image and get *kids* interested in it,' according to the musician. 'That's why I used them in my soundtrack to the video game *The Sims Medieval*. That was totally at odds with what a baroque purist would have done. I want to do things to bring lute music up to date and not play the same piece by Bach for the thousandth time. Something like that no longer challenges me.'

Jozef van Wissem's musical taste varies from blues to post-industrial music and from baroque to avant-garde, but he refuses to slot the genres into any sort of hierarchy. To him, playing the lute is a contemplative activity that, certainly on stage, invariably results in a kind of trance. His concerts are intense and intimate events in which dialogue with the audience is of paramount importance. 'The audience must get the feeling I am playing solely for them. It sometimes has such a profound effect they shed tears of emotion.' Van Wissem has performed more than eight hundred lute concerts worldwide and likes to compare himself to the medieval troubadours or itinerant bluesmen. Unlike the harpsichord, the lute was a light instrument that could be taken anywhere, which enhanced the spread of lute music throughout Europe. 'I don't get why today's conservatories elevate it into something so special, because the lute used to be everywhere: at the court, in pubs, people's homes,' Van Wissem states. 'I want to fetch it from the museums and give it back to the people.'

That explains why Jozef van Wissem also ventures among the audience while playing. In one respect, he wants the lute to be regarded as an instrument that can hold its own with a concert grand piano, while at the same being one on which he can experiment.

'The pieces I play sound different every night, because lutes resound differently in different spaces', he says. 'You can't just buy an instrument like this anywhere. All my lutes have been especially designed and built for me by Michael Schreiner, a perfectionist who spent a great deal of time considering how they ought to sound and which guarantees an exceptional acoustic experience. You'd best not spoil it with any electronic gadgetry.'

DIRK STEENHAUT
Translated by Scott Rollins

www.jozefvanwissem.com

Religion

Lutherans in the Low Countries
Self-Imposed Thresholds and Calvinist Clout

In 2017, it is 500 years since Martin Luther nailed his 95 theses to the door of the Castle Church in Wittenberg. The movement for reform that Luther set in motion got off to a rapid and forceful start in the Netherlands. It was above all in the cosmopolitan trading metropolis of Antwerp that the influence of this church reformer made itself felt. German merchants brought not only goods with them, but also new religious ideas. Luther also found an important foothold in the Augustine monastery that had just been established in Antwerp. Several of the monks had studied with their fellow monk in Wittenberg and started propounding his views from the pulpit. However, the emperor Charles V and his central government reacted with a series of increasingly stricter edicts denouncing this as heresy. In 1522, the monks of the Augustine monastery were imprisoned. Two obstinate monks who refused to retract their erroneous views were burnt at the stake on the Grand Place in Brussels in 1523.

The vigorous repression by the central government and the dismantling of the Augustine monastery in Antwerp were serious blows to the young Lutheran reform movement. A small Lutheran community remained in Antwerp, which maintained contacts with Wittenberg. Small groups of believers met in private homes. However, some Antwerp Lutherans wanted to take it a step further and set up a real underground church organisation, but this clearly met with resistance from Martin Luther. He informed the Antwerp Lutherans that secret preaching and secret baptisms and marriages were absolutely not allowed. According to him, such activities were reminiscent of the work of rebellious sects, and in his view they were the work of the devil. Believers were however allowed to gather together in the privacy of their homes and quietly celebrate their faith. Those who were not able to resign themselves to this had to move to another place where it was possible to practise openly. Luther's rigid approach was related to his views on the secular government, which he considered had to be strictly obeyed. In his opinion, an underground community life with preachers who were not officially tolerated was going too far. In the Dutch context, however, this sort of attitude put up serious barriers to the growth and power of the Lutheran movement.

By contrast, the Calvinism that began to grow more strongly in the Netherlands from the mid-sixteenth century onward was well equipped to enter into the fray with a hostile government. From the mid-1550s, the Calvinists began to set up well-organised underground congregations in a number of Walloon, Flemish and Brabant towns and cities. In the 1560s, when opposition to Spanish policy in the Netherlands was on the increase, the leaders of the Calvinist Church did not hesitate to let their voice be heard. During the Wonderyear – the year of the Petition and the Iconoclasm (1566-67)[1] – they even took the lead in the armed resistance. By contrast, the Lutherans adopted a far more cautious position. When an army of Protestants was crushed by royal troops in March 1567, the Calvinists tried to take power in the city. They were however defeated by a coalition of Catholics *and* Lutherans. The Calvinists saw this as a betrayal of the Protestant cause. Together with their doctrinal differences, this carved a deep rift between the two Protestant groups.

After the Wonderyear, the Calvinists resolutely allied themselves with the Revolt launched by William of Orange. When, from 1572 onward, he achieved his first successes in Holland and Zeeland, and after 1577 was also able to win several towns and cities in Flanders and Brabant over to his policy of rebellion, the Calvinists had the wind in their sails. They had after all shown themselves to be unconditional supporters of the Revolt. In the meantime, the influence of Lutheranism remained mostly confined to Antwerp. In that city they were able to build up a well-organised church between 1578 and 1585, but even then, the political distrust shown by the Calvinists worked against them.

Alexander Farnese's conquest of the rebellious towns and cities of Flanders and Brabant in the 1580s was accompanied by a mass migration of Protestants to the rebellious north. In the Republic of the Netherlands, the Calvinist Church did

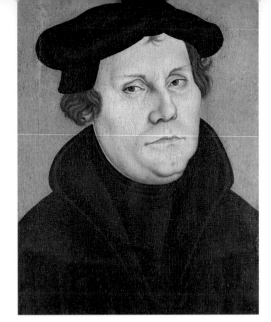

Lucas Cranach the Elder, *Portrait of Martin Luther*, 1528, Lutherhaus, Wittenberg

not gain a religious monopoly, but it did become the privileged public church. It picked the fruits of its good organisation and strong commitment to the Revolt, assets the Lutheran Church could not lay claim to. For that matter, in the Republic Lutheranism initially remained mainly associated with migrants from Antwerp, who in the seventeenth century were joined by German and Danish immigrants. The rich congregation of Amsterdam built up a prominent position in Dutch Lutheranism, but in this case too, the Lutheran Church, which in religious terms was very much oriented towards Germany, also had to play second fiddle to the public Calvinist Church.

GUIDO MARNEF

Translated by Gregory Ball

Willem Frijhoff and Marijke Spies, *1650: Hard-won Unity* (Dutch Culture in a European Perspective, vol.1), Palgrave Macmillan, Basingstoke, 2004.

Guido Marnef, *Antwerp in the Age of Reformation. Underground Protestantism in a Commercial Metropolis 1550-1577*, John Hopkins University Press, Baltimore / London, 1996.

1 See *The Low Countries*, XXIV, 2016, pp. 287-288.

Theatre

A Theatre Icon from the Lowlands
International Appreciation for Ivo Van Hove

If such a thing as a Nobel Prize for theatre direction existed, then anno 2017 Ivo Van Hove (b. 1958) would stand an excellent chance of winning. Not only has Van Hove gained world renown with his Toneelgroep Amsterdam, he has also achieved global recognition in his stints as guest director in Germany, France, England and the United States.

Van Hove's international reputation has risen spectacularly especially in the last year and a half, a provisional highpoint of which was his collaboration with global star David Bowie who passed away on January 10, 2016. In Manhattan's New York Theatre Workshop Van Hove directed *Lazarus*, a psychedelic rock musical based on Bowie's cult film *The Man Who Fell to Earth*, with existing Bowie repertoire and new songs he wrote especially for the production.

A deluge of articles and reviews in the international press and a partnership with such a pop icon: so much recognition for a man in his fifties from a Flemish village in Limburg, is to say the least, quite remarkable.

When Van Hove took the reins as artistic director of Toneelgroep Amsterdam on January 1, 2001,

Kings of War © J. Versweyveld

such a glorious future still seemed very far-off indeed. In both artistic and business terms, there were initial problems to overcome, but within a few years Van Hove was able not only to turn things around for the company, but also with the press and his audiences. In the meantime, Toneelgroep Amsterdam has become an absolute top-notch national and international theatre company.

Formerly successful productions are regularly re-staged, co-productions are made with companies from both home and abroad and such laurelled theatre makers as Katie Mitchell, Simon Stone and Sam Gold are brought to Amsterdam as guest directors. Furthermore, in the meantime, foreign demand for Van Hove productions has risen more sharply than the company can accommodate in logistical and organisational terms: approximately sixty percent of requests from abroad have to be declined.

The majority of cultural subsidies come from Dutch government authorities, and that fact alone gives priority to productions for Dutch audiences. On the other hand: there is large-scale foreign investment in major productions, and without the collaboration of companies that include London's Barbican, the Wiener Festwochen and Parisian Théâtre national de Chaillot such a monster production as *Kings of War* (première June 2015) would not have seen the light of day. Playing outside the Netherlands is not only a privilege; it has also become an obligation.

Modern techniques, straightforward stage designs, costumes and attributes that refer to topical subjects, but also radical adaptations of texts, artful *mise-en-scènes* and physically stylized forms of performance are characteristic of a Van Hove production. The realization of the stage setting always involves his life partner Jan Versweyveld, who almost always opts for a functional and pragmatic approach.

Illustrative of this duo's innovative style is *Roman Tragedies*, a nearly six-hour-long production based on three Shakespeare tragedies that premiered in July 2007. A magisterial *tour de force*, an epic constellation, played without intermissions, in open surroundings in which the fourth wall between the playing area and hall was abandoned allowing the audience to move freely from the ground floor and balcony to the foyer and even the stage.

Other great successes, in international circles as well, were *Angels in America* (première March 2008), a diptych by Tony Kushner about the aids epidemic of the 1980s, and *The Fountainhead* (première June 2014) based on the eponymous novel of ideas by the American writer and philosopher Ayn Rand.

The celebrated *Kings of War*, a Shakespeare marathon in which the historical plays *Henry V*, *Henry VI* and *Richard III* were combined into a universal metaphor about power and lust for power premiered the year after *The Fountainhead*. Van Hove brought this production to London's Barbican in the spring of 2016, Shakespeare's quatercentenary year, and in November 2016, just prior to the American presidential elections, to the Brooklyn Academy of Music (BAM) in New York.

The headlines in *The Daily Beast* read, 'A Cautionary Tale for Election Day', which confirmed Van Hove's intentions. He takes extreme interest in the demons that besiege the human spirit, the unforeseen consequences of which determine the course of history. *Kings of War* is a gorgeous example of that fascination, but so are *The Crucible* and *A View from the Bridge*, the Arthur Miller plays Van Hove staged on Broadway in 2015 and 2016.

One can scarcely keep pace with the speed of nominations and prizes that Van Hove has received of late. On May 20, 2016 he won the Founders Award for Excellence in Directing in New York, an award that one can only receive once and that was awarded to a non-English-speaking director for the first time.

He had already received Tony Awards as Best Director of a Play (*The Crucible*) and Best Revival of a Play (*A View from the Bridge*). In his acceptance speech, Van Hove reminded his audience of the initial scepticism that had befallen him as the 'bad boy of Belgian avant-garde theatre' and the demanding route he had subsequently travelled in New York.

On the threshold of 2017, it was announced that Van Hove had been included in the prestigious American magazine *Foreign Policy* list of 100 Leading Global Thinkers of 2016: the director was praised 'for unmasking fear from the stage'.

In April 2017, Van Hove will be leaving for London with Toneelgroep Amsterdam to take part in a co-production with the Barbican of *Obsessione*, an adaptation for the stage of Luchino Visconti's 1943 debut film (based on James McCain's novel *The Postman Always Rings Twice*). Two actors from Toneelgroep Amsterdam will be sharing the lead roles, together with (film) actor Jude Law.

A striking aspect of the high status that Van Hove has achieved is his lack of divulging details regarding his private life. It wasn't until David Bowie's death, that the public was allowed a temporary view into the man Van Hove himself, and was able to see how moved he was at that moment. It generated a kind of intimacy that felt out of place for such an apparently inaccessible man who – like all great artists – is constantly searching for the great story behind the small, the universal behind the personal, and depth behind the superficial.

JOS NIJHOF
Translated by Scott Rollins

Michael S. Hall in *Lazarus*, 2016 © J. Versweyveld

Visual Arts

Light and Balance
Museum Voorlinden

Light and balance are the two cornerstones of Museum Voorlinden, which opened its doors in Wassenaar, just outside The Hague, in September 2016. The art collector Joop van Caldenborgh (b. 1940), a former chemical industry magnate, commissioned a building to house his extensive collection of contemporary art in a setting characterised by clarity and clean lines. Tucked just behind the dunes of the Dutch coast, Museum Voorlinden sits almost unnoticed in a park landscape. It is a large building covering an area the size of a football field and with the proportions of a Greek temple. But its single-story construction from sand-coloured travertine limestone, and its elegant steel pillars and wide expanses of glass, give the building an aura of almost ethereal lightness. Transparency and soothing simplicity also characterise the interior of the building, which provides a welcome setting for both the art collections and the visitor. It is all in marked contrast to some of the loud, showy museums which seem to have been designed only for the greater glory of the architect.

Until five years ago, Joop van Caldenborgh did not even want his own museum. He felt there were already enough. Moreover, his generous lending policy meant his art could be seen all over the world. However, when he built an exhibition from his personal collection in the Kunsthal in Rotterdam in 2011, he liked it so much that he decided to commission a building of his own. At that time, Van Caldenborgh had already built up the biggest private collection of contemporary art in the Netherlands, with thousands of works by artists ranging from Giorgio Morandi, Andy Warhol and Marcel Broodthaers to James Turrell, Richard Serra and Roni Horn. He has no time for great theories of art. 'Artists have taught me to look at the world differently, to think more freely', he said in an interview with Dutch newspaper de Volkskrant, adding, 'a work of art is either good or it isn't. A good work of art evokes an emotion, anything from revulsion to joy'.

Van Caldenborgh, who according to the Dutch business magazine Quote is worth 300 million euros, likes to describe himself as 'a simple seller of chemicals with a passion for art'. As a teenager, his talent for drawing prompted dreams of becoming an artist. It was a talent he had probably inherited from his grandfather, who was a good amateur artist and frequently took the young Joop along to exhibitions. Van Caldenborgh bought his first work of art at the age of sixteen. Yet collecting art was not a carefully considered decision. 'Looking back, I would say that I began buying art when I realised that I would probably never be a really good artist myself', he said in an interview with the Dutch newspaper Trouw. Van Caldenborgh studied economics and chemistry and at the age of twenty-nine founded the Rotterdam chemical company Caldic. He has built up his art collection over a period of fifty years. When his son took over as CEO of Caldic, he was able to devote himself to his collection again. He purchased the Voorlinden estate in Wassenaar in 2011 for 15.5 million euros; it is a landscaped park where Hugo Loudon built a stately English mansion in 1912. The house is now home to the museum restaurant. The new museum building, designed by the Rotterdam firm, Kraaijvanger Architects, stands no more than a hundred metres away.

The pavilion-style architecture is reminiscent of the Neue Nationalgalerie in Berlin, designed by Mies van der Rohe. 'Other sources of inspiration were the Beyeler Foundation in Basel and the Menil Collection in Houston, both designed by the architect Renzo Piano', says Suzanne Swarts, artistic director of Museum Voorlinden. 'Another example is the Louisiana Museum in Humlebaek, near Copenhagen; they are all museums which allow daylight in and which create a dialogue with their environment.'

What immediately strikes the visitor on entering the building is the lightness, transparency and clarity of the generous space. There is no signage. Even electrical sockets, fire extinguishers and emergency lighting have been almost manically hidden away. The result is that the white box remains a perfect, virgin white. 'We want to remove any disruptive elements and ensure that nothing gets in the way of experiencing the art', explains Suzanne Swarts.

© Museum Voorlinden, Wassenaar

The first temporary exhibition was dedicated to the American minimalist painter Ellsworth Kelly, one of Van Caldenborgh's earliest favourites. The fact that top museums such as the Museum of Modern Art, Tate Modern and the Centre Pompidou in Paris have loaned works to the museum says something about the reputation that Joop van Caldenborgh has built up in the international art world.

ERIC RINCKHOUT
Translated by Julian Ross

The temporary exhibition *Say Cheese!* can be seen in Museum Voorlinden until 7 May 2017. This exhibition brings together around 40 works to form a coherent reflection of the versatile and characteristic oeuvre of the British artist Martin Creed. It has been realised in close collaboration with the artist (see www.voorlinden.nl).

The museum is laid out in a way that is both simple and easy to read. Two visual axes run across the building, which is divided into three parts: one housing a collection presentation, another for a temporary exhibition and the third containing a handful of large, permanent art works. The latter include the specially built *Skyspace* by James Turrell, a maze sculpted from over 200 tonnes of steel by Richard Serra, the hyperrealistic, more than life-size *Couple under an Umbrella* by Ron Mueck, and the trompe l'oeil swimming pool by the Argentinian artist Leandro Erlich. Works such as these are not easily relocated.

The first collection presentation is entitled *Full Moon* and starts with a confrontation between the canvas *Moonnight* by the Dutch artist Jan Sluijters (1912), a fragile painting by the Belgo-Mexican artist Francis Alÿs (2012) and an abstract landscape of brightly coloured panels, an installation by the Dutch artist Esther Tielemans, created in 2011. The display plays emphatically on correspondences in colour, form, theme and genre between Rineke Dijkstra and Michaël Borremans, Marcel Broodthaers and René Magritte (all Low Countries artists), Yves Klein and Katja Mater. Information on the labels is kept to a minimum; a visitor guide provides all the information, once again illustrating the museum's desire not to distract visitors from the works of art. The art on display is given lots of space, though the collection presentation is perhaps slightly too serene and could benefit from a little more fire, sharpness and dissonance.

Rocky Mountain Landscapes, Vast Distances and Mysterious Valleys
Hercules Segers and his 'Printed Paintings'

The work of the painter and etcher Hercules Segers (1589/90-1633/40) has always appealed to the imagination. This is chiefly because of his painted and etched landscapes, which make no attempt to depict the reality of the surroundings, but are founded largely on fantasy. For most of his life Segers worked in Amsterdam and probably never travelled abroad. It is most likely that he owed his penchant for landscapes to his studies under the Flemish landscape painter Gillis van Coninxloo. His influence is apparent in the early painting *River Valley*, which is built up using shades of green, yellowish-brown and greyish-blue oil paint. The dark foreground with the traveller leads into a desolate rocky landscape through which a river meanders.

Segers presents a more individual and unconventional face in his landscape etchings. He was born in Haarlem and became familiar with the innovative printmaking of his fellow artists Willem Buytewech and Esaias van de Velde, who, like Seger, enrolled in the Guild of St Luke in Haarlem in 1612. These were the artists who discovered that etching was the best method by which to depict landscapes. The artist can after all draw in the etching ground with a point as spontaneously as with a pen or pencil on paper. The prints these *peintres-graveurs* did were to be decisive in the emancipation and appreciation of the art of printmaking. Segers played a unique role in this development. He was more than anyone the undisputed master in experimenting with and manipulating the potential of the etching technique to create individual works of art. It is largely the subjects he chose, mainly rocky mountain landscapes, vast distances and mysterious valleys encircled by fantastic rock formations, woodland landscapes and existing or imagined ruins, that contribute to the present fascination with his prints, even though they are sometimes no larger than a postcard. And although the printing technique was actually invented so as to reproduce many copies of a single work of art, Segers used etching to experiment freely and to try out a variety of effects. He sometimes took eight different prints from a single etching plate. His work has become extremely rare. At present, 184 prints from 53 etching plates are known, almost all of them unique.

A thorough study of Segers's technique was carried out on the occasion of the special exhibition that was on at the Rijksmuseum in Amsterdam until early January 2017 and is now at the Metropolitan Museum of Art in New York. He printed in a variety of coloured inks - black, yellow, blue and green - on linen and cotton, to which he applied a thin coat of pink, brown or another colour by hand. Sometimes

Hercules Segers, *Distant View with Branch of a Pine Tree*, etching, hand coloured with brown, greenish, blue and white, printed on pale brown prepared linen, 14.3 x 19.5 cm.
© Rijksmuseum, Amsterdam

he even used two separate copper plates for one print. In addition, he was the first artist in Europe to use paper from the Far East, twenty years before Rembrandt printed a number of etchings on Japanese paper. Segers then worked on the print with brush and ink or with oil paint in several colours. What is more, he experimented with the etching technique itself, by working on the finished etching plate with a dry point or by drawing on the plate with a brush dipped in ink mixed with gum Arabic or a sugar solution to create a range of tones.

Because Segers printed his etchings onto prepared paper or linen and then continued working on them with paint or ink, Samuel van Hoogstraten called them 'printed paintings' in his *Introduction to the Academy of Painting* (1678). In Segers's day, there was an increase in demand for affordable painted landscapes and it may be that he cleverly took advantage of this. However, the majority of the etchings shown in the exhibition originate from his estate and only came into circulation after his death, so some of them may be works in progress.

It is no surprise that Rembrandt, who was himself a master in the repeated reworking and reprinting of his etching plates, was a great admirer of Segers. Rembrandt owned no less than eight of his paintings and undoubtedly some prints too. In addition, from Segers's estate he acquired an etching

Hercules Segers, *River Valley*, panel, 29.8 x 53.2 cm.
© Rijksmuseum, Amsterdam

plate portraying Tobias and the Angel. Rembrandt replaced the existing figures by the Holy Family on their flight to Egypt, though they are made barely visible in the bushes so that all the emphasis is on Segers's mysterious and picturesque landscape. Van Hoogstraten tells us that Segers, lacking success, in despair and drunk, suffered a fatal fall from the stairs, but this is probably a romantic legend. He had no need to complain about any lack of success, since, in addition to Rembrandt, the steward Frederik Hendrik and the king of Denmark also purchased his work.

As a pioneer of etching, Segers was an example to many twentieth-century artists who thought they recognised a contrary personality in his fanciful fantasy landscapes, one who attempted to transcend the limits of printmaking. The exhibition presents virtually all his known work. In addition to 110 different prints from 54 etching plates, it also includes 16 paintings and two sketches in oils. Three of these additional works are privately owned and have hardly ever been seen, if at all.

ILJA VELDMAN
Translated by Gregory Ball

The Mysterious Landscapes of Hercules Segers, at the Metropolitan Museum of Art in New York until 21 May 2017 (www.metmuseum.org).

Olivier Schrauwen
The First True Internationalist of Flemish Comics

Olivier Schrauwen (b. 1977) may not be a household name in international art circles yet, but this Flemish cartoonist is slowly gathering acclaim from general media and specialized comics circles all around the globe. Recently, his colourful work as an illustrator has regularly been featured in *The New York Times*, but his comics work has enjoyed an even better reception in the United States. His most recent graphic novel *Arsène Schrauwen*, a fictional account of his grandfather's stay in Congo when it was still a Belgian colony, was featured in several 'best of' lists in American media at the end of 2014 and the publication of the book by Seattle-based publisher Fantagraphics Books even preceded the edition of Schrauwen's book in his mother tongue Dutch.

Schrauwen has been slowly developing an international career since 2006. That year, the animation and comics alumnus from art schools in Ghent and Brussels published his debut book *My Boy* in English and French. Several other translations ensued, but the book was never published in Dutch. *My Boy* is a comical tragedy about a father and his son, who has not grown since the tragic day when his mother died giving birth to him. Technically, the book can be seen as a collection of short stories about the father and the songbird-sized son. Together, they visit Bruges and admire paintings by Flemish primitives in one story and find entertainment in the zoo in the next. The book stands out because of its stylistic maturity. The prologue, in which the mother dies, was drawn in a style reminiscent of old-fashioned puppet theatre. The rest of the book evokes the art nouveau sensibility of the best representatives of the American newspaper comic strip, such as Winsor McCay of *Little Nemo in Slumberland* fame. The mixture of a modern sensibility and old styles results in an interesting and funny contrast.

My Boy got Schrauwen critical acclaim immediately. It won him the biannual prize for the first comic by a Dutch-speaking cartoonist at Turnhout's comics festival (Flanders) and his first nomination for the album prizes at the International Comics Festival in Angoulême, France – later, three more would follow. The book was printed in seven languages and the English version got a second, enhanced edition in 2014. When the Flemish Literature Fund promoted young Flemish cartoonists at the Angoulême festival in 2009, Schrauwen was asked to design the poster. Thus, his status as a leading young talent was confirmed.

The appreciation in his native Flanders did not change his international approach to his work. In 2007, Schrauwen left Belgium to go and live in Berlin, where he currently resides. His second book, *The Man Who Grew His Beard* (2010), was a collection of short stories published in the American anthology *Mome* and the Italian *Canicola* and marked his choice of Fantagraphics Books as his English-language publisher. The short stories in the book are thematically and graphically so different that they seem to have been drawn by different cartoonists. The only things that connect the stories are a character sporting a beard and a wild imagination. Colourful and cruel colonial stories are juxtaposed with stylistically more sober stories referring to pseudo-scientific theories about the link between hairdos and psychological characteristics. Again, Schrauwen's book was nominated for several international prizes.

Instead of always aiming for more ambitious graphic novels, Schrauwen retreated in minicomics and self-publishing for a while after *The Man Who Grew His Beard*. The 38-page booklet *Mowgli's Mirror*, a sequel to *The Jungle Book* originally only published by a small French publisher, and *Greys*, a self-published auto-fiction in English about an abduction by aliens, only reached a very small audience until they were translated or nominated. In addition to being named for the Angoulême prizes in 2012, *Mowgli's Mirror* was his first book nominated for the Eisner awards at the Comicon in San Diego in 2016. In these projects, Schrauwen appreciated the sheer liberty, meaning the total lack of an editorial influence. He subsequently decided to self-publish his next big book, *Arsène Schrauwen*, in instalments before presenting it to his usual publishers.

Compared to *My Boy* and *The Man Who Grew His Beard*, *Arsène Schrauwen* is a less lush book, in two colours only, a choice inspired by printing on a Risograph. After pushing visual narration to the extreme in the wordless *Mowgli's Mirror*, in *Arsène Schrauwen*, much like in *Greys*, Olivier Schrauwen relies on textual narration, with the images serving as illustrations rather than essential vectors of the story. *Arsène Schrauwen* is Olivier Schrauwen's most ambitious work so far: 260 pages of one continuous story. The red and blue colours acknowledge the legacy of classic Flemish newspaper comic *Bob and Bobette* by Willy Vandersteen (1913-1990) that was long printed in these colours, and the imaginative colonial story, entirely fictional though presented as factual, makes fun of international trends in cartooning: Schrauwen replaces factual biography, reportage, travelogue by their fictional counterpart, while succeeding in mixing the dark atmosphere of Joseph Conrad's *Heart of Darkness* with clichés from classic European comics about so-called leopard men and dangerous parasites. By creatively digesting international comics history, Schrauwen has found a unique style for his idiosyncratic imagination. His uniqueness partially explains his success with prize juries and critics. The more the reader knows about comics, the better he or she will be able to appreciate Schrauwen's rich voice.

GERT MEESTERS

ollieschrauwen.blogspot.be

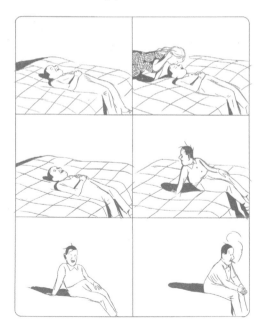

Contributors

Dirk Van Assche
Deputy Editor Ons Erfdeel vzw
dirkvanassche@onserfdeel.be

Paul Binding
Writer and Critic
paulbinding@yahoo.co.uk

Derek Blyth
Journalist
derekblyth@lycos.com

Karl van den Broeck
Journalist
kvdbroec@me.com

Geert Buelens
Professor of Dutch Literature
(Utrecht University)
gbuelens@gmail.com

Piet Chielens
Director In Flanders Fields Museum
(Ypres)
Piet.chielens@ieper.be

Wim Chielens
Director Academy of Arts
(Poperinge)
wimchielens@gmail.com

Tom Christiaens
New Media Editor
(*De Morgen*)
Tom.christiaens@demorgen.be

Maarten Dessing
Freelance Journalist
mdessing@yahoo.com

Luc Devoldere
Chief Editor Ons Erfdeel vzw
luc.devoldere@onserfdeel.be

Jeroen Dewulf
Associate Professor / Director of
the Dutch Studies Program
(Berkeley, University of California)
jdewulf@berkeley.edu

Elsbeth Etty
Critic
E.etty@nrc.nl

Jane Fenoulhet
Professor Em. of Modern Dutch Studies
(University College London)
J.fenoulhet@ucl.ac.uk

Stefanie van Gemert
Critic
svangemert@gmail.com

Ger Groot
Critic
Ger.groot@skynet.be

Kees 't Hart
Writer and Critic
keeshart@planet.nl

Rob Hartmans
Writer
rhhistor@xs4all.nl

Wim D'Haveloose
Critic
wimdhaveloose@hotmail.com

Marc Holthof
Art Critic
Marc.holthof@gmail.com

Joris D'hooghe
Art Critic
jorisdhooghe@gmail.com

Geert van Istendael
Writer
Geert.van.istendael@telenet.be

Ivo De Kock
Film Critic
ivo.de.kock@hotmail.com

Pieter Leroy
Professor of Political Sciences of
the Environment
(Radboud University, Nijmegen)
p.leroy@fm.ru.nl

Dirk Leyman
Critic
Dirk.leyman@skynet.be

Patrick Loobuyck
Professor
(University of Antwerp)
Patrick.loobuyck@uantwerpen.be

Guido Marnef
Professor of History
(University of Antwerp)
guido.marnef@uantwerpen.be

Marita Mathijsen
Professor Em. of Dutch Literature
(University of Amsterdam)
M.T.C.Mathijsen-Verkooijen@uva.nl

Gert Meesters
Maître de conférences in Dutch
(University of Lille 3, France)
gert.meesters@univ-lille3.fr

Philip Mosley
Professor of English and
Comparative Literature
(Pennsylvania State University, USA)
Jpm11@psu.edu

Jos Nijhof
Theatre Critic
nijhof@xs4all.nl

Cyrille Offermans
Writer and Critic
cyrilleoffermans@home.nl

Emanuel Overbeeke
Music Critic
overbeekemanuel@gmail.com

Lut Pil
Professor in the Arts
(KU Leuven)
lutpil@hotmail.com

Tineke Reijnders
Critic
tineker@xs4all.nl

Eric Rinckhout
Art Critic
Eric.rinckhout@gmail.com

Beatrijs Ritsema
Writer and Critic
britsema@xs4all.nl

Reinier Salverda
Honorary Professor of Dutch Language
and Literature
(University College London)
reiniersalverda@yahoo.co.uk

Jelle Schot
Film Critic
jelleschot@hotmail.com

Dirk Steenhaut
Critic
Dirk_steenhaut@hotmail.com

David Stroband
Art Critic
davidstroband@versatel.nl

Casper Thomas
Journalist
thomas@groene.nl

Tomas Vanheste
Deputy Editor Ons Erfdeel vzw
t.vanheste@proximus.be

Ilja Veldman
Art Historian
Ilja.veldman@gmail.com

Jeroen Vullings
Critic
jeroen.vullings@me.com

Judith van der Wel
Writer
info@judithvanderwel.nl

Rudi Wester
Writer and Cultural Advisor
r.i.wester@upcmail.nl

Translators

Anna Asbury
Gregory Ball
Pleuke Boyce
Sheila M. Dale
Lindsay Edwards
Chris Emery
Yvette Mead
Scott Rollins
Julian Ross
Jon Swan
Paul Vincent
Laura Watkinson

Advisor on English usage
Elisabeth Salverda (United Kingdom)

Colophon

Institution

This twenty-fifth yearbook is published by the Flemish-Dutch cultural institution 'Ons Erfdeel vzw', with the support of the Dutch Ministry of Education, Culture and Science (The Hague), the Flemish Authorities (Brussels) and the Provinces of West and East Flanders.

'Ons Erfdeel vzw' also publishes the Dutch-language periodical *Ons Erfdeel* and the French-language periodical *Septentrion. Arts, lettres et culture de Flandre et des Pays-Bas*, the bilingual yearbook *De Franse Nederlanden – Les Pays-Bas Français* and a series of books in several languages covering various aspects of the culture of the Low Countries.

Address of the Editorial Board and the Administration

'Ons Erfdeel vzw', Murissonstraat 260,
8930 Rekkem, Flanders, Belgium
T +32 56 41 12 01, F +32 56 41 47 07
www.onserfdeel.be, www.onserfdeel.nl
thelowcountriesblog.onserfdeel.be
VAT BE 0410.723.635

Philippe Vanwalleghem *Head of Administration*
Dorothee Cappelle *Administrative Secretary*

Aims

With *The Low Countries*, a yearbook founded by Jozef Deleu (Chief Editor from 1993 until 2002), the editors and publisher aim to present to the world the culture and society of the Dutch-speaking area which embraces both the Netherlands and Flanders, the northern part of Belgium.

The articles in this yearbook survey the living, contemporary culture of the Low Countries as well as their cultural heritage. In its words and pictures *The Low Countries* provides information about literature and the arts, but also about broad social and historical developments in Flanders and the Netherlands.

The culture of Flanders and the Netherlands is not an isolated phenomenon; its development over the centuries has been one of continuous interaction with the outside world. In consequence the yearbook also pays due attention to the centuries-old continuing cultural interplay between the Low Countries and the world beyond their borders.

By drawing attention to the diversity, vitality and international dimension of the culture of Flanders and the Netherlands, *The Low Countries* hopes to contribute to a lively dialogue between them and other cultures.

ISSN 0779-5815
ISBN 978-90-79705-276
Statutory deposit no. D/2017/3006/2
NUR 612

Copyright © 2017 'Ons Erfdeel vzw' and SABAM Belgium 2017
Printed by die Keure, Bruges, Flanders, Belgium
Design by Stelvio D'Houst (die Keure)

Prices for the yearbook 2017, no. 25

Belgium € 37, The Netherlands € 39, Europe € 39

Other Countries: € 45
All prices inclusive of shipping costs

You can order this book from our webshop at www.onserfdeel.be and pay by credit card

As well as the yearbook The Low Countries, the Flemish-Dutch cultural institution 'Ons Erfdeel vzw' publishes a number of books covering various aspects of the culture of Flanders and the Netherlands.

Wim Daniëls
Talking Dutch.
Illustrated; 80 pp.

J.A. Kossmann-Putto &
E.H. Kossmann
*The Low Countries.
History of the Northern
and Southern Netherlands.*
Illustrated; 64 pp.

Isabella Lanz &
Katie Verstockt,
*Contemporary Dance
in the Low Countries.*
Illustrated; 128 pp.

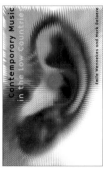

Mark Delaere &
Emile Wennekes,
*Contemporary Music in
the Low Countries.*
Illustrated; 128 pp.

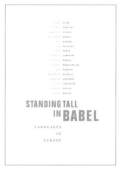

*Standing Tall in Babel.
Languages in Europe.*
Sixteen European writers
about their mother tongues.
Hardcover; 144 pp.

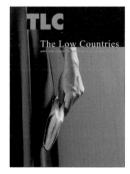

Between 1993 and 2016
twenty-four issues of the
yearbook *The Low Countries*
have been published.

EUROPE

NORTH SEA

GRONINGEN
•Groningen
Leeuwarden
FRIESLAND
•Assen
DRENTHE

NORTH HOLLAND
FLEVOLAND
Lelystad
•Zwolle
Haarlem
AMSTERDAM
OVERIJSSEL

The Hague
Utrecht
SOUTH HOLLAND
UTRECHT
GELDERLAND
Arnhem

ZEELAND
Middelburg
's-Hertogenbosch
NORTH BRABANT

Bruges•
EAST FLANDERS
Antwerp
ANTWERP
LIMBURG

WEST FLANDERS
Ghent•
FLANDERS
FLEMISH BRABANT
LIMBURG
Hasselt•
GERMANY

BRUSSELS•
•Leuven
Maastricht

•Wavre
WALLOON BRABANT
•Liège

HAINAUT
Mons•
Namur•
LIÈGE

FRANCE
NAMUR

LUXEMBOURG

LUX.
Arlon•

0   km   50

© Carto

▨	Dutch language area
▢	French language area in Belgium
▥	Brussels bilingual area: Dutch and French
▨	German language area in Belgium
▨	Bilingual area: Dutch and Frisian
◉	Capital city
•	Provincial capital
——	National frontier
······	Provincial Boundary